P9-APH-056

Maxime Rodinson was born in Paris in 1915 of a radical Jewish working-class family. After working for several years as an errand boy, he took advanced studies in the École des Langues Orientales Vivantes and at the Sorbonne, where he studied Semitic languages, ethnography, and sociology. In the forties, he spent seven years in Lebanon, teaching in a Muslim high school. He had joined the French Communist Party in 1937 and made many contacts with Communists and leftists throughout the Middle East during his years there. On his return to France in 1947 he took charge of oriental printed books in the National Library. He later became a professor of Middle Eastern Ethnology and Old South Arabian languages at the Sorbonne. He left the Communist Party in 1958 but remained in the left, as an independent Marxist writer and theoretician. He has had dozens of articles published in scholarly journals, magazines, and encyclopaedias, and is the author of *Israel and the Arabs, Mohammed, Marxism and the Muslim World,* and *Islam and Capitalism*, which won the Isaac Deutscher Memorial Prize for 1974.

AL SAQI
BOOKS

Maxime Rodinson

Al Saqi Books

U.S. Distribution: Humanities Press

Cult, Ghetto, and State

The Persistence of the Jewish Question

Translated by Jon Rothschild

Introduction and chapters 1, 2, 3, 5, 6, and 8 taken from the collection
Peuple juif ou problème juif?, first published by François Maspero,
Paris 1981.
© Librairie François Maspero 1981.

Chapter 4 first published as 'Nation et Idéologie', in *Encyclopaedia
Universalis*, Paris 1971.
© Maxime Rodinson 1971.

Chapter 7 first published as 'Quelques idées simples sur l'antisémitisme',
in *Revue d'Études Palestiniennes*, Beirut 1981.
© *Revue d'Études Palestiniennes* 1981.

Chapter 9 first published as 'Les conditions de la coexistence' in
Intervention, Paris 1982.
© Maxime Rodinson 1982.

This edition first published 1983.
Al Saqi Books, 26 Westbourne Grove, London W2.
© Al Saqi Books 1983.

Typeset by Comset Graphic Designs
Singapore

Printed in Great Britain by
The Thetford Press Ltd
Thetford, Norfolk

ISBN 0 86356 110 1 Hbk
ISBN 0 86356 020 2 Paperback

Contents

Introduction

It is my hope that this collection of essays, both new and old, written over a period of fifteen years, will arouse some interest if for only one reason, for the thread that runs through them is a rare phenomenon indeed: reflection about Jewish problems that is not Judeo-centric, and even sets out to criticize the Judeo-centric outlook.

This phenomenon used not to be rare, but it has become so, for quite human and understandable reasons. Judeo-centrism is now characteristic of Jews and non-Jews alike. And the very same conviction moves me now, as it did in the past, to argue against ideas and political options that are derived, in my view, from Judeo-centric assumptions. I have always been and remain convinced that such attitudes—whether Franco-centric, Americo-centric, Christiano-centric, Arabo-centric, or whatever—are extremely harmful, as pernicious for the comprehension of facts and situations as they are for one's ability to influence the facts. This deep conviction has impelled me to deal with Jewish problems for three decades now, despite my initial reluctance. But I could not stand by and watch the spread of an unparalleled spate of assertions taken for good coin by a broad audience despite their highly questionable character and disastrous effects, especially when the only counter-reactions were embarrassed silence or anti-Semitic diatribes, generally repressed and therefore especially dangerous.

Judeo-centrists have found this rejection of Judeo-centrism so shocking that they have sought any number of far-fetched explanations for it. One author has even published an analysis seeking to resolve the mystery, which his own Judeo-centrism (although not of the most virulent variety) prevented him from penetrating.[1] In 1967, the late Jean-Paul Sartre asked his friends to 'psychoanalyse' me from this point of view.

On the whole, these various explanations have been pretty unkind. It has been suggested that I am in the pay of the Arab League, and it was even added that my supposed employers had supplied me with a bodyguard. A somewhat more agreeable version was that I was suffering from a fixation on medieval Arab civilization so enthusiastic that it had clouded my mind and inclined me to hatred of the Jews. The most common explanation, one also applied to other Jews of more or less similar outlook, diagnosed a psychological disorder commonly known by its German name: *Selbsthass*, or self-hatred. (Others, doubtless with somewhat greater justification, have accused me of self-love.)

The perplexity is itself yet another index of the prevalence of Judeo-centrism. No one was scandalized, for example (or at least no one but a few fascists), when Sartre and many others criticized the attitude of the French state, as well as of French masses and organizations, during the war in Algeria. But I am constantly asked about a Jewish journalist who criticizes the state of Israel, 'Why does he take this position, when he is a Jew himself?' It reminds me of my Arab pupils (Christian and Muslim) when I taught French literature in Lebanon some forty years ago. 'Sir', they would ask, 'how come Voltaire attacked Christianity, when he was Christian himself?' Their attitude was a product of their deep internalization of the

---

[1] W. Rabi, 'Les Ambiguïtes d'un Juif diasporique: le cas Rodinson', in *Dispersion et Unité*, Jerusalem, no. 15 (1975), pp. 177–192. I had held out some hope that Rabi might come to understand the dolorous effects of his Judeo-centrism after his stomach turned at the unconditional support for anything Israel might do that he encountered from his audience during a conference, in Brussels I believe. It was for this reason that when he asked me for materials about myself, including some unavailable articles and autobiographical information, I gladly supplied him with these documents, few of which he understood. His wilful ignorance and practical disdain for the Arab factor, something I see every day (and simply an aspect of his Judeo-centrism), closed them to him with locks that are nevertheless not so inaccessible. Nevertheless, hope rises anew, for the mustard-seed has sprouted. As evidence I may cite his article on Elie Wiesel (*Esprit*, new series, no. 45, September 1980, pp. 79–93), in which he correctly and courageously demystifies a collection of the ethnocentric attitudes and unwarranted mystico-literary procedures of this star of letters. Likewise, his book *Un peuple de trop sur la terre?* (Paris 1979) often courageously contests the Jewish establishment.

system of religious communities—or more accurately, of religious identification—that prevails in the Muslim world, where one belongs to such a community as to a sub-nation or quasi-nation (more about this later).

Everything has an explanation, at least potentially. Even Judeo-centrism. Among the Jews themselves it has passed into humour in the shape of 'old jokes', like the one about the old Jew who was told that there had been an earthquake in South America and asked, 'Is that good or bad for the Jews?' This kind of reaction is understand-able among groups of people who have been treated as inferior, scorned, tormented, and sometimes massacred. But it is of no help at all in the study of earthquakes, or of anything else.

Among European non-Jews, Judeo-centrism is a form of European ethnocentrism (this goes for Americans too). All attention is focused on things that happened within Euro-American society, or in the Christian world. Contempt for or massacre of white Jews by white Europeans is not looked at the same way as the massacre of Armenians by Turks, of blacks by slave traders, or of Gypsies, of Chinese in Indonesia, and so on. Auschwitz is elevated to a meta-physical phenomenon, but not the butchery other peoples have suf-fered. I would be the last to minimize the atrocity of Auschwitz, where my father and mother perished. But don't the tears of others count? Must I turn a blind eye to the tears caused by those who call themselves—and are to some degree—my congeners, even if they too are survivors of Auschwitz? Is there anything more common than the transformation of persecuted into persecutor, or at least com-plicity with the persecutions from which one benefits? I am not say-ing (although some will no doubt claim that I am) that it has attained the dimensions of Auschwitz, but many Jews have made many tears flow in the land of Palestine—the fact is incontestable.

I neither hate nor despise myself. I have never denied my Jewish origin. But nor have I ever regarded it as a mark of glory that auto-matically makes me superior to others, that suffices to protect me from intellectual or moral error. I have tried to study the facts and to judge on the basis of them, setting aside the circumstance of my origins when making my judgements, as is the duty of any analyst who claims to be impartial. I was born to a de-Judaized family, which has probably afforded me the advantages and disadvantages of outlook so well expounded by Isaac Deutscher.[2] Indeed, I confess a repugnance for Jewish nationalism (common among very many Jews of my generation) even stronger than the repugnance I feel for other nationalisms, as strong as it is. The reason for this is simple, and to discover it does not require the contortions my attitude seems to have provoked in some quarters. It is simply that this particular nationalism interests me more than any other, that one must put one's own house in order first, and that I hardly have any special qualifications for speaking out against the excesses of, say, Chinese nationalism. Moreover, this particular nationalism claims me and innumerable other 'Jews' (the quotation marks are justifiable without cowardice and hypocrisy, whatever Rabi may say) who have no desire to adhere to specifically Jewish groupings in which hypocrisy does indeed prevail. It is closely linked—although the bond is recent—to a religion that also claims us, despite our aversion to its dogmas and practices. (The present atmosphere makes it necessary to recall that adherence to a religion means belief in dogmas and in the validity of certain practices.) Nationalism and religion proclaim our duty to rally to their banners, and accuse us of treason and cowardice if we fail to do so. For various reasons, often good ones, many who find themselves in this position put up with it, gritting their teeth and holding their tongue. I, along with a few others, have become their spokesman.[3]

I have defended nationalisms when they were fighting for the

---

[2]Isaac Deutscher, *The Non-Jewish Jew*, London 1968.

[3]It is amusing that Rabi takes me to task for daring to talk about Jewish questions in spite of my aversion to catalogued and sacred Jewish identities. 'Nobody forces a Jew to remain one, there is no internal constraint; the door is open', he writes (*Dispersion et Unité*, p. 182). As an example he names Lévi-Strauss, 'the son of a great rabbi [who] also walked out the door' but now deals primarily (he says) with the Bororos. Then, in the same breath, Rabi associates himself with those who accuse me of 'treason'. He thus begrudges me the right to speak, a curious accusation considering the ideas he claims to uphold. Sorry, dear Mr Rabi, but I deal with Arabs, not Bororos. I don't know whether the latter are in need of support from Lévi-Strauss, nor whether they may have received it. But I do know that among European public opinion, and even more so among Jewish public opinion, the Arabs need people who are aware of their problems, who take account of their grievances (without exaggerating them), and who express them. There are a small number of Jews like me who feel that they have a special duty towards this people despoiled by *some* Jews, towards that portion of it directly oppressed by *some* Jews. I prefer to link myself to Judaism in this manner rather than others.

rights of exploited or oppressed populations. I have great affection for the cultural traditions of the French people, among whom I was born, for the French songs that soothed my childhood, for the French literature that contributed more than any other to shaping the intellectual milieu in which my thought matured, for the French language, which is the only one natural to me, the only one all of whose subtleties I grasp effortlessly. But none of this blinds me to the negative features that French history and society may exhibit, nor does it move me to complicity with the errors or crimes of French people or of French groups. When it goes beyond the stage of defence, French nationalism, like any other, easily becomes collective narcissism, a perfectly disgusting contempt for others. Nationalism is a mental disease, perhaps necessary in certain situations, but which must then be disposed of as fast as possible.

Jewish nationalism has special peculiarities. For one thing, it applies to a very disparate human group,[4] whose members have possibilities of self-understanding and action other than those afforded by the ideology of the nation. The best proof of this is the persistent, recurrent, and obstinate effort of Jewish nationalists to rally the mass of their potential adherents behind them, often by dubious means. Not to mention their myriad complaints about the insufficiency of the response. Listening to them—and this is just a simple observation—one gets the impression that they are harnessed to a kind of labour of Sisyphus that must forever begin anew, as they gain a broad audience through great efforts only to lose a large part of it in subsequent years.

I have allowed myself to be drawn by passion further than was necessary. In particular, I have provided here a personal account of my past, in a long self-criticism whose length I believe is justified, because it goes well beyond my own personal case. But I have tried

---

[4]W. Rabi denounces my tentative attempts to delineate the sociological categories into which those who call themselves 'Jews' or are so called by others may be divided, as well as my quotation marks to designate certain 'Jews'. I would have liked very much to have readily hit upon the words and definitions required to designate a unit that would include King David, Einstein, Jesus of Nazareth, Maimonides, Moses Mendelssohn, Karl Marx, Menachem Begin, Jacques Offenbach, Benjamin Disraeli, Michel Debré, Tristan Bernard, and others—not to mention Rabi and me. I refer the reader to the first essay of this collection, 'A Bit of Clarity at the Outset'.

to remain faithful to my initial commitment: as far as is humanly possible, not to allow my origins and situation to influence my analyses and judgements, to ask myself not 'is it good or bad for the Jews?', but 'is it good or bad for people?'. Anyone who thinks this stance is wrong should say so frankly, should proclaim openly before the world that it is a good thing to sacrifice other people, other human groups—and the freedom of one's own mind—for the good of the Jews, which in any case will always mean the good of *some* Jews. It would be equally dishonest to claim that the attitude I am upholding here amounts to sacrificing the Jews, or some Jews, for the good of others.

W. Rabi maintains that I am insensitive to the misfortunes of the Jews. A slanderous accusation that he cannot sustain. He is unacquainted with my intimate thoughts, and it is thus completely gratuitous for him to claim that I never felt 'any doubt', 'not the slightest tremor', in my political options, with which I will deal later on. It may be that he feels that I have not written much about the great massacre. That is true, but there are enough writers, good and bad, who have dealt with it, many of them in the mystical-lyrical tones that Rabi himself finally found repulsive enough to denounce in someone like Elie Wiesel. What would my own cry of pain among the millions of others have accomplished had it been published? What specific contribution would it have made? But in reality, his reproach is directed solely at my failure to draw from this trauma the same conclusions as he and many others, which I do indeed find repugnant: that the tragedy of the Jews of Europe justifies the infliction by *some* Jews of undeserved (albeit less) misfortune on others and that this tragedy renders any apologetic insanity to the glory of the Jews intellectually sacrosanct. Since he has had the merit of reacting to the most outrageous of these insanities, would I be entitled to say that Rabi insensitively supported, without doubt or tremor, the pain inflicted by *some* Jews on others?

This insensitivity is equalled only by irritability at the slightest reproach addressed to *any* Jews. Rabi complacently parrots the time-honoured practices of polemical discussion, Stalinist among others, calling attention to certain of my formulations. Thus do Communists howl against the slightest analogy between Soviet and Nazi concentration camps (or at least they used to), and even (at one time) against any suggestion that Soviet camps even existed. 'Supreme slander, inadmissible outrage against the valiant soldiers who liberated Europe, against the fallen', and so on. Vociferation of this type prevents examination of the facts, and often silences one's opponent. Likewise, Rabi claims 'amalgam bordering on infamy' and 'dishonesty' if I speak of people who are Jews only in the Hitlerite and Zionist sense of the word. I can well imagine that this is deeply shocking to some honest Zionist militants who are unaware of the calamities they have inflicted on the Arabs of Palestine, and I was wrong to express myself so crudely in an interview.

But in the end, who is it that claims that the Jews are eternally rooted in their Jewishness despite all the efforts of those who do not desire to belong to a Judaic religion or a Jewish people? Don't Zionists do this? Don't anti-Semites do it too? And who is it that affirms that the Jews (including those who are 'Jews' between quotation marks, by descent or, as they say, by race) are aliens in the countries outside Israel in which they live and that they must return to this, their only 'homeland'? Don't anti-Semites say this? Don't Zionists say it too? Rabi and his ilk know very well that the answer is 'yes'. Herzl, the founder of political Zionism, said so without embarrassment.[5] So why is it an 'amalgam bordering on infamy' (thanks, by the way, for the 'bordering'), why is it dishonest, simply to note this, to compare these two sets of assertions? If the similitude is displeasing, it might be better to ignore it than to slander those who notice it.[6]

---

[5]See Maxime Rodinson, *Israel: A Colonial-Settler State?*, New York 1973, n. 29, pp. 102-3, for the relevant quotations from Herzl.
[6]Just as he is irritated by my tentative search for the proper terms by which to define sets of so-called Jews, Rabi likewise reproaches me for the complexity of my comments on my commitment to Stalinism in the past. He finds them 'contorted', evidence that in other circumstances I might have made a 'formidable Talmudist' (if I wrote that, people like him would call it anti-Semitic). Are my behaviour and attitudes inexplicable? And is the explanation of deviations of this type so simple? The self-criticism that appears in this volume will probably seem even more complex to him. It is not my fault if realities of this kind are complicated. But everything is simple to the simple-minded. Apparently, Rabi has always known the 'true truth', always understood everything, and always joined up with the good guys. I hope that some day he will discover the lies and atrocities with which his prose has made him complicit, and will realize that simplistic explanations (and there is no shortage of them) do not suffice to account for his own blindness either.

Contrary to what is said in some quarters—and is sincerely believed by the many people who are unable to read perceptively a text that contains an assertion they find outrageous—I am not an unconditional lover of Arab causes. My admiration for the civilization of the Muslim Middle Ages has never lured me in that direction. I admire ancient Hellenism even more, but that has not made me an apologist for Greek claims on Constantinople. I simply say, and will not cease to reiterate, that plenty of Arabs have grievances against *some* Jews the gravity of which cannot be doubted. But I have never subscribed to all the political attitudes, tactics, and strategies of the Arabs, nor to all the programmes of their governments and movements. I have always refused to bind myself to the Arab side by the slightest chain, gilded or otherwise.

Arab intellectuals are well aware of this, and some of them have accused me (this may astonish many readers, but I could cite published references) of being anti-Arab, anti-Islam, and even guilty of a crypto-Zionism all the more dangerous for its subtlety. The parallel between the apologetic methods (both defensive and offensive) of Zionism and those of the extreme forms of Arab nationalism, or of any nationalism for that matter, is striking. I have been no more obliging to the one than to the other.

Except that my uncompromising condemnation of the errors and crimes committed under the aegis of the Zionist movement, in contradistinction to the apologies for these things by my opponents, has given me the right to criticize more or less analogous ideas and practices among the Arabs, who understandably are not interested in obviously biased discourse. For my part, I have been able to try to explain to Arab audiences, to Arab public opinion, that the behaviour of the Zionists, although surely meriting criticism, does belong to the gamut of human conduct. I have said and reiterated, for example before three commissions convoked by the Egyptian Popular Assembly in late 1969, that Zionists are not demons, nor beasts with a human face. I said and explained—not without arousing sharp reactions, but they did listen to me—that I deplored the historical error of the creation of the state of Israel on Arab land, but that a new nationality or ethnic group with a culture of its own now exists there, and not a religious community that could as well adopt the Arabic language and Arab culture, not a heterogeneous collection of gangs of occupiers who could be sent back where they came from with the greatest of ease. My explanations, which were not very easy to formulate with all the necessary subtlety, were often heeded and understood.

On the other hand, even the Zionists might perhaps be able to understand, with a bit of effort, that the Arabs will hardly listen to anyone who simply comes along to tell them how right it was, by virtue of admirable 'Jewish values' or 'inalienable' rights dating back to Solomon, to attack them, drive them out, and take their lands.

I would also add that the attitude I have adopted is actually far less rare than may seem, judging by the press, the printed word, and the mass media. Many Jews and non-Jews are deeply convinced of its validity. But they remain silent, either because they are not in a position to write or speak publicly, or because they fear the reactions of their immediate environment or of the broader public. I understand them very well. Moreover, publishers, newspaper editors, and radio and television producers also tend to be afraid to let them speak; they suffer constant blackmail from Judeo-centrists. And finally, it is unhappily the case that speaking the truth does not always lead to fortunate results. But nor does hiding it.

In short, I am not as isolated as one might think. But I have acted as the spokesman of those who cannot or dare not speak, as I have also done in those of my works directed largely at audiences in the Muslim world.

At this point I ought perhaps to reassure my readers. Although I was initially quite ignorant of the Jewish religion, I have since inquired into it studiously and at length. In fact, I have studied Jewish history rather more closely than most of the Zionist publicists who use it as an argument at every turn. I am familiar with biblical literature. One of my passions has been and remains studies of this literature, the scholarly studies of the many generations of specialists who have illuminated so many problems, whereas most of those who produce brilliant essays on biblical thought or on the role of Hebrew concepts in world history seem to be unaware even of their existence. Unconsciously, however—leaving aside the obvious presumption that they know very well what they are doing—they may nonetheless suspect that something is lacking, for they try to compensate with tricks of hair-do and dress designed to catch the eye of television viewers and others. The assurance afforded by philosophical training—I speak not of real philosophers—in virtuosity in the manipulation of concepts does the rest.

I have studied Semitic (and some other) languages for quite a few years, as well as the cultures and histories of the peoples that speak them. I have specialized in the Arab and Muslim world and in Ethiopian culture. But unlike the para-philosophical clique of which I have just spoken, I have always tried to keep abreast of advances in scientific research about the history and culture of the Hebrews and the Jews; this research has been going on for centuries, and its achievements are of capital importance, whatever these essayists, publicists, and polemicists may think of them, or not think of them. I have occasionally tried to contribute to this too, alongside my studies of related populations, especially the Arabs and Ethiopians, within the general framework of studies of the history of religion, anthropology, and sociology. I therefore believe that I am better qualified than many to say something about the problems raised by the evolution of Jewish cultural and social formations.

I say all this not to parade my credentials, but to respond in advance to those who will no doubt seek to heap discredit on my analyses by explaining that I might be able to say something accurate about the Arabs and Islam, but not about the Jews.

Some of the studies, sketches, and essays in this volume are articles that have appeared in French or other languages. It has not been possible for me to update them all, particularly from the bibliographical point of view.[7] I have, however, made some small additions. These and other alterations are signalled by brackets.

---

[7]Nevertheless, let me list some general works on Zionism, Israel, and the Arab resistance that have appeared since most of the essays in this collection were drafted. My own book *Israel and the Arabs* (Penguin Books, second edition 1982) is a history of the conflict in the context of the struggles of the region; the new edition brings the chronology up to date. Walter Laqueur's *History of Zionism* (London 1971), very detailed and well documented, is a work by a Zionist who has become critical and conscious of the Arab problem, which has led him to some disenchanted conclusions. Nathan Weinstock's *Zionism: False Messiah* (London 1979), of Trotskyist, anti-Zionist but not anti-Israeli outlook, is a mine of documents and critical reflection. In

Other essays were written especially for this collection. It will be obvious which ones these are.

Readers are asked to excuse the inevitable repetitions that occur in a work of this type. And the nature of the collection should account for some incongruities. The date of each essay is indicated; the overall approach is the same throughout, but my appreciation of some particular points may have changed to some extent.

All the essays dealing directly with the Arab-Israeli conflict (except the last) were written before the October War of 1973, Sadat's trip to Jerusalem (November 1977), and the Camp David Accords (September 1978). Whatever some may say, I do not believe that these events—as important as they undoubtedly are—change anything in the basic problem. As I noted in 1969 (see page 219), the Arab world remains generally irredentist. Acceptance of the *fait accompli* of a new Israeli nation, even recognition of its legitimacy, is becoming less unthinkable. But the preconditions for such recognition remain very difficult to fulfil; they require Israeli concessions, and whatever the succession of governments, Israeli public opinion still seems little inclined to move in that direction.

Israël, la fin des mythes (Paris 1975), Amnon Kapeliouk, a very well informed Israeli journalist, offers a lucid analysis of the victorious euphoria that gripped Israel between 1967 and 1973, up to the October War and its aftermath. Olivier Carré's *Le Mouvement national palestinien* (Paris 1977) is a concise and confident guide containing many original documents. Worthy of special recommendation is *La Terra troppo promessa: sionismo, imperialismo e nazionalismo arabo in Palestina* (Milan 1979), a very well documented and judicious book by Massimo Massara, who is also responsible for the large collection of texts and long introductory analysis entitled *Il Marxismo e la questione ebraica* (Milan 1972), which possesses the same qualities. Those who want to keep informed about these problems while avoiding the constant distortions of publications that are either Zionist or influenced by Zionism may consult the following specialized periodicals: the Israeli bulletin *Israleft*, which offers significant extracts from the Israeli press translated into English (bimonthly, POB 9013 Jerusalem); the courageous little review *Israel and Palestine* (monthly, B.P. 130-10, 75463 Paris Cedex 10), published in English in Paris by dissident Israeli journalists; *Khamsin,* a journal of revolutionary socialists of the Middle East, published in English (BM Khamsin, London WC1N 3XX). Israel Shahak, professor at the Hebrew University of Jerusalem, also translates into English and comments on enlightening extracts from the Israeli press. This non-conformist information from resolutely dissident Israelis can be usefully complemented by the review *New Outlook* (monthly, in English, 8 Karl Netter Street, Tel Aviv), most of whose collaborators are members of Mapam or close to this party. The review does not deviate much from the party apparatus, but is often courageous in its denunciation of the excesses of Israeli chauvinism and in its search for peaceful solutions.

I would have liked to add to my polemic against the Judeo-centric outlook a criticism of its most recent manifestation in the form of apologetic works by authors gifted with some verbal virtuosity, expert at handling concepts, and deeply ignorant of history. But unfortunately there was not sufficient time to complete this criticism.

I extend warm thanks to all those who have assisted me. But the most precious aid has come from people whose efforts have exasperated me. *Indignatio fecit versus.* They have contributed to lending quite a few of these essays a more lively, and, I hope, a more convincing tone. In view of the harm they do, I cannot thank them, nor do I therefore wish them to continue. I would rather that my next writings were of a more sedate style.

1
A Bit of Clarity at the Outset

'The Jews don't eat pork.' 'The Jews are circumcised.' 'Jews are greedy.' 'Jews stick together.' 'The native land of the Jews is Israel.' 'All the Jews are now mobilized for Israel.' And so on. Claims about 'the Jews' abound. Some are laudatory, some defamatory, some even neutral. Some are radically false, but none is totally true. And for very good reason: the word 'Jews' is applied to very different collections of men and women. Even the classical distinction between those considered Jews by others and those who consider themselves Jews does not suffice to exhaust all the forms of diversity.

If we are to gain some understanding of the problems involving the Jews (in the various senses of the word), if we are to reason soundly, then we must constantly bear in mind that various sets of individuals are more or less commonly designated as Jews. One or another (and often two or three) of the following sets is usually meant.

1. The adherents of a well-defined religion, Judaism. Like any religion, it has its dogmas (the oneness of god, his selection of a chosen people, etc.), its sacred history (Moses receiving the Law on Mount Sinai, the passage across the Red Sea, etc.), its multifarious and complex practices or rites (circumcision, sanctified holidays, dietary laws, etc.). As is the case with every religion nowadays, many adherents do not believe in this or that dogma, do not practice this or that rite, but nevertheless consider themselves among the faithful of the religion, part of a community historically formed on the basis of it, and not as part of any other. As in Christianity and other religions, many people practice only those 'rites of passage' which, they believe, are sufficient to establish their adherence: rites of birth,

marriage, and death, and often accession to adulthood as well.

2. Descendants of adherents of Judaism who no longer consider themselves faithful to the religion and who on the contrary subscribe in practice to simply deist or even atheist ideas, who sometimes have even converted to other religions, but who nevertheless desire to maintain some link with the adherents of religious Judaism and thus regard themselves as forming a sort of ethnic-national community along with them—a people, to use the most common term. It is especially easy for Jews to adopt this attitude, since unlike purely universalist religions like Christianity, Islam, or Buddhism, Judaism, despite powerful universalist tendencies during certain periods, has also retained many traces of its origin as an ethnic religion specific to a particular people of the ancient Middle East: the people of Israel, also called the Hebrew people. The boundary is therefore evanescent between Jews in the religious sense, who are often not very religious but attribute an ethnic-national connotation to their adherence to the faith, and Jews who consider themselves members of a people to which religious Jews belong as well; in any case, the latter are often motivated, perhaps even in spite of their convictions, by a sentimentalism that ascribes an ethnic-national significance to Jewish rites, traditions, and even dogmas.

3. Other descendants of adherents of Judaism who have rejected any affiliation either to the religion or to a 'Jewish people' and who consider themselves atheists, deists, Christians, or whatever on the one hand, and French, Turkish, English, Arab, or whatever on the other. But despite this, since the memory of their descent from religious Jews has been preserved, others still consider them Jewish, at least on certain occasions and in certain contexts.

4. Yet other descendants of adherents of Judaism whose ancestry is unknown by others and often by themselves; they can only be called 'unknown Jews', as suggested by Roger Peyrefitte in a thick book whose only valid point was probably this designation and his insistence on the importance of the category, which is most often forgotten.

Transitions from one category to another are frequent. Sometimes they occur during the lifetime of a single individual; they occur quite often if we consider groups of lineages over time. In our epoch they are facilitated by the disappearance in a great part of the world of the religious communities of times gone by. In the Muslim world, transitions are hampered by the fact that the Jews of the first three categories are institutionally considered members of a 'Jewish community' (also called 'Mosaic') unless they have formally converted to another religion. One belongs to this community by virtue of one's birth, and remains in it (barring conversion) until death, regardless of one's inner convictions, just as one is a member of a given nationality even if one lacks the slightest inkling of patriotism. Jews born in the Muslim world have internalized this conception quite profoundly, and have carried it with them in their migrations, like the North African Jews who have recently immigrated to France, where a wholly different conception has held sway since the revolution of 1789: a religion is only a religion, and if you no longer believe in its dogmas, no longer practise its rites, and no longer participate in its cultural organizations, then you are no longer a member of it, but are a French deist or atheist or whatever, regardless of your Catholic, Protestant or Jewish ancestry.

Between thse two antipodal conceptions, of course, there are many mixed forms. The United States tends to approximate the Muslim model, though less rigorously, because of the multiplicity of groupings which reflects the formation of this nation of immigrants, the competition among them, and the attachment of most of them (after a period of attempted fusion in the great melting pot) to a cultural specificity of their own, in addition to their membership of the greater American nation.

In the Soviet Union and in some of the People's Democracies, the term 'Jew' defines membership of a 'nationality', like 'Uzbek', 'Ukrainian', or 'Russian'. In practice, this membership, which is recognized by law, amounts to approximately a religious community of the Muslim type. Except that the officially recognized criterion in the Soviet Union is not the Jewish religion (which the state combats along with all others), but the Yiddish language, which is considered a 'national language'. Nevertheless, this Germanic dialect, mingled with Slavic and Hebrew vocabulary, is spoken by only about one-fifth of the members of this Jewish 'nationality'. Most Jews in the USSR are well assimilated to Russian culture, even though they are descended from people whose religion was Judaism and whose language was Yiddish. But there are some who still practise this religion but whose ancestors never spoke the language. The Jews of Georgia, Dagestan, and the Bukhara region—who speak Georgian or Turkish or Iranian dialects—have never known Yiddish.

In the rest of this book, I will try always to define the sense in which the term 'Jews' is being used, unless the meaning is clear from the context. Wherever this is not done, the set of people in question consists of the first three categories.

2
Self-Criticism

They say that crime doesn't pay. Sometimes, maybe not. But intellectual dishonesty does, as experience confirms every day. It can even become the source of a regular income. Striking proof is provided by salaried or aspiring ideologues, venal journalists, and the intellectual functionaries of various party apparatuses.

I do not know whether I am the most famous anti-Zionist in France, as is claimed in a hateful little polemical pamphlet published, probably by mistake, by an imprint normally inclined to impartiality and scientific rigour.[1] But I am probably the most frequently attacked. Naturally, this does not mean that my arguments are rationally refuted. It is often not polemically effective to do so, and also requires the expenditure of intellectual efforts that might better be saved. They are often neither quoted nor analysed, or else it is simply claimed that they have been triumphantly refuted by public or scientific opinion. Arguments that I have criticized are repeated without the slightest allusion to this criticism, and therefore without answering it.[2] The unsuspecting reader is thus led to believe that good minds have shed all necessary light on the inanity of my efforts. No need to take a closer look. And since many readers indeed seek only to persuade themselves of the validity of their preconceived ideas, they do not in fact go any further.

It has long been known that intellectual dishonesty pays big dividends in polemics. That is why thinkers committed to reasoning

---

[1] Claude Franck and Michel Herszlikowicz, *Le Sionisme*, Paris 1980, in the *Que sais-je?* series published by Presses Universitaires de France, p. 89.
[2] Albert Memmi, for example, has done this.

as rigorously as possible have always warned against polemics, whereas masters of rhetoric, who offer their readers and disciples no more than recipes for success, have always recommended them. One of their most cherished procedures is the so-called argument *ad hominem*: assault the personality, character, origin, or morals of the person who sets forth an assertion, in order to avoid responding to the assertion itself.

Intellectual dishonesty is further accentuated when the objections of authors are parried by invoking not even what they now are, but what they used to be and used to say, even though they have broken with their past. But people do evolve and change, and at least some learn something from their experience. As I have.

Taking full advantage of the millennial lessons of professors and practitioners of mendacity, the authors of the unscrupulous work of propaganda cited above, following in the footsteps of many other Zionists, have hurled at me an article I wrote in 1953 entitled 'Sionisme et socialisme'.[3] At the time this article was written and published, I was (and would remain for another five years) a member of the French Communist Party. They quote from it several passages that are, indeed, odious. Until now I have responded only very briefly here and there. I now gratefully take the opportunity of this volume to expound the necessary explanations at somewhat greater length. They concern far more than my own personal case, and permit some fundamental problems at least to be broached, if not examined in depth.

I was a member of the French Communist Party from 1937 to 1958. At the time, this definitely required a state of mind that has correctly been called Stalinist.

I was not alone. Millions of people throughout the world—and I refer not to the cadres or militants enrolled by force or by strong pressure in the so-called socialist countries—opted for the same commitment. Some of them, even in the capitalist countries, were acting out of self-interest, ambition, or similar motives. In an engagement of this kind, however, it is always difficult to disentangle the various underlying motivations, both conscious and unconscious. It is never-

---

[3] *La Nouvelle Critique*, no. 43, February 1953, pp. 18–49.

theless undeniable that at least a good number of these millions of members joined because they dreamed of devoting themselves to an admirable ideal, and that at the very least most of them were neither scoundrels nor imbeciles.

Today even the most anti-communist are willing to admit this in the case of people who have come over to their side or who have at least manifested their recantation in a striking manner in the domain most dear to them. George Orwell, Arthur Koestler, and Ignazio Silone, for example, like André Gide, Boris Souvarine, and, much later, many anti-communist shock troops, were themselves Communists for varying periods, something younger generations are often surprised to learn (when, that is, dissimulation of the past, so frequently practised, does not prevent them from ever finding out). After their defection, these 'converted' figures have sometimes tried, as I shall do here, to explain their blindness.[4] I do not believe that a single one of them has confessed to having been moved by motives of a criminal type, even when they have decided that their past conduct was weak, cowardly, or even marred by passive complicity with acts worthy of condemnation.

Some boast that they remained ever clear-sighted, and that they stayed in the party in order to work behind the scenes for a line less offensive to their hearts and minds. There is at least a strong dose of retrospective illusion in this view of their past.[5] In reality, things were more complicated.[6] With the exception of the total 'believers', whose mental age was on the low side, most of us had our areas of blindness

---

[4]An excellent and exceptional example is the collection entitled *The God That Failed: Six Studies in Communism*, by Arthur Koestler, Ignazio Silone, André Gide, Richard Wright, Louis Fischer, and Stephen Spender, with an introduction by Richard Crossman, London 1950. Also a must is the review by Isaac Deutscher, 'The Ex-Communist's Conscience', in C. Wright Mills, *The Marxists*, New York 1962, pp. 353–363.

[5]Jeanine Verdès-Leroux, who conducted, for a work now in preparation, a punctilious inquiry among several dozen ex-Stalinist French intellectuals, tells me that she encountered only four (myself among them) who acknowledge having really believed in all the Stalinist myths and having acted on that belief. Could we have been the sole cause of it all, this 'gang of four'?

[6]Among the testimonial works that have analysed this complexity most subtly, I would cite, apart from the contributions of the collection mentioned in note 4 above, many passages of *The Seizure of Power* (London 1983), the excellent novel by Czeslaw Milosz, and *The Captive Mind* (London 1953) by the same author; the analysis of his own past experiences by Manes Sperber, especially in the second volume of his

and others of lucidity, their relative proportion varying according to the fluctuations of personal situation and general conditions. I do not seek to exaggerate my own share of lucidity.

The thesis of the 'vulgate' widely diffused thanks to the talent of Edgar Morin[7] is not generally valid, contrary to what some people who never lived through the experience have thought. Morin speaks for the generation of intellectuals who joined the party during the Second World War. The layer to which he belongs had its own 'intelligent' interpretation of the directives of the party, which the latter expressed in crude formulations accessible and even attractive to the masses.[8] This was exactly the technique of Christian, Muslim, and Jewish philosophers (not to go any further back than that), who had their own 'enlightened' religion, which the masses could never understand, and agreed that the various myths and rites were only the crude translations of it required by simple-minded and ignorant beings. Such are the visions to which people cling whenever faith begins to crumble and waver; it is always a step towards cynical resignation or disengagement.

For my part, I, like many others, accepted these kinds of explanations only partially and belatedly. Perhaps Morin and his ilk were as lucid as they claim, but I was far more profoundly blind. My party membership began earlier—having its roots in participation in mythology and ritual from early childhood, for I was born to a Communist family[9]—and I did not consider myself an intellectual, at least

---

memoirs, *Le Pont inachevé* (*Ces Temps-là*); the few pages added as a postscript by Jean-Toussaint Desanti to the book of his wife, Dominique Desanti, *Les Stalinjens, un expérience politique (1944-1956)*, Paris 1975, pp. 361-69, a work far more contestable in many respects. In *Parcours immobile* (Paris 1980), Edmond A. El Maleh also gives a good, even lyrical, account of the mentality of the 'committed', including the colonial dimension as well. And the memoirs of Jorge Semprun, Marcel Thourel, Claude Roy, Jean Recanati, Renaud de Jouvenel, Ignazio Silone, etc. are also recommended. But I am far from having read everything on the subject.

[7] Edgar Morin, *Autocritique*, Paris 1959.

[8] I can still remember being told of Maurice Thorez's anger (understandable, after all) at a party economist who suggested, with unfathomable naïveté, that the party's thesis about the 'absolute impoverishment' of the proletariat, unacceptable and supported by infantile arguments, be translated into 'intelligent' terms. Every Communist leader feels himself obliged to publish apparently profound 'theoretical' works, to imitate Lenin and Stalin. The results are often pitiable. The same practice is now common among the 'chiefs' of some of today's far-left Marxist sects.

[9] A rather similar atmosphere thirty years later is vividly described in the childhood

not of the same type as Morin's companions. I found my proletarian origins flattering, and was proud never to have availed myself of the facilities offered by the bourgeoisie, unlike the many young people in the party with secondary education (at least).[10] Suspicious of their double language, I sensed that it represented infidelity to the aspirations of the humiliated and oppressed, among whom I counted myself.

To sum it all up (too briefly, but this is not the place to dwell on the point), the origin of my party membership was a general moral indignation leading to a commitment to self-sacrifice. Except in the (rare) cases of conscious and cynical careerism, this attitude exists in a more or less pure form. Bourgeois intellectuals, who may seem the most disinterested, nevertheless (sometimes) have in the back of their minds the idea of playing on their party membership in various rivalries among the scribbling elite,[11] of defying a strictly conservative family, or something of the sort. On the other hand, workers who may seem to be acting for selfish reasons, joining an organiza-

---

memoirs of Nina Kéhayan, in Jean and Nina Kéhayan, *Rue du Prolétaire rouge*, Paris 1978, chapter 1.

[10] I long felt the weight of bitterness at having been unable to attend secondary school (you had to pay for it in those days) and at having had to work as an errand boy from the age of fourteen to seventeen. In the Communist Party I got my revenge, and I savoured the imaginary privilege of an orientation less inclined towards a treacherous petty-bourgeois slope than those of my comrades who had climbed the traditional ladder of the children of the bourgeoisie. I took a sensual delight both in my far easier contacts with poorly paid employees and the popular layers and in my manner of speech, which was closer to theirs. At least so I believed. But the 'full-timers' nevertheless considered me an intellectual, a carrier of all the vices inherent in the category, in accordance with the (true) 'vulgate' of the party.

[11] It is this factor—the simulacrum of power afforded by party membership—that Jean-Toussaint Desanti emphasizes in his self-criticism, cited above. He speaks for a certain category of intellectuals, but it would be wrong to generalize in the manner suggested by his formulations. The party did indeed afford some writers, philosophers, and essayists a broader audience than they would otherwise have expected, or at least another audience, in which their words elicited a deep response, and some action. For specialists in domains unlikely to be of much interest to wide audiences or to lead to any action, like the linguists and orientalists among whom I counted myself (remember that at the time, the world of Islam was of only very slight concern to the public at large), there was hardly any power to be gained, fictitious or otherwise. At the most there could be some response from an incompetent audience of good will, for ideological reasons. That could console us for the moroseness of our daily relations with our colleagues, but it weakened our reputation in the scholarly circles that read our publications, without offering much in the way of compensa-

tion that is defending their wages and living conditions, quite commonly display genuine devotion. It would be far easier for them to benefit from the advantages won by the action of others without compromising themselves or making any effort. Granted, in Western Europe and North America, we are well past the time when working-class militancy involved terrible dangers in the form of fierce repression by the 'forces of order' and the employers' militias. But it usually does entail stubborn efforts that compromise personal life, as well as difficulties and quite a few obstacles. True enough, it is also a road to upward mobility (for those who work their way up the ladder of the party and the trade-union apparatuses). But this ascension is dearly bought; it can often be purchased more cheaply, and in any case, many of those who take this road do so at first in a spirit of self-denial of some depth.

How does it happen that from this more or less pure beginning, we arrive at what later seems to be inadmissible complicity in tragic and criminal manoeuvres? The problem is that the initial indignation is invested in action, this action is framed within an organization, and the intellectual justification for the indignation congeals into ideology. Organization has its own laws of structure and evolution, as does ideology.

Devotion to certain values is translated into commitment to an organization that seems to be the propitious instrument, whether the only one or the best, specially capable of defending these values and bringing about their victory. Pure devotion to the values is not enough. Some degree of development, of intellectual elaboration, is required even by the crudest minds: how can these values be concretized, which people and structures embody them, what acts and attitudes should they inspire?

The organization must also answer these questions by presenting its members with a doctrine, which its intellectuals strive to elaborate. This doctrine determines a programme: the goals to be aimed at, the stages to be set, the paths and means by which to assure

---

tion. In general, we looked askance at the extra time fruitlessly expended on the articles requested by the party, and produced them out of a sense of duty. Moreover, within the party itself we were generally just rank-and-file militants. For my part, I had always evaded any post other than cell treasurer. I was criticized for this, and I felt guilty about it, seeing it as a mark of insufficient aptitude for militant activity.

this advance in a hostile or indifferent world. Quite clearly, this means the recruitment of members and the attraction of sympathizers in numbers as massive as possible.

If the whole history and study of societies dictates at least one conclusion, it is that any organization has an irresistible tendency to become an end in itself. If, as is usual, the organization considers itself the prime instrument for the promotion of some good, namely the defence, illustration, and advance of the values it upholds, then it must constantly defend and strengthen itself. At the same time, the organization is composed of individuals to whom different roles are assigned. It needs bodies of leadership and orientation, more or less specialized committees, loyal activists. Each member assumes some role or other, the organization presses everyone to adopt some position or other, depending in part on individual aptitudes, but also, and increasingly, on the directives of those who have been placed, or have placed themselves, in leadership posts. The full weight of human passions and interests is brought to bear on those directives.

The members trust the organization to define and lead actions (including intellectual actions) along the lines of their aspirations. The leaders determine the actions to undertake. On both sides it increasingly seems that the prime tasks concern the defence and advance of the organization, and consequently its struggle against its rivals, opponents, and competitors. Since there is a constant tendency for tasks to become autonomous, the application of these tangible objectives tends to overshadow the values whose realization these objectives are supposed to serve, for it has been decided once and for all that these amount to the same thing. But the values are a long way off, and their concretization, their translation into more precise ideas and actions, pose dark and difficult problems, whereas the tasks are near to hand and clearly defined. People cannot constantly question their own thoughts and purposes.

Once they hold power over a country, even those governments most devoted to the cause of their people—including those that are at first sincerely committed to strict rules of personal morality, sometimes even religiously attentive to securing eternal salvation —very soon convince themselves that the administration, defence, and progress of the country in question cannot be effectively pursued without resorting to means contrary to their own supreme values. In many cases, this is even true, but the ultimate laudable objective will always purify impure means, and in any event soothes consciences. The governed, ignorant as they are of the requisites of government and absurdly wedded to the values of individual morality, cannot always be told the whole truth. That would even be dangerous for state security. 'Nobody can rule guiltlessly', said Saint-Just, demanding the head of Louis XVI. But he soon understood that more than the monarchy was at stake. He wrote in a draft: 'One strives for rigour in principles when destroying an evil government; but if one comes to govern oneself, it is rare that one does not soon abandon these same principles in favour of one's will.'[12]

The same process holds for organizations that aspire to political power, or share in it, or even want to share in it or at least influence it, whatever their deeper inclinations. Today's political parties for example.

In practice, you cannot get involved in the problems of power without losing your innocence. No group, no social layer, can take action without dirtying its hands, even if it hurts to do so, as it did the jurors of the revolutionary tribunal who broke into sobs when condemning Cazotte to death and asked him to sympathize with their unhappy fate.[13] But this kind of suffering does not last long.

For those governed by a state power, the problem of conscience does not remain very serious for long. Their conscience is protected by their impotence. Revolt is no small thing; it is dangerous, and requires a lot of effort, a lot of organization. They can be satisfied with official explanations, take pleasure in an increasingly wilful ignorance, hide behind the imperious necessities of politics, behind the facts, unknown to them, which motivate their governments and which the latter cannot divulge.

---

[12]*Institutions républicaines*, in *Oeuvres de Saint-Just*, introduction by Jean Gratien, Paris 1946, p. 296.
[13]According to Albert Ollivier (*Saint-Just et la force des choses*, Paris 1954, p. 156) who confuses the novels of Cazotte and Lesage. In fact in his final address, 'which flabbergasted part of the gallery', Lavau, the president of the tribunal that tried Cazotte (it was one of the first revolutionary tribunals, holding sessions in August and September 1792), called upon the defendant 'to lament the fate of those who had just condemned' him. (See J. Cazotte, *Oeuvres badines et morales*, Paris 1817, vol. 1, pp. 127 ff.)

This is more difficult for the members of an opposition party, since those who hold power spare no effort to make sure that they know all about the errors of their leaders. But for that very reason, how can one refuse them confidence, when everyone knows that the government would not hesitate to accuse them falsely? The accusers cannot be blindly credited. How can one judge, be informed impartially, sort out the true from the false? It is especially difficult in that many members, even if they possess the intellectual capacities and information necessary to make these judgements, are engaged in an absorbing personal or professional life. They are normally under pressure to postpone as long as possible any challenge to a commitment that has often cost them dear.

But let us abandon the heights of abstraction and descend to the Stalinist commitment itself. Adherence to Communism entailed, and still entails, commitment to a struggle that is supposed to enable humanity to accomplish an essential and eminently beneficial leap: to put an end to a system that permanently produces poverty and crime, that subjugates and condemns millions of people throughout the world to an atrocious life, or even to death. The intent is to create a liberated humanity in which all can blossom to the full extent of their best potential, in which the collective of free beings will control the administration of things and will lay down the minimum of rules indispensable for harmonizing relations among human beings. It is true enough that those who made this gamble can be accused—correctly, I would now say—of inadmissible naïveté, perhaps for having believed such an ideal realizable in the first place, and surely for having believed that enrolment in the ranks of the parties of the Communist International would bring it about.

If we were guilty of such naïveté, and of blindness to the structures and people in whom we placed our confidence, then so have many others been at one time or another since 1917. A long list could be made (barely begun above), and on it we would find no shortage of people who now haughtily condemn my aberration or that of my companions, who now combat their former faith with the zeal of the neophyte, and who, moreover, employ just the same sort of reasoning, the same virulent tone and lack of subtlety, that they had formerly placed in the service of the cause they now combat. They speak with great assurance, as if they had been imbeciles or scoundrels for a certain period of their lives, to use these terms yet again. To reject any such suspicion it is sufficient simply to listen to them or to read their writings. But some explanation is needed, and for the most part they carefully avoid presenting one.

'You didn't use to talk this way.' 'Yes, but since then war has broken out—or maybe you've forgotten.' No one who lived in France before the Second World War could forget this slogan, which was printed every day in the newspaper of Gustave Hervé, who was famous for his anti-patriotic zeal before 1914 ('plant the flag in the dunghill'), and for his hyperbolic chauvinism afterwards. There were, we will be told in the same spirit, terrible events that should have opened your eyes. How could you have joined this party at such and such a date, stayed in it after this or that date, when you had abundant evidence of its faults, and its support for errors, inadmissible political lines, and unpardonable crimes?

When, then, should we have definitively awakened? At what point did support for the Communist Party become criminal? Copious documentation on Soviet Russia has always been available in the capitalist world. A 1931 bibliography listing only works in French notes 1,312 books written on the subject since the revolution, aside from the innumerable articles in magazines and newspapers. From the very first years, it was possible to know all about the authoritarianism of the Bolshevik Party, the inhuman treatment to which its opponents were subjected, the contempt for the right of peoples to self-determination, the stifling of any critical voice, the atrocities of the repression inflicted on protesting workers and peasants as well as members of the working classes.

How could you have forgiven the dissolution of the Constituent Assembly, the repression of Kronstadt, the annexation of Georgia? it was asked towards 1925. How could you have failed to see the ignominy of the Moscow frame-up trials? it was asked in 1939. How could you have tolerated the trial of Slansky, Rajk, and others? it was asked around 1955. The list could easily be extended and amply filled out.

At each stage, moreover, we find among the indignant accusers people who, ten, twenty, or thirty years before, were themselves being denounced for similar acts, for unsavoury and tortuous manoeuvres, disgusting statements, and brutal deeds in the service of 'the cause'. A thick anthology could be compiled of the judgements pronounced about the acts and words of people who subsequently became famous for the rigour of their condemnation of similar acts and words. Here I will be kind enough not to mention any names.

It is difficult to escape the conclusion that some permanent mechanism lies behind all these apparent twists and turns. Deviation is the inevitable fate that awaits anyone who climbs aboard such a galley. 'Pay heed, Philippe, you who thought of the good of humanity', exclaimed Lorenzaccio in the play by Alfred de Musset, whose lucidity had been sharpened by the consequences of the revolution of 1830.

The deeper reasons for deviation from the ideal that originally motivated commitment lie in the dynamics characteristic of organization and ideology, in the requisites of maintaining them, defending them, and extending their influence. The initial aspirations are subjugated by the exigencies of realism; indolent resignation is easily attained once the inevitable impurities of the process are noticed; and finally, for some, after more time or less, there are the personal advantages that can be gleaned from the situation. 'Action is not sister to the dream', the future seems grim, there is no longer any hope for something grand or beautiful, and you have to live. Once this stage is reached, nothing prevents you from drawing—unevenly, depending on the individual—some benefit, at least some solace, at most some pleasure (sometimes sadistic), from the conditions that have arisen. For the most part, however, the deeper reason for the delay in registering disillusionment is simply the visceral need not to renounce a commitment that has illuminated one's life, given it meaning, and for which many sacrifices have often been made. Hence the reluctance to recognize the most obvious facts, the desperate paralogical guile to which one resorts in an effort to avoid the required conclusions, the passionate and obstinate blindness with which the idea of any change is rejected, the refusal even to examine any document, any argument, that could imperil the delicate balance one has achieved in one's inner being. How many party militants have I known who refused to read an opponent's texts, the expositions of divergent points of view, or even neutral studies, often stating quite flatly that it was a matter of preserving their mental tranquillity! Astonishing behaviour for people who often boast of their contempt for the obscurantism of religious conviction. But the fear of being unable to withstand the shock is often justified. The choice is easily made if one is blessed with a weak will, megalomaniacal pride in refusing to admit error, or great ignorance. For others, after many detours, much backsliding, the time comes when you simply have to bow to the truth.

This moment comes slowly. It is like the moment at which you finally admit that someone you loved does not deserve your love, and it is painful for the same reasons.

I am charged with having waited until 1958 before quitting. But chronology has little to do with the matter. Different people resist the evidence for different lengths of time, and even now others are still awaiting the moment when their innermost being will give up the ghost. But in my case, the attacks come from a single quarter: Jewish nationalists, and more precisely, Zionists. The sin for which they will never forgive me is not so much having written against Zionism in 1953 (others did so and are now praised to the skies by the same people), but having formulated reasonable objections, although framed at the time within the architecture of Stalinist activism, and having maintained the essence of them, which had nothing to do with Stalinism, after my de-Stalinization.

What was the context of my 1953 article? I borrow the portrait from a historian of icy impartiality:

'From 1949 to 1952, the people's democracies underwent two successive waves of purges....The first was directed against "bourgeois nationalism", the second, as in the USSR, against "cosmopolitanism". ...At the end of 1951, another trend could be seen in the purges. ...In the trial which was to lead to the death of Slansky and his collaborators [in Czechoslovakia], there were eleven Jews among the fourteen accused. In this second phase of the purges,...*cosmopolitanism* was the key word on which people were questioned and condemned. ....Parallel to these arrests and trials...the situation in the USSR suddenly grew more tense at the beginning of 1953...On 13 January 1953, *Pravda* announced the arrest of nine doctors accused of crimes similar to those imputed to the accused in former times; they had murdered Zhdanov, prepared the murder of several marshals:...General Shtemenko, etc. ...One of the nine doctors...had been called as an expert in 1938 in the trial of Bukharin and had accused the whole group of the Right of having murdered Gorky and of having prepared the murder of Stalin; he himself was now accused of the crimes of which he had accused those who were on trial, and this transition from the position of accuser to that of accused was a repetition of something which had already been seen many times. But what also characterized the "doctors' plot" was that...seven out of the nine were Jews, and as regards the accused in Eastern Europe, one fact emerged from the charges established against them: they had taken part in a Zionist plot, and had acted at the instigation of the international Jewish organization, the Joint. No sooner was Stalin dead than in March 1953 *Pravda* published the news of the liberation and rehabilitation of the doctors, who had been the victims of a "machination".'[14]

Naturally, clear-sighted people of the time, as well as systematic anti-communists—many of whom had at least gone along with similar affairs, of communist origin or otherwise—immediately understood that all these mythical accusations were fabricated. They exposed the frame-up to the public, itemized the evidence of the deception, and undertook a legitimate campaign to mobilize public opinion against the trials. No less naturally, most Communists adopted the opposite attitude. For them it was not a matter of studying the files on the various defendants, but of defending the Soviet Union and its leader, who was their leader too.

The world over, Communist militants were either fully convinced, or not quite fully convinced, or in some rare cases sceptical. In any event, they needed no instructions from Moscow to know what to think and do. Their leaders in each country, who often knew scarcely any more about the facts than they did and were not overly concerned with them anyway, also required no more than some advice about the details of what they should do.

The Soviet Union had been accused by the coryphaei of 'bourgeois' opinion, left and right. Perhaps it was admitted to the most reliable party members and sympathizers that all was not for the

[14]H. Carrère d'Encausse, *Stalin: Order Through Terror*, trans. by Valence Ionescu, vol. 2 of *A History of the Soviet Union 1917-1953*, London 1981, pp. 180-81.

best everywhere in that great country. Perhaps there were even judicial errors, abuses of power. But in the view of Communist militants, the Soviet Union was nevertheless that part of the earth where a new world was being forged, a world without oppression, exploitation, or internal forces driving towards war. That was why this country was always attacked and slandered by profiteers and exploiters, by the rich, the powerful, the selfish, the warmongers. Attacks in the press and in books were clearly no more than elements in a vast arsenal of aggression, the inevitable outcome of which, once the ground had been carefully prepared, would be direct military attack.

To us, combatants engaged in the struggle to realize the ideal of which the USSR represented the model, our duty was clear: to defend the Soviet Union intellectually in order to aid in its material defence. Since the attack was temporarily being waged at the level of public opinion, a response in kind was required. That was the task for us, men of the pen. Just as our manual comrades were making their contribution to the same battle by pasting up posters and distributing newspapers and leaflets (which we did too out of self-sacrifice and solidarity), by encouraging strikes and carrying out the most humble tasks, so we had to wage our kind of fight, while overcoming our own repulsion, disgust, and shame.

Thus we answered the call of the party cadres who asked us to mobilize to answer the 'anti-Soviet campaign'. We considered ourselves soldiers, and everyone hurried to his post.

How could we do our duty and respond to what could only be slander? Obviously, by employing the classic resources of any apologetic (and of any counsel's plea): to show that the assertions of our friends were just, and, since everyone knows that the best defence is a good offense, to attack our enemies for similar crimes or abuses. It may not testify to the glory of the human spirit, but denunciation of a crime (whether real or not) committed by one party often seems convincing evidence that the opposing party is innocent.

In Paris we had no way of examining the Russian files, of getting to know the ins and outs of the charges against the defendants. Of course, careful and critical study of the official publications about the Czech trial could have enlightened us, but that seemed an inordinate and, above all, wasteful effort, since in any case our party was concerned with much broader issues: indeed nothing less than the future and the good of humanity. What we could do was to demonstrate that the charges were plausible.

This was a fall-back position which I myself had long since adopted, as did many other members of this and other parties. Once you have risen somewhat above the mental level of the innocent who believes everything that comes out of the headquarters of the organization without the shadow of a doubt, what else can you do—apart from take the rational and critical step of studying the files close up, which was beyond the practical means of most people? The only option is to have confidence in the seasoned leaders of the struggle in which one is engaged so long as they give no obvious sign of incompetence or treachery, to persuade oneself that the explanations they offer are at least plausible. My article of 1953 thus began with this sentence, which was meant to be ironic: 'To begin with, as usual, no defendant in these countries [the USSR and the People's Democracies] could possibly be guilty.' The possibility of guilt could not be ruled out, and in my efforts to convince myself during the previous years, I had accumulated a file of genuine political crimes (or that I definitely believed to be genuine) commited by oppositionists 'in these countries'. Who could deny their existence? And if political crimes were possible, why couldn't these be instances of them?[15] And if that was the case, then did it not all

---

[15]The model of the French revolution, obsession of the revolutionaries of 1917 and their rivals alike, played a great part in convincing us. Did not many of the most sincere revolutionaries of 1789 subsequently dissociate themselves from the more consistent (as we saw it) course taken by the revolution after 1792? Did not some of them go over to surrender, indulge in conspiracies with counter-revolutionary elements and even with other countries, enemies of revolutionary France? In some cases, official historiography itself acknowledged this. In others, the historian Albert Mathiez (who happened to be pro-Communist at the time, just at the beginnings of the Russian revolution) had opportunely demonstrated, around 1921, that terror is necessary in a revolutionary country under attack, and that the most determined of the Jacobin leaders really had been targeted by a conspiracy directed from abroad, with the complicity of corrupted revolutionaries. He had shown that Danton, considered a pure glorious revolutionary by Mathiez's predecessors, who believed his guilt unthinkable, had actually been in the pay of both royalty and foreigners. He had contradicted Anatole France, who had accepted 'the legend and portrayed the judges and jurors of the [Revolutionary] Tribunal as either mystical imbeciles killing without reason or servile butchers killing on orders'. There was at least considerable truth, Mathiez pro-

boil down to a matter of confidence? The immense army of profiteers of capitalism, the people they abused, the intellectuals who followed them out of self-interest or because they were themselves duped, all had confidence in their leaders, the governments of the bourgeois states. Well then, we also had the same confidence in our leaders, and above all in our supreme leader, Joseph Stalin. Had he not demonstrated his superiority as wise, expert, and vigilant guide, defeating the enemies of the revolution, turning a backward country in ruins into one of the strongest powers in the world, deceiving and finally winning victory over Hitler, victoriously resisting all plots, whether based on force or perfidy, a man who had been right against all others? Thus we reasoned, thus we deceived ourselves.

The priority, then, was to demonstrate that there was nothing implausible about the plots of the enemy. In an article entitled 'Judéosabotage' and published in the *Observateur* of 15 January 1953, Claude Bourdet had written that 'one can only heave a shrug at the idea of leading physicians conspiring to shorten the lives of patients. ...Doctors, who are trained to save lives at all cost and apply this principle even to the enemy on the field of battle, would have enormous difficulty renouncing their education and training, in any country.' The rare exceptions were 'tainted individuals, failures in their profession', or, in the well-known cases of Nazi doctors who engaged in criminal 'experiments' in the concentration

---

claimed, in the charges of the previously ridiculed Robespierrist tribunals, and he expressly compared Jacobinism and Bolshevism. It was difficult not to follow the analogy through. Those who considered such treachery implausible were bourgeois imbeciles! Why wait another hundred years for a new Mathiez to demonstrate, evidence in hand, the reality of the plots woven against Bolshevik Russia? Why accept a priori that no such plots existed? Like many Communist intellectuals, I made use of Mathiez's published writings against Danton and his consorts, in particular his collection of articles *La Conspiration de l'étranger* (*Études robespierristes*, vol. 2), Paris 1918, and *Robespierre terroriste*, Paris 1921, from p. 140 of which I was quoting above. On the attitude of Mathiez, see J. Godechot, *Un jury pour la Révolution*, Paris 1974, pp. 293–311. In any case, towards 1930, shortly before his death, Mathiez had come to understand the real nature of Stalinism, but we were unaware of this change in his views and made no effort to find out about it. Anyway, it could always be attributed to senility or to a resurgence of his petty-bourgeois upbringing. For a much wider-ranging study of this model of the French revolution, see the book of my old companion in these deviations, François Furet, *Penser la Révolution française*, Paris 1978, and Alice Girard, *La Révolution française, mythes et interprétations, 1789-1970*, Paris 1970.

camps, 'warped and blinkered functionaries acting on the orders of
military commanders'.

A doctor was needed to answer arguments dealing with the
medical profession. An eminent practitioner and Communist militant came forward. He was Dr Louis Le Guillant, a well-known
psychiatrist, head of service at the psychiatric hospital of Villejuif.
In the March 1953 issue of *La Nouvelle Critique* (no. 44), which
opened with the emotional announcement of the death of Stalin (a
stop-press item), Le Guillant attacked Claude Bourdet and
others.[16] He had no trouble demonstrating that 'leading physicians'
in Germany had directed, conceived, and sanctioned criminal 'experiments'. To this excellent argument, he added others, far more
debatable. He pointed out that many doctors, outside Germany,
had 'performed or allowed' experiments on people; he denounced
the advocates of sterilization and birth-control; he stigmatized
plans for bacteriological warfare, which the Communist world
(with the support of some unimpeachable scholars of the Western
world) claimed that the Americans had applied in Korea.

Membership of the opposition was not a guarantee of innocence.
Nor was membership of the medical profession, even at its highest
levels. Nor was membership of the Jewish people, community,
group, collectivity, or whatever term one preferred to use (see
below). Such was our line of defence and attack; its basis was incontestable, its subsequent development foolhardy.

Against the proclamation of the inevitable innocence of the
medical profession, we put up an eminent Communist doctor, well
placed to know his colleagues intimately and to have a less idealized
view of them. It was good policy to call upon Jews to answer the
proclamation of the inevitable innocence of Jews. Several were
found whose discordant subsequent trajectories may perhaps be instructive. Articles were published by Annie Besse, who later
became Annie Kriegel, a virulent anti-communist, Zionist, and pro-
Israeli fanatic; by Francis Crémieux, who has remained faithful to

---

[16]Dr Louis Le Guillant, 'Les Médecins criminels ou la science pervertie', *La Nouvelle
Critique*, no. 44, March 1953, pp. 32–66. Le Guillant was badly traumatized by the
revelation of the error into which he had fallen. On 9 April Claude Bourdet published
an article in the *Observateur*, that, he said, he had considered entitling 'Hang Yourself,
My Good Guillant'.

the party; and by Maxime Rodinson, whom you are now reading, who was expelled from the party five years later, and who is not content merely to acknowledge his errors (which is already more than most anti-communist 'converts' do), but also would like to analyse the mechanism that produced them, and to avoid falling into a similar mechanism, even if in the interest of another 'good cause'.

I must admit that although the article in question was requested of me, I was not displeased by the request. Ever since my return from the Middle East, where I had spent seven years, I had resented with exasperation the predominance among French public opinion of an inaccurate picture of the problems of this region. As a man of the left, I expected no better from the right. But I was indignant to see the left allow itself to be taken in by the same picture, and even to circulate it. Even my own party, the Communist Party, whose principles should have immunized it against such fantasies, sometimes drifted in their direction and scarcely reacted to them, contradicting them but feebly.

Indeed, at the time it was accepted as a series of axioms that Israel was a pole of socialism in the Middle East, that the Jews had an incontestable right to Palestinian land, that they had found it a desert and had made the land blossom for the first time in nearly twenty centuries, that Arab intellectuals, officials, and leaders (the Arab people, irremediable idiots, did not count) opposed Zionism out of a mixture of religious fanaticism and Hitlerite racism. This opposition of theirs was just one more entry on the lamentable list of persecutions of which the people of Israel had always been the victims. An identical inspiration linked Mesha', King of Moab, Antiochus Epiphanes, Apion of Alexandria, John Chrysostom, Tomás de Torquemada, the Mufti al-Hajj Amin al-Husaini, King Farouk, and Gamal Abdel Nasser: unreasoned hatred of the Jews.

Because of this unchallenged common image—even anti-Semites rallied to it, or at least pretended to do so, out of hatred for the revolt of the colonized—it was impossible to publish an article or book, or to make a film, in which the Arabs appeared as at least having some grounds for complaint about Zionist Jews. To emphasize that their grievances were not totally irrational was allegedly to erect obstacles to the necessary entente between (ordinary) Arabs and

Jews. This reconciliation was considered from only one angle: the Arabs had finally to become rational, to understand the grandeur and beauty of the Zionist project, and to rally to it, contribute to it, and support it.

This portrayal of things set my teeth on edge. I am the sort of person who cannot stand to hear a passer-by give someone wrong directions on the street, and I tend to butt in even at the risk of appearing indiscreet. So much the more so when it was a matter of a very serious problem, one that affected me personally in at least three respects: as a Frenchman of Jewish origin, as a member of a party dedicated in principle to an anti-Zionism that it applied badly, and as someone who knew something about the problems of the Middle East because of my studies and my long stay in the region, where I had struck up strong friendships with people of the left.

If memory serves, on several occasions I had proposed that the party publish articles on this subject. I was always rebuffed. Contrary to what some may believe, the party at the time had no desire to take positions on these delicate problems. As always, their eyes were fixed essentially on their French clientele, and the party leaders believed that any position that diverged from the 'vulgate' that held sway among French public opinion could only cost them members, sympathizers, and votes among the Jewish population and beyond. The tiny Communist Parties of the Arab countries did not merit such a sacrifice.

The only thing that could alter this attitude was 'imperative number one', the one that had led the party even to approve the German-Soviet Pact of 1939, at the risk of destroying the party's popularity in France for a long time to come. And that was unconditional support for the Soviet Union. Until then, the Soviet Union had not demanded anything of the kind. (In 1948 the USSR had supported the new state of Israel, and it was the Arab Communist Parties that paid the price. Since then, of course, relations had cooled, but that could always be blamed on the pro-Western policy of the Israeli leaders.)

Moreover, none of us could admit that Soviet anti-Semitism existed. Certain 'prejudices' might still persist among the most backward layers of the population, but the regime was doing all it could to uproot them—which in fact was true until 1939. The Jews condemned from time to time were denounced because of their 'counter-revolutionary' acts and not because of their Jewishness. Nationalist tendencies were repressed among Jews as among others. Beyond all these benevolent interpretations, our image of the Soviet Union—without which we would not have been Communists—could not be reconciled with the idea that a current like anti-Semitism could be fostered or even tolerated by the Soviet leaders. How could such a deviation be possible in a country in which democracy and the most complete freedom prevailed, a land governed scientifically by enlightened minds acting for the good of all and with their assent, building a new type of humanity free of the vulgar passions of the epoch of dog-eat-dog struggle?

Before the charges against the doctors in the Ussr, the trial of Slansky, Rajk, and others in the People's Democracies had touched off a wave of denunciation of this beautiful country of our dreams. The accusation of anti-Semitism was prominent in this attack. The official Communist indictment had cited a Zionist conspiracy. The duty of all Communists throughout the world was to respond, to defend the Ussr, to show, as we were indeed convinced, that there was nothing implausible about the conspiracies that had been denounced, that the Zionists were certainly capable of weaving or inspiring anti-Communist conspiracies. And if they were capable of it, why wouldn't they have done it? Why question information released by the official organs of the Communist state? Since the party was under attack, the time had finally come to deal head on with the thorny question of Israel, Zionism, and the Israeli-Arab conflict, to distinguish clearly between justified anti-Zionism and inadmissible anti-Semitism, of which the Ussr had to be innocent. I was well informed about the Jewish question and the problems of the Middle East, an ardent Communist militant (although without any post in the apparatus) with a minor reputation for erudition (I was not yet at the University, but was a librarian at the Bibliothèque Nationale). It was inevitable that I would be called upon.

La Pensée was a review whose dependence on the Communist Party was barely concealed, edited, under the somewhat distant control of the apparatchik ideologue Georges Cogniot, by the honest and modest René Maublanc, a professor of philosophy who held the unenviable post of secretary of the editorial board. At first, *La Penseé* was content to publish a three-page article by the writer Pol Gaillard, who showed, with the aid of three American quotations, that there was nothing implausible about the confessions of Slansky and the others. A postscript asserted the 'stupidity' of the charge of anti-Semitism hurled against the USSR and the Communist movement.[17] This and subsequent issues devoted far more space to apparently quite untopical articles by Claude Cahen, myself, and others on Avicenna, the great Muslim philosopher and scholar whose millennium it was by the Muslim calendar. But the Soviet ideological leadership had decided to commemorate several thinkers, artists, writers, and scholars of the past each year, most of them from the Third World. This initiative can only be applauded. I began my article on Avicenna with a passionate attack on bourgeois scholars and a quotation from Stalin. Louis Massignon tells me that he was surprised that I considered Stalin a philosopher, but he added that after all he could understand my need for provocation.

In the *Cahiers du communisme*, the theoretical organ of the party meant to supply members with somewhat more reflective ideological materials, Annie Besse (now Annie Kriegel), who then played a leading role in the party's ideological section, produced a heavy attack on the 'typically social-democratic slander that anti-Semitism reigns in the Soviet Union and among Communists..., intoned out loud' by Claude Bourdet. In classic fashion, she explained how 'the key to the correct analysis of the Jewish question and to the discovery of its just solution can only be the class struggle'. Bourgeois Jews were in solidarity with bourgeois non-Jews, just as workers of Jewish origin were in solidarity with 'all the workers of the entire world'. 'Hitler', she wrote, 'refrained from harming the Jews of the big bourgeoisie.... Who will ever forget that Léon Blum, his wife at his side, contemplated from the windows of his villa the smoke from the ovens of the crematoria!' Zionism, employing the thesis of 'Jewish solidarity', which is 'a subjective illusion', had 'a nationalist and racist foundation' and 'has become a mere ideological instrument in the hands of the State Department..., a mask behind which to conceal espionage operations against the Soviet Union.' That was

---

[17]Pol Gaillard, 'A propos des condemnations de Prague', *La Pensée*, no. 46, January-February 1953, pp. 87–89.

'the substance of the Slansky trial' and of the 'conspiracy of the criminal doctors in the Soviet Union'.[18]

La Nouvelle Critique had been founded alongside *La Pensée*, considered too soft and academic, in order to supply a more juvenile, ardent, and militant tone. It was edited and tightly controlled by an ambitious young man of philosophical training, Jean Kanapa, who wanted to mount the rungs of the apparatus (which he subsequently succeeded very well in doing), which does not necessarily rule out genuine conviction. On Zionism and the polemic against the charge of Soviet anti-Semitism, there was, besides the article by Louis Le Guillant cited earlier, a more specifically political piece by Georges Cogniot; and Kanapa got two 'Jews', Francis Crémieux and myself, to contribute two slightly more elaborate articles.[19]

Leaving to authorities in whom I had confidence the task of taking care of the repression of those they declared counter-revolutionaries, I saw all this agitation primarily as an opportunity to put forward my theoretical analyses of Jewish problems. Towards the end of 1952, I had begun drafting a long article tentatively entitled The Jewish Question and Marxism. I probably meant to have it published in *La Nouvelle Critique* or *La Pensée*. In December 1952 René Maublanc had asked me for 'a documented study of Zionism, about which there was so much talk in connection with the Slansky business' (letter of 15 December), to be printed in *La Pensée*.

As often happened, what I had written was too long, too encyc-

---

[18]Annie Besse, 'A propos du sionisme et de l'antisémitisme', *Cahiers du communisme*, February 1953, pp. 241–49.

[19]Georges Cogniot, 'Les communistes et le sionisme', *La Nouvelle Critique*, no. 44, March 1953, pp. 3–9 (an extract will give an idea of the tone: 'The Soviet Union answered Tel Aviv's abominable provocation in the way that was necessary: the Soviet Union picked off the murderers in white coats, the secret agents recruited among the Zionists and Jewish nationalists, exactly as a Polish tribunal picked off..., at the same date, the agents of espionage and diversion garbed in the cassocks of Catholic priests.'); Francis Crémieux, 'Le Sionisme et la question juive', ibid., pp. 10–31 (central idea: 'The campaign about alleged Soviet anti-Semitism is no more than a call to war, to an Atlantic crusade', p. 30). The issue opened with a black border ringing the news of the death of Stalin, announced by Jacques Duclos 'in a voice choked with grief' at the national conference of the French Communist Party in Gennevilliers on 7 March. My article in the preceding issue (see above) opened the series, and was based primarily on the trials in the People's Democracies, with last-minutes additions about the story of the Soviet doctors, which had just broken.

lopaedic, too theoretical, and too detailed to be a good review article, even for *La Pensée*, famous as it was for its rather heavy and
often indigestible content. When it was later typed up, my piece filled
forty-six large pages of about fifty lines each. The way I reconstruct
the course of events from the documents I still have, Kanapa must
have asked me to distil a shorter and more direct text out of the draft
of my article, one more attuned to the polemic then under way. I
must have protested that this would be difficult, especially because
of time pressure. Kanapa then said that he would trim the article
down himself, promising to respect my formulations and to show me
the results before publication. I then gave him my text, in manuscript
form. But my handwriting is quite readable, and can even be sent
directly to typesetters.

The axis of the bulky article I had written consisted in a few broad
ideas which events had afforded me an opportunity to expound: that
Marxist (and therefore scientific) analysis was fundamentally opposed to the Zionist view of Jewish problems; that the Soviet Union had
combatted anti-Semitism; that Zionism and anti-Semitism had in
common an analysis of the Jews as a special alien nation implanted
by misfortune in the midst of other nations, and which should break
from these foreigners and return to its ancient and new-found homeland; that Zionism and the state of Israel are not socialist in
character, do not offer the Jews of the world a magic solution to the
evils besetting them, and would not halt the spread of anti-Semitism.
However regrettable the creation of the state, and however unfairly it
had been formed, Israel was now a fact of life, its Jewish inhabitants
could not be cast into·the sea, and the progressive forces within it,
those exerting pressure for a democratic evolution towards an egalitarian state, had to be supported. On the basis of these theses—the
essence of which I am still convinced of (except for the assessment of
Marxism), since the events of the past twenty-seven years seem to me
to confirm their correctness—I drew the most unfortunate and contestable extrapolations, following one of the most persistent procedures of ideological thought.

Thus, contrary to what I thought and wrote, neither Marxist
analysis nor the Soviet attitude during the first two decades of the
regime's existence necessarily implied the pursuance of an attitude of
energetic struggle against popular anti-Semitism, nor were they a

guarantee against underhanded anti-Semitic measures. Although I still maintain that 'the state of Israel is endowed with no particular virtue just because it is made up of Jews' (p. 37), my description of its enfeoffment to the United States was marred by exaggerated claims. But the inadmissible abuses occurred above all in several slashing and crude formulations and the few phrases alluding to Slansky and the Soviet doctors.

Annie Kriegel recently told André Harris and Alain de Sédouy: 'I wonder... to what extent I have forgotten certain things, because one of my pupils spitefully told me last week that in 1947 I had written an article on "Zionism and Anti-Semitism". You could have knocked me over with a feather, I did not remember any more.'[20] I, however, have never forgotten, and I do not seek to evade my responsibility for what happened then. But I do not consider myself a criminal on that account.

It is true that at the time Annie Besse and the other contributors were hardly interested in the problems of Israel (as she correctly says), nor in those of the Jews. I vaguely recollect that she asked me a question or two on the subject. Like me, they rushed into the fray as militants, principally interested in the central problems of the Communist movement: the situation in Europe, America, Eastern Europe, and especially France.

In no way did I disdain these problems. As was my duty as a Communist, I tried to study them within the framework of the main lines set out by doctrine and the party; I was enthusiastic for the good cause, mobilized to defend the right positions. But for reasons of character, the study of which I leave to those so inclined, I have always had a passion for the non-topical and the theoretical, although I had no desire to ignore the present (as many of my colleagues do), nor could I do so. I was preoccupied with my erudite studies as an orientalist, and I was always passionately interested in the situation in the Arab East, where I had lived for seven years and had so many friends, a situation that held no great interest for the

---

[20]A. Harris and A. de Sédouy, *Juifs et Français*, Paris 1979, p. 145; published in the Livre de Poche collection of Grasset, no. 5348, p. 156. It is probably by mistake that Annie Kriegel speaks of an article in *L'Humanité* and dates it from 1947. But I have no way of checking. In any case, the *Cahiers du communisme* article of 1953 quite obviously fell victim to her forgetfulness as well.

cadres and militants of the party. Beyond my own sphere of interests, and to verify and frame them, I had long sought to erect a sociological theory of the Jewish case from the point of view of historical materialism, which I also sought to define.[21] In this case that theory was connected to the problems of the Middle East. Let me add that my daily work as a librarian in the Bibliothèque Nationale and my family life left me little extra time to extend my inquiries in all directions.

On occasion, I had been upbraided in the party for this penchant for the non-topical. Imbued with party ideology, which on the contrary accorded primacy to immediate action, I considered it a defect, at least if it was exaggerated and exclusive. But I was convinced, with justifications drawn from the lives of the revered masters of the movement, that one had to keep abreast of both aspects. East European affairs afforded me an opportunity to develop some general ideas and analyses that were little represented in the intellectual activity of the party.

That is why my initial text (the draft manuscript of which I still have) was centred on these general analyses. Into it I had also inserted some convinced but relatively cautious phrases about the subjects under ardent debate in 1952–53. They seemed quite inadequate to the editorial boards of the party organs.

As I said, the text I had drafted was called 'The Jewish Question and Marxism'. The title was an accurate reflection of its theoretical ambitions and its slightly encyclopaedic aspiration. After an introduction that ritually related the piece to the topicality of the Slansky trial (the business about the Soviet doctors must not yet have come up when I was writing that first page), the section headings were: From the Hebrew People to the Jewish Religion; Anti-Semitism and Judaism; What Is a Jew?; Zionism; Are Marxists Anti-Semitic?; the USSR and the Jews; The State of Israel and

---

[21] Beginning in 1944, I had given general courses in Marxism to small circles in Beirut every year. I had written down many sections of these courses and had conceived the unbounded ambition of expanding and publishing them as a complete manual, the outline of which I had also presented to Éditions Sociales (the party publishing company). I had already abandoned or indefinitely postponed the completion of this vast and juvenile project. But my reflection on the fundamental theses of what was called historical materialism (which formed one of the draft chapters of my projected book) continued, and is still continuing.

Its Problems; Conclusion.

I thus consigned this long text to the editorial scissors of Jean Kanapa, who was anxious to respond to the 'anti-Soviet campaign' not only with directly political and polemical articles like those of Georges Cogniot, Annie Besse, and Francis Crémieux, but also with a text having at least the appearance of a more fundamental effort, documented and detailed.

Kanapa had the text typeset after deleting all the passages dealing with Jewish history, the history of anti-Semitism, the characteristics of the Jews, the analysis of the position of Marx, and the details on the situation of the Jews in the USSR, in particular a paragraph on anti-Semitism, the existence of which I acknowledged, though I confidently declared that it subsisted only in the form of residues, and called it 'cringing, spiteful, and ineffective'. Then he sent me the galleys for final adjustments. The package was accompanied by his handwritten letter, unfortunately not dated, the essential and significant passages of which ran as follows.

'Dear Comrade,

'Enclosed are your proofs and the manuscript (chopped up, but I have carefully saved the rest, don't worry!). It is necessary:

'—in general, never to use the expression "Jewish question" or "Jewish problem"

'—to do a beginning that, after taking note of the adverse campaign in a few words [my introduction was thus judged inadequate], comes directly to this: "Lenin, like Marx, always denounced anti-Semitism *and also* nationalism in all its forms, Jewish included"...

'—to insist on the fact that Washington and London have made the *state* of Israel a centre of espionage and sabotage. A while back, *L'Huma* [the party newspaper, *L'Humanité*] quoted the confession of a member of the government of the fact that American officers were *officially* kept informed.

'It is absolutely necessary to insist on, and to lead the reader to grasp, the rapprochement between Tito and Israel, as two "state-instruments" in the hands of the USA. That is decisive.

'—to indicate, around galley 11, that the real enemies of the *Jewish workers* of Israel are the same as those of the French workers, the American workers, and the Soviet people; these enemies are *both* the Israeli government *and* the Slanskys *and* the traitor doctors. "Our enemies are the same." This call must be issued—we are very widely read over there.

'Finally, *I must ask you* to get to work *this very night* if necessary, since we are in a real hurry. Your article came on top of everything else (I'm not complaining!); so we must move terribly quickly....All the best.'

The underlinings are Kanapa's. And indeed, I had to make some very rapid adjustments in the press proofs. I tried to take account of Kanapa's directives without modifying my text too much. I drafted a new brief introduction. I do not know which of these additions, adjustments, and corrections were mine, and which came directly from him. I do recall that he still found it insufficiently 'topical', 'political', and 'hard-hitting', and that he added a few lines, words, or phrases more to his liking. Moreover, he 'faithfully' informed me of these, but using a trick common to many editors of reviews, political or otherwise. I could have seen the final version of the text, but to do so I would have had to have gone to the (far-away) printshop within the hour, in view of the exigencies of the printing schedule.

In fact, much later Kanapa admitted his use of this trick, which had become habitual with him. Myriad nuances would be required to analyse the ideologically committed man, Stalinist or otherwise. He has his periods of doubt and introspection, although they are not always long-lasting or cumulative. In 1968, during one of these phases, Kanapa confided to a seminar of the editorial board of *La Nouvelle Critique*—a confidence recorded on tape—that his use of such procedures was systematic. He would 'correct' the articles given to him, introducing modifications of varying subtlety, cuts and additions, 'not for reasons of style, but for reasons of substance, reasons I believed just', and would first confront the author with a *fait accompli* and then make it impossible for him or her to see the text, by erecting practically insurmountable obstacles. He also relied, quite effectively, on the resignation of the militant in the face of what was portrayed as the higher interest of the party, and consequently of the great cause to which the writer was devoted.

In autumn 1978, during one of those recurrent periods in the history of the French Communist Party when some party militants, under the pressure of events, suddenly give vent to thoughts and feelings too long pent-up, Francis Cohen, Kanapa's successor as editor of *La Nouvelle Critique*, revealed these confidences in an obituary of Kanapa.[22] His intention was not to disparage. Cohen himself was only too well aware of the dilemmas faced by a convinced militant entrusted with such responsibilities. But it was the beginning of a denunciation of the system that had placed us all in such situations. To repeat an expression used very often in party documents, 'it is no accident' that the party authorities shut down *La Nouvelle Critique* (and several other journals) shortly afterwards.

I remember shuddering at some of these formulations that had been printed over my by-line. But I could not prevent their publication, and to have protested later—necessarily in a 'bourgeois' periodical—would have damaged the party, the Soviet Union, and the forces struggling (as I then believed) for peace and socialism, and for the future happiness of all humanity.

The ideologically committed person, especially the committed intellectual, is humble. One is always persuaded that one's personal view of things is distorted, partially mistaken, at best one-sided. True, real, and adequate consciousness, one believes, is forged at the level of the collective organism, be it party or church, which combines all the various partial and limited views, subjects them to criticism, and thus distils the deeper truth, with the higher aid of Marxist science (embodied in its supreme leadership) or the Holy Spirit. The entirely correct perception of the limits of the thought of any individual thus leads to the quite false concept of collective infallibility, mystical in the final analysis.

My comparison with the church is not meant to be a polemical device. Some day I hope to return to it in a far more elaborate and detailed form. All organisms of this type face a common set of problems, regardless of the content of their doctrines, the difference in which I do not at all intend to minimize. The best way to under-

---

[22]F. Cohen, 'Jean Kanapa, un homme sans relâche', *La Nouvelle Critique*, no. 117, October 1978, pp. 2–5.

stand the reactions of individuals in a Communist Party is to compare them to those encountered in a religious order, the Jesuits for
example, who also opt for total self-denial in the pursuit of a cause
that stands above them: *ad majorem Dei gloriam.*

In both cases humility is the essential virtue, pride the principal
vice to be feared: I try to think as clearly as I can, and thus to make
my contribution to the intellectual treasury of the organism. But
ultimately, the party knows best, the church knows best. Especially
since the thought of each individual is dulled by original sin and the
insinuations of Satan, or by the weight of bourgeois ideology,
which seeps in through our every pore. For intellectuals it is even
worse, since they have a natural propensity to believe in the pro-
ducts of solitary thought, and to contemplate the extraordinary
presumption of claiming to be right against all others.

Obviously, I must have felt bad about the pages of my exposition
that were deleted from the article in *La Nouvelle Critique.* In a
similar manner, *La Pensée* never printed the article I had been asked for. One way or another, it had been decided to turn the deleted
pages into an article for *La Pensée,* provided some adjustment was
made. This article was entitled 'The Myth of the Jewish Nation and
Reactionary Zionism'. René Maublanc advised me of his receipt of
the manuscript on 9 March 1953 and sent it along to the typesetter.
I still have the proofs. But because of lack of space (taken up in
part by the final instalment of my article on Avicenna), it was postponed to the June issue, and then put off again. It never appeared.
In the meantime Stalin had died, it had been acknowledged that the
doctors were innocent, and an unpredictable evolution was under
way in the land of socialism and its satellites—and also in the hearts
and minds of its bruised admirers.

In any event, sometime earlier I had decided that the time was
ripe to pull all these elements together and to go further, drafting a
basic book that could be called something like The Jewish Question
and Marxism. I could make use of the conjuncture—over which I
had no practical control—to finally get the party publishers to
agree to produce such a book. Remember that until then the party
much preferred that this question not be treated under its imprint.
At the end of January 1953, I therefore presented an outline of this
prospective book to Éditions Sociales. On 27 February the directors

of the company sent me some observations on my fifteen-page 'synopsis'.

It is interesting to quote the letter containing these observations, because it is rather typical of the point of view from which intellectual work was guided in the French Communist Party, as in the rest of the Stalinist universe. The book on this subject now being prepared by Jeannine Verdès-Leroux,[23] after a detailed and scrupulous investigation, will, I believe, shed more light on this outlook and on the methods employed than the many books—hastily written, ill-documented, full of errors of fact, and marked by analytical debility (often the result of an inverted Stalinism)—that have been on the market for some time now.[24]

My outline was considered good, but it was demanded that I follow '*very closely*' (the words were underscored twice) the line indicated in this or that Soviet article; it was necessary to denounce 'all espionage agents: both the Catholic priests in Poland and the Zionist agents in the USSR'; 'stick strictly to the line of the *capital* [underscored twice] text on the question', the article by M. Mitin, 'L'Officine sioniste de l'impérialisme américain' [The Zionist Den of American Imperialism], a translation of which had appeared in the 20 February 1953 issue of *Paix et Démocratie*. I had been wrong to 'falsely give the idea' that anti-Semitism had 'eased since 1918'. 'There had been pogroms' in Liverpool and Glasgow. I had to 'emphasize discrimination in the United States', and I had 'insufficiently stressed' the 'role of Social Democracy'. On the ancient history of the Hebrews, I had to 'take account more clearly of the works of Soviet historians'.[25] Was it 'really useful to dwell on the psychological analysis of anti-Semitism by Sartre'? One section of

---

[23]Since I wanted to analyse the mechanism of my errors and not to conceal them, I opened all my archives and made all the resources of my memory available to her. See note 5 above.

[24]For some exceptions, see note 6 above.

[25]This was a constant concern of our intellectual leaders. Here is another example. In his letter of 9 March acknowledging receipt of my article on Zionism for *La Pensée*, René Maublanc had this to say about my other article, on Avicenna: 'Cogniot asks me to pass this request on to you: he would like to see "more emphasis on Soviet sources." Do you have any precise references on this point? If you cannot indicate any Soviet work known in France, he would like you—and I quote—"to eliminate at least some of your lavish references to Thomist sources, etc."' The honest Maublanc, less ideological and still faithful to the ordinary criteria of more or less scientific publica-

the synopsis on historical evolution was headed, 'The Jews Are No Longer Only a Religion', thus characterizing a phase of this evolution. It was commented: 'Perhaps it might be necessary to explain in detail what may remain of Jewish cultural particularity in other respects.'

I wrote about thirty pages of this book and then abandoned it. I suppose I was somewhat discouraged by the demands of Éditions Sociales. However deranged I was by the ideology of militant commitment, I remember very well that I was exasperated by the restrictions imposed on our thought and research by the intellectual and other cadres of the party, who were often unsympathetic, ignorant, and blinkered. I remember in particular shrugging my shoulders at Cogniot's demand for Soviet references. It was the root of future schisms, but for the time being I submitted, hoping that an *aggiornamento* would not be long in coming. Quite consciously, I imitated the exegetic Catholic scholars who yielded to the edicts of the Papal Bible Commission while awaiting the blessed day when the Pope would finally decide to let them say that the Pentateuch was not the work of Moses. I must also have realized that the party would not long have sponsored such a project, now that the situation no longer demanded that the dangerous Jewish problem be dealt with head on, and it would have been impossible to find a 'bourgeois' publisher. Finally, and possibly most important to me, I had many other projects in the works.

---

tions, immediately added a conciliatory proposal: 'For my part, since I find this bibliography very useful, I hope that you will be able either to cite some titles of Soviet works or to add a note indicating that Soviet works on the subject have not yet appeared in France.' For Maublanc this was mainly a matter of appeasing Cogniot, a party honcho who not only scorned Maublanc as a narrow-minded old professor lumbered with outmoded scruples and lacking in militant vigour—in short, just not with it—but also had no compunction about browbeating him in front of witnesses. That said, however, we all felt that Soviet scholars, at least potentially, had to be superior to us, because they enjoyed the great material possibilities offered by the state in the service of a Marxist outlook that was encouraged, and since they were close to the centre where the guiding theory was being elaborated. In comparison, the few European Marxist scholars were marginal, isolated, put at a disadvantage by all the ambient structures and the entire social milieu, lacking in material resources, and in addition saw their time devoured by the tasks of party militancy. It was only later that Marxism was recognized as a legitimate orientation at least compatible with serious research.

Most of those so totally and blindly committed to the Communist Party at that time have long since quit. Some (like Le Guillant) died in despair, while others took refuge in various other activities, whether selfish or altruistic, abandoning active politics or finding other causes. In general, no one reminds them of their utterances of yesteryear, rather like those septembriseurs of 1792 who remained or became honest shopkeepers and to whom surviving aristocrats came to buy their bread or meat under the Empire and the Restoration. As we have seen, many have themselves forgotten, and many say they have forgotten.

If I, exceptionally, am reminded of my phrases (or of those of Kanapa printed under my signature) of twenty-seven years ago, it is because people now engaged in a similar procedure in the service of other causes have an interest in doing so. They use the same techniques we used to employ in the service of Stalinist Communism. For instance, we readily dredged up the chauvinist declarations that escaped Socialist lips in 1914–18, during the patriotic delirium that had gripped all of France. But what we rebuked Léon Blum for, we refrained from hurling in the face of Marcel Cachin, who had in the meantime become one of the leading lights of the Communist Party, thanks precisely to the grip these 'errors' of the past enabled the Comintern to exercise on the man, as none other than Annie Kriegel has very well demonstrated.

I dare say that those who have merely switched ideological systems while indulging in the same methods have not really drawn the lesson of our errors, even if they now vigorously denounce the theses they once defended. I dare say that in detaching myself from these systems in themselves I am the one who has learned the lessons of this engagement, even though I still maintain that some of the theses I once defended, in part with methods worthy of condemnation, were valid.

The systems to which some of my former comrades and companions have rallied—to varying degrees and alongside many others too young to have gone through our experience—are Zionism and an ideological variety of what I would call monopolar anti-communism. They are different in structure, but are now converging and pointing many minds in the same direction, most often under the impetus of the most laudable motivations. Just as laudable as those that impelled us to devote ourselves to the future good of humanity.

Zionism constitutes an ideological movement very similar to Communism in many respects. The ideal state is no longer the Soviet Union, but Israel. Some are driven to exaggerated formulations by faith in the Jewish religion (revised to adapt itself to political Zionism) or by that mode of reasoning fostered by familiarity with unbridled philosophical speculation. The Zionist philosopher Robert Misrahi, for instance, embarrassing even many Israelis, once said that the state of Israel is a perfect state. He went on to explain— unaware of the connotations of his comparison for Israel's victims —that he meant perfection in the Aristotelian sense: a knife is perfect when it performs its proper knife-function and cuts well. Thus also those non-Jewish philosophers who proclaim that a Jew can do no wrong (it has really been said!). But there are also many who admit that Israel can be rebuked for many things. Likewise, the most subtle of us admitted that the Soviet Union might have its defects.

But these reservations of the less deranged are quickly bracketed. We felt that despite everything, the Soviet state had to be defended by whatever means were necessary, because it represented humanity's only chance to break out of the infernal cycle of oppression, exploitation, and war. The Zionists and those who follow them believe that, despite everything, Israel represents the only chance for the Jewish people to escape the infernal cycle of the hatred of other peoples, persecution, and massacre. Here I will not dwell on the difference between the two ideals, nor on the fact that these arguments are far removed from rational evidence.

Around its central idea, Zionism has created a number of interlinked apparatuses which defend their own existence and have become ends in themselves just like Stalinist apparatuses. By the same means, they seek to mobilize the largest possible number of sympathizers, beckoning them to lean ever further into a vortex that draws them into increasingly unconditional engagement. Once again, the grandeur of the goal, in the eyes of the adherents, renders the means sacred. Likewise, a whole gamut of ideological constructions prescribe action and legitimate it. An entire arsenal of ideological instruments (both apologetic and polemical, for use against opponents) is developed, without much concern for rational or moral scruples, which are of little moment given the enormous stakes.

There are many examples of the dubious manoeuvres of the Zionist apparatuses in their efforts to mobilize opinion in their favour, to win the support of other apparatuses throughout the world, and primarily to assure their supremacy over Jewish apparatuses and public opinion of all colorations. Many volumes and teams of researchers would be required to enumerate them all.[26] Their success has been spectacular, particularly on this last point. Whereas before 1939 the Zionists represented only a small percentage of the Jewish masses, and whereas before 1967 the Jewish masses remained at least lukewarm and relatively passive, the subsequent rallying to Zion has been massive. Those who have not joined in, keep silent. Their estrangement from any sort of Jewish identity is often invoked to demonstrate that their protests are not to be taken into consideration, whereas on the other hand they are included among those over whom the Zionists claim to have influence and jurisdiction, and in whose name they speak, with no mandate whatever. Above all, the religious apparatus of Judaism has been conquered almost entirely. Nevertheless, not so long ago the Zionist movement had no greater enemy than the rabbis, of whatever tendency.

The most effective ideological instrument in this conquest of Jewish and non-Jewish public opinion, and of the various apparatuses as well, has been the identification, repeated *ad infinitum*, of Zionism and Judaism, of Jews and Zionists, and consequently the assimilation of anti-Zionism, and of criticism of Zionism, to the essentialist Judeophobia commonly called anti-Semitism. Many of those who were revolted by massacres and persecution of Jews, and who feel guilty for at least having reacted insufficiently to them, have rallied to this identification. The mechanism of ideological investment in the cult of the 'Maximal Victim' has worked well. It matters

---

[26]An American Jew, notably, has long devoted considerable time and effort to describing and denouncing some of these manoeuvres in the United States. He is Alfred Lilienthal, whose two principal works are *What Price Israel?*, Chicago 1953, and *The Other Side of the Coin*, New York 1965. Similar denunciations have proliferated since then, sometimes ruined by clearly 'anti-Semitic' overtones. Nevertheless, many of the facts reported are true. But the unconditional backers of the other side cry anti-Semitism in any case. Moreover, as they see it, no operation of benefit to Zionism could be contestable. If it is too difficult to justify, its existence is simply denied without further examination.

little to the manipulators that the enemies of Israel are thus encouraged (and other factors have this same effect, too) to translate their anti-Israeli attitudes into anti-Judaism or, once again, into anti-Semitism. Naturally, here as elsewhere, propaganda and ideological apparatuses are not everything, and cannot do everything. I do not at all mean to claim that the Zionist movement was a purely artificial creation, launched by a few individuals with ulterior motives, the way a new brand of soap is put on the market. It was the systematized, ideologized, and organized reprise of spontaneous feelings, both widespread and confused, for which it provided a form and an orientation. Later, during each of its phases of development, the movement continued to be based on such sentiments, to which it afforded an expression and an outlet. The dissatisfactions of the Jews were powerful. In an ideological atmosphere in which nationalism is an extremely widespread value, for many of those who are at least attached in some way to the Jewish identity, or are attached to it by others, the channelling of these identifications towards a Jewish nationalist claim is natural, and attracts greater or lesser numbers of Jews in varying forms depending on the circumstances. Later, solidarity also plays a role. In a world in which national and charitable solidarity are exalted at every turn, people and structures that pride themselves on having the same ethnic-national identity and who have been victims—even often victims, at least individually—easily attain broad support and solidarity. The shame associated with not sustaining one's 'brothers' and 'victims' plays a decisive role.

This is indeed the very same process of identification by which the Communist apparatuses tried, and still try, to assimilate their cause to that of any progress of humanity, to that of the victims of exploitation and capitalist oppression, to the struggle against fascist barbarism, and so on. And once again, the consequence is that any criticism of their programme, initiatives, or methods is stigmatized under the label of 'anti-communist', functionally equivalent to the label of anti-Semitism as applied by the Zionists. Any criticism of Zionism or Communism as the case may be is assimilated to the ideas and acts of Nazism. Was not Nazism the enemy of Communism and of the Jews?[27]

---

[27]Of course, during periods in which anti-Semitism is looked at askance by general

Of course, anti-Communism does exist, and in itself there is nothing reprehensible about it. The number of those now living in capitalist societies who would prefer to live in Communist societies is minute. It is not even very large in the ranks of mass Communist parties like the French, since the reasons for joining relate far more to the desire to struggle for better living conditions on the part of disadvantaged layers, and at most to struggle against the capitalist system, of which these living conditions are seen as the manifestation. Most people are now aware that the Communist system is extremely tyrannical, that the advantages it may achieve—in the best of cases—are not commensurate with the consequences of this tyranny, that its drawbacks, on the contrary, are manifest, and that the prospects for its improvement are dubious at best.

If one has this perception of Communism, then there are good reasons for not joining the organizations that claim allegiance to Communism. And not to be a Communist is, in some sense, to be 'anti-Communist'. A sentiment as diffuse as this, consisting primarily in the rejection of something, does not constitute an ideological movement of the type of Communism, fascism, Zionism, and so on, all of which entail positive options for the realization of a perspective, programme, and structure. It would rather resemble anti-imperialist Third Worldism (which most often denounces only capitalist imperialism), a diffuse sentiment widespread among the masses of the Third World and among those concerned with their suffering.

Nevertheless, within this vast current of rejection of Communism, there are structures of thought and organization that do approximate the models exhibited by Communism and Zionism. In fact, it is rather a question of ideas, of concepts, that correspond to spontaneous tendencies but are then shaped and systematized by certain anti-Communist organizations of struggle and certain ideologues of that struggle. The universal propensity of the ideological mode of thought is to concentrate and extrapolate. In a manner that parallels

public opinion, genuine Judeophobes, 'anti-Semites', disguise their Judeophobia as mere anti-Zionism or anti-Israeli sentiment. Likewise, genuine fascists disguise their opinions as mere criticism of Communism. But this does not change the fact that criticism of Israel, Zionism, or Communism cannot be discredited simply by assimilating it to manifestations of anti-Semitism or fascism respectively.

the individual tendency of paranoia, it sees the enemy everywhere, perceives only perversity in that enemy, and ascribes all setbacks, all vices, and all the defects that afflict the universe to which it belongs to the enemy's diabolical manoeuvres. One of the major fantasies of this type of thought is that of the enemy's unity of purpose. All blows dealt the representatives of Good are seen to be orchestrated by a malevolent centre. To this united front a no less monolithic front must be counterposed. The slightest nuance in support to the front of Good, or in denunciation of the front of Evil, signifies complicity with the latter—at least unconscious complicity, but more probably we have to do with agents, paid or otherwise manipulated by the malefic centre.

Naturally, in each case, some centres of organization and propaganda do exist. But it is rare that they command the universal power, boundless ramification, and omniscience attributed to them by ideological thought. It is unlikely that all the incidents that tend to favour one of the adversaries are wilfully produced by its action. Many events in the world take a course desired by the leaders of the bloc of Communist states and those who follow them. Many actions undertaken by one or another group, or by one or another state, seem (at least) to point in the same direction. Any action taken against the structures of the capitalist world can therefore be interpreted in this way, even though the Communist leaders do not always desire to weaken this or that capitalist partner. But to see the hand of Moscow in actions of this type always and everywhere is a phantasm analogous to Communist and far-leftist myths denouncing, at all times and all places, the occult manoeuvres, the 'plots' (a favourite word in the Middle East) of 'Imperialism' (with a capital *I*), Wall Street, and the CIA. Usually these actions attacking capitalist structures or the world dominated by capitalism have a locally justified basis. Many people may see this and act to support legitimate organizations without adhering to the extreme conceptions of the ideological and organizational centre that has proclaimed itself their defender. It is not at all certain that this action, which partially points in the same direction, will ensure the triumph of the hard core in question, with its oppressive implications, just as it is not true that all those who enter struggles are agents of potential or actual oppressors.

Those who once adhered to the ideology and ideologically centralized organization of Communism and now adhere to the ideology and ideological organizations (less or not at all centralized) of Zionism and of systematic, monopolar anti-Communism have merely changed their banner, altered the content of their system of thought and action. Absolute Good is no longer Moscow Communism but the Jewish state and the struggle against Communism. These two causes, though actually quite distinct, are claimed to be necessarily linked, the connection established through paralogism, phantasm, and delirium, which thereby raise their contingent convergence to the level of myth. All other concerns have to be subordinated to this new absolute. Everything must be interpreted in the light of it. Anything that might impede its forward march is regarded as a diabolical manifestation of the centre of Evil, which has also changed, of course. Now it has become the Kremlin and its occult action. Any revolt, any strike, any incident, any local war that might be to Moscow's advantage must be explained quite simply as a manoeuvre organized by the Kremlin. Any nuance is suspect, any acknowledgement that some of its ideological foundations or initiatives are justified is treason.

In face of these Manichaean visions, the only weapon of the critic, no matter how lately converted, is lucidity, subtle analysis of the facts, conviction that reality is multifarious and contradictory, and recognition that it is always necessary when dealing with ideological representations to sort out the rationally founded elements from the extrapolations, distortions, and unwarranted concatenations.

We all draw our own lessons from those of history's revelations that traumatize entire societies or single individuals. From the trauma of the great massacres, to which I refuse to ascribe the religious term 'holocaust', some have concluded that 'the Jews' are henceforward always justified in any action and idea. My conclusion was primarily that we had to struggle against the return of regimes of that type; this was legitimate enough, but initially marred by the concept that 'regimes of that type' could only be fascist ones spawned in the compost of liberal capitalism. From the revelation of the horrors of the Stalinist period and of Stalinism's ideological extremism, some have concluded that any criticism of liberal capitalist society, any rebellion against the structures it fosters (at least), in one's own country and throughout the world, has to be regarded as a dangerous manoeuvre by the Kremlin and nothing more. When those 'some' were Jews (or enthusiasts of the Jewish cause), they appended to this credo the notion that the state of Israel and the Zionist movement are impeccable by nature and that any criticism or action directed against them or their policy is illegitimate and maleficent in essence.

You do not have to be a Communist or a Communist sympathizer to understand the futility of these latter conceptions. When I was in the Communist Party I sought—using arguments that were extravagant in part but also valid in part (in large part, in my opinion), seasoned with a few little phrases about the deplorable news of the day (the sauce completed by Kanapa) that were meant to discharge my duty as a militant—to demonstrate two major ideas.

1. Zionism is not the inevitable, fatal corollary of the continued existence of a Jewish identity. It is only one option, and merits criticism, first of all because in general it presents a nationalist project and ideology as the sole solution to the problems of the Jews, heaps anathema upon any other project, ideology, or option, whether individual or collective, declares them sacrilege, and combats them in word and deed with an ardour that easily drifts towards fanaticism. But it merits far more severe criticism because of its claim upon an Arab territory that could be Judaized (or re-Judaized if you prefer, it changes nothing) only through the subordination and expulsion of the indigenous populace.

2. The state of Israel is not an ideal state; it is not a socialist state in any sense of the word, whatever the international left may have thought at that time (islands of collectivism do not make a socialist state); its internal policy has always—perforce—entailed the subordination of those Arabs not evicted from the territory; the—inevitable—hostility of the Arab states and peoples has impelled it fatally towards frequently deplorable foreign-policy options;[28] these options, supported by many non-Israeli Jews for reasons of

---

[28] At the risk of getting myself denounced once more by Arab extremists as a crypto-Zionist (and therefore especially dangerous), which has already happened not infrequently, I must mention that in my article of 1953 I firmly endorsed the opinion of the Communist movement that the state of Israel was legitimate (within the borders set by

'solidarity', have in turn driven the latter into inevitable dead-ends, often with respect to the state in which they were living, their homeland, or with respect to the political or social movements to which they adhered.

I continue to maintain these two essential ideas. I do not see how they are necessarily linked to adherence to Communism. The Communist movement has adopted them, but so have many non-Communists. In fact, they fall within the compass of liberal, progressive, leftist, and in general internationalist thought, supported in principle by many Jews. In continuing to uphold them, I am simply following the thread of this thought, more consistently than many who apply this sort of orientation everywhere except when it comes to Jewish questions. I defended these theses as a Communist; as a non-Communist, I still uphold them. The Communist Parties, as is customary for them, argued for them while deducing extravagant, false, deplorable, and sometimes criminal corollaries from them. Thus did many Christians once conclude from the Incarnation that heretics ought to be burned at the stake. In itself, this neither confirms nor refutes the Incarnation, and their present-day descendants have preserved their faith in it while condemning the outrages of their ancestors. Thus—a closer comparison—Christians, Muslims, and Jews have absorbed into their faith the idea that one ought not to kill one's neighbour; they have been able to shed their belief in the dogmas of their former religion without renouncing this idea and moral duty on that account.

This self-criticism is therefore both genuine and profound. I have renounced the systems of thought that channel an existential engagement into subordination to ideological constructions, programmes

the United Nations in 1947). For example (p. 47): 'Must any Israeli or Zionist thus be treated as an agent of imperialism, as a traitor to the cause of progress? Should holy war be preached against Israel, or the expulsion of this alien body from Asian land demanded? Stupidities. ...The Zionist leaders must not be confused...with the Israeli-Jewish masses still deceived by their propaganda. Nor must it be forgotten that while we condemn the manner in which this state was created, the state of Israel is now a fact, a million and a half Jews live there, and there can be no question of casting them into the sea.' I have confirmed that these lines were indeed my own. Except that my 'not at all' was changed to 'stupidities'. This was most probably due to Kanapa, who was anxious to make the text as lively as possible.

of action, and the initiatives of a central organization. I have likewise renounced similar sorts of ideological constructions that invent guiding myths and then subject reality to them by means of unwarranted extrapolation and concatenation. In short, I have renounced, in my personal case, the narrow subordination of efforts at lucidity to the exigencies of mobilization, even for just causes.

But this self-criticism is also limited and partial. I was wrong to mobilize for a system that proclaimed itself the sole road to a just cause, when in fact this cause can be approached (if at all) only by very different means. But I do not think I was wrong to be attracted by this cause in itself. I do not think I was wrong to adopt as guidelines principles of sociological analysis that were justified (albeit integrated into a system that was far less justified), and modes of apprehension of reality that are legitimate, even though I was wrong to allow myself to drift into the unwarranted consequences deduced from them by the ideology and organization in question. I have now dedicated myself to the elucidation of the mechanisms that pull in that direction, and in doing this I benefit from the inestimable experience of my own errors.

I do not regret not having chosen the path of smug apology for the social system under which I lived, and of its practical consequences and the ideas it inspires. Nor do I regret my indignation and rebellion against them. I do not accept the pharisaic condemnations of those who have been led by acceptance or resignation to complicity with the pernicious consequences, the crimes, of the existing system. I accept only the lessons of those who have proven themselves more clear-sighted by better directing their indignation and rebellion.

Since this book is centred on Jewish problems, let me add that I do not regret not having closed my eyes, because of my Jewish origin, to the errors, faults, and sometimes crimes of certain Jews, groups of Jews, and Jewish institutions. I do not regret never having accepted the repugnant and insalubrious idea that these individuals, groups, and institutions are incapable of error, fault or crime. I do not regret always having combatted that idea, albeit under a sullied banner. I do not accept the pharisaic condemnations of its advocates, whose silence, and sometimes enthusiastic approval, has shrouded the errors, faults, and crimes of Jewish nationalists just because they were Jewish. I do not consider myself a criminal for not having wallowed in the muddy pools of Jewish chauvinism, whether moderate or extremist, nor for having rejected and denounced the narcissistic cult of my supposed collective identity, while never neglecting also to criticize analogous instances of narcissism, including that of the Arabs (which is quite pronounced). I am proud that I never participated in the nauseating litany of insanities intoned these days more than ever about 'the Jews', about some abstract Jew who has never existed, composed with the aid of the most sophisticated systems of thought (the defects of which are in any case revealed by their utilization for this purpose). The defence of groups and individuals massacred in the past and threatened in the present can never offer the slightest justification for a rash of absurdities that can only be classed among the many varieties of human phantasms, in the category of racism and ethnism when they come from Jews, and of delirious ideological concoctions requiring more subtle specification when they come from others. I am particularly honoured that my knowledge of the Middle East has enabled me to open the eyes of many (among them some Israeli dissidents whose thanks I have received) to the mistakes, lies, errors, and impasses to which Zionist ideology has led and is still leading.

Least of all do I regret my attitude at a time when the blind alleys of Zionism are becoming more evident day by day, when hundreds of thousands of Israeli Jews are leaving Israel, when this country, groaning under the weight of its immense military spending, without which it could not maintain itself, is heading towards tragic economic bankruptcy, when its almost complete diplomatic isolation allows it recourse only to fragile American support, with all the consequences this entails. Zionism has succeeded in attracting only a small proportion of the world's Jews to Palestinian land, despite the many verbal professions of support to Zionism and even struggles in its favour by many Jews who nevertheless obstinately persist in living in New York, London, Paris, and even Berlin, tacitly voting with their feet and thus giving the lie to their vocal, and even physical, outbursts. Contrary to what many Zionists predicted, Zionism has not had the effect of preventing anti-Semitism from flourishing in a number of countries, and has even spread Judeophobia into regions where it did not exist, or nearly did not exist. I frankly fail to see why this impressive balance-sheet should induce me to repent in this year

1980.

More broadly, I am willing to accept criticism, but not ethical condemnation, from those—more clear-sighted in many respects, more pessimistic about the possibilities of radically improving social relations among people—who have never contemplated sacrificing a bit of their material and moral comfort, ambitions, or vanities to some human goal larger than themselves. All of us accursed Stalinists tried, at least for a while, to set these things aside. Those of us who were intellectuals sacrificed at least some possibilites of advantages in prestige, honour, and money; we accepted work that retarded or prevented the advance of our studies (not to mention those who sacrificed even their lives); we swallowed many an insult from our leaders, all, or so we believed, in order to make our modest contribution to the future good fortune of humanity. Let those who were right but who were never even tempted by the self-denial of commitment keep silent before the thousands of fighters who died crying—wrongly, of course—'Long live Stalin!'. Quite apart from the sadistic tyrant whose name they invoked before the firing squads of the fascist armies, they thought they were striving for an ideal that was itself full of purity and greatness.

'Pay heed, Philippe, you who thought of the good of humanity', says Lorenzo de Medici to Filippo Strozzi in Alfred de Musset's *Lorenzaccio*. 'There are many demons, Philippe; the one that tempts you now is not the least frightful of all....Beware; it is a demon far more beautiful than Gabriel: liberty, fatherland, the happiness of the people, all these words resound at his approach like the chords of a lyre; it is the sound of the silver scales of his dazzling wings. The tears of his eyes nurture the earth, and he holds in his hand the palm of martyrs.' We who paid heed to this demon must blush at our naïveté and at having been unable to gauge accurately the point at which we crossed the threshold into the realm of tyranny. But we have no reason to be ashamed of having been lured by that song, which awakened all that was best in us.

Now, when others younger than us, at first full of joy and then of pain, are also taking that road that left us flayed, we have finally come to know Soviet Stalinism in all its perversion. But it is not unique. Russia provides a paradigmatic instance of a phenomenon that is indeed present in all revolutions, but also in all forms of reaction and conservatism. We can clearly perceive the abyss into which leftist movements can so easily plunge when they come to power, and sometimes even when they do not. But the self-proclaimed or shame-faced conservatives, proud of their clean hands, ought not to believe, as they so often do these days, sometimes even with 'left ideas', that the Stalinists who must be fought consist only of those now germinating or in full bloom in the Third World (particularly in the Muslim world), the post-Stalinist Stalinisms (if I may use the term) of the Communist world, and the micro-Stalinisms germinating among the far-left groups.

Not everything can be indifferently mixed together, as is done so often in the ambit of far-left thought. The situation of inferiority, narrow dependence, more or less accentuated poverty, and permanent consignment to unrewarding jobs not freely chosen, which are now suffered by many social layers in the developed societies, constitute neither Nazism nor Stalinism, even taking account of the more or less repressive institutional sanctions. Even the toughest factory is not an extermination camp, nor even a 'strict regime' labour camp, in which any guard who feels the urge can kill with impunity. At the very least, the possibility of open protest against the injustices one suffers is a precious guarantee that cannot be disdained. The effects of its elimination abundantly demonstrated this to slightly older generations.

It is nevertheless quite true that we cannot lull ourselves in complacent good conscience and joy at belonging to a 'free world' this side of Stalinism and fascism. This quietude is obtained, at least in part, by the export of constraints and poverty, and by the development of multiple 'creeping Stalinisms' within our societies. Conservatives ought not to forget that their choices, in the struggle against what is now called destabilization, led people like them, not so long ago, to at least complacency in the face of the horrors of Mussolini's fascism and Hitlerite Nazism, not to mention all the South American regimes of this type. This is just what we were aware of, even with all our deviations, and it remains our merit and honour to have mobilized to do something about it.

That despite such intentions we erred so deplorably should be a lesson to us all. There is no guarantee against the traps of self-satisfaction and collective narcissism, nor against the ideological delirium and moral lapses to which even the most admirable of commitments can lead.

So? There is no better conclusion than the one drawn by a Czech Communist of pure heart, Julius Fucik, who throughout his short life waged a struggle full of courage and illusions, inspired by ideas for which he suffered torture and death at the hands of the Gestapo and the executioners of the Third Reich. Had he lived, I have no doubt that he would have applied to these ideas themselves this slogan, which he bequeathed to us all: 'People, be vigilant!'

3
From the Jewish Nation to the Jewish Problem

This text was written as a preface for a new edition of La Conception matérialiste de la question juive, *the book written by the Belgian Trotskyist Abram Léon and published in Paris in 1968 by Études et Documentation internationales (EDI). Léon, who died in Auschwitz in 1944 at the age of twenty-six, had abandoned his earlier Marxist-leaning Zionism for Trotskyism. He drafted this work between 1940 and 1942, under the atrocious conditions of occupied Belgium, in the midst of the terrible difficulties of his clandestine militant activity in the resistance. His primary intention in it was to demonstrate that the entity constituted by the set of all Jews had not been preserved through history for religious reasons, nor as the result of some national will to live, but because of the specialization of the Jews in certain professions, particularly in credit. One can only admire Abram Léon's ability, in the circumstances in which he lived, to collect such extensive documentation on Jewish history, to build his theoretical 'model' on the basis of it, and to produce a historical portrait corresponding to it. Nevertheless, he had no historical training, and he did not know the sources first hand. His argumentation suffers from this, and from the schematism so often inseparable from youthful political activism. His book was first published in 1946, probably from manuscript notebooks, by a Trotskyist group in Paris (Éditions Pionniers, Collection marxiste), with a preface and postface by E. Germain (then a pseudonym of Ernest Mandel).*

This posthumous edition was marred by many typographical errors, mistakes, and bibliographical inaccuracies. In 1968 I worked on correcting these errors and rectifying these inadequacies for the EDI. I was also asked to contribute a preface, which I expanded into the long study printed below. As will be clear, I tried, without renouncing a Marxist orientation and an anti-nationalist point of view, to introduce some nuances into Abram Léon's too-schematic views, and to propose other explanations. Naturally, I made use of recent documentation to which the author could not have had access.

The second edition of the work duly appeared, including my introduction, the 1946 preface by E. Germain, a 1937 interview with Trotsky, and the text of an address on the Jewish question in the USSR given by Isaac Deutscher at a conference in 1964. The volume has since been reprinted frequently.

My preface was also published in the review L'Homme et la Société *(no. 9, July-September 1968, pp. 141-183), in the form of an article. For this printing I have made only minimal corrections and additions.*

*[An English translation of Léon's book—*The Jewish Question: A Marxist Interpretation—*was published by Pathfinder Press, New York, in 1970. It does not contain Rodinson's introduction—Translator's note.]*

The republication of Abram Léon's long out-of-print and virtually unavailable book is a political act, an important contribution to a nearly deserted 'ideological front', an instance of serious sociological reflection about a problem in which mythopoeic ideological delirium has long had free rein. For all these reasons, the publishers deserve full credit for affording the public access to such a remarkable and enriching work once again.

An abandoned ideological front? There is no doubt about it, and if this expression, so employed for dubious purposes, has any validity whatever, it is in this case. Indeed, the works on sale in bookshops which fall within the ideological and scientific current of which Léon was part can easily be counted on the fingers of one hand, even if that current is construed very broadly. One does not have to share Léon's political positions—especially twenty years on—to pay homage nonetheless to the clear-sightedness and courage they evince. On the other hand, I do not much like the equivocal term 'materialist', which Marx never used to designate his position in the realm of socio-historical analysis. But the history of the past century and a half of ideological semantics has provided us (to my knowledge) with no better one by which to designate that which stands opposed to historical idealism. I would even prefer the term 'Marxist', but here it would immediately be necessary to exclude about twenty different varieties of mythpoeic Marxism. Whatever word is used, the important thing is to understand what it means. One may well decline to accept all the aspects of Léon's ideological orientation. But nevertheless, all those who would strive to consider the structure and development of the Jewish question otherwise than by resorting to the myths of idealist nationalism can agree with him on his essential message.

Let us try to define this common position, which is situated in a line of descent from Marx, with a bit more precision. If the 'Jewish problem' has been a privileged terrain for ideological delirium, it may also afford us a similar opportunity for delimiting, here more clearly than elsewhere, what this 'materialist' position consists of and what defines that of its opponents.

The existence of most of the ethnic groups, peoples, and nations with which historians deal is circumscribed, usually over many centuries, by specific factors that are lasting, stable, and even permanent: community of territory, language, history, culture, and so on. Even the most idealist of theorists cannot ignore this solid material base, which at least imposes limits on idealist theorization.

The category of Jews, on the contrary, has for millennia been defined by constantly varying criteria. For the greater part of this historical span, the concrete base just mentioned has been lacking. It can be denied—correctly in my view—that the Jews have possessed the quality of an ethnic group, people,[1] or nation in the full sense of these terms for the past two thousand years. What is more, the category in question can be defined in various ways, from within and without. Ardent and arcane discussions have raged among the Jews, their enemies, and their friends alike to determine 'who is Jewish?',

---

[1] I would be less categorical about this today, and in fact am more nuanced even in the rest of this article (see below, pp. 99 ff.). We are dealing here with a highly complex reality, and words are often ambiguous. But obviously, the Jews of the Diaspora (dispersion), after the fall of the Palestinian centre and before the Emancipation in Eastern Europe, formed a people or ethnic group of a very exceptional type, even if we insist on adopting these designations. That is why I said 'in the full sense of these terms'.

usually without any clear conclusion being reached.

This ambiguity has left a particularly favourable field for idealist theories. Obviously, any theory that postulates the existence of a Jewish people as a necessity or a norm may be called idealist. Since no one envisages, for example, the radical destruction of the objective bases of the French people (common language, history, culture, territory, and so on), no matter how difficult it may be to delimit them, no one would dream of completely detaching the existence of this people from its material base and consider it instead a transcendent necessity or a pure categorical imperative. Since the concrete bases of a Jewish entity have on the contrary varied through the ages, and since on several occasions they have been almost entirely lacking, this entity having come close to dissolution several times, the idea that its perpetuation is a necessity can be deduced only as an a priori exercise of the will of hypostatized history, or as a moral obligation capable of being imposed, if necessary, against contrary circumstances.

The shifting character of the objectively existing Jewish entity at various epochs normally leads, once the necessity of its perpetuation through history is postulated, to the search for some substratum common to these diverse forms of its existence, a substratum devoid of the objective bases listed above. And that means, in other words, to attribute an essence to it. Since this essence is ascribed a necessary character, refusal to subject it to the ordinary laws of history normally follows. Thus arise the various conceptions of Jewish history that may be called teleological nationalist. One of the ends of history is supposedly to preserve the existence of the Jewish people in spite of all historical laws, if such trangression be required to assure this end.

This notion crops up even in the conception of the author most inclined to take the entire set of objective factors into consideration, the erudite and unfortunate Simon Dubnov.[2] He correctly criticizes

---

[2] I am referring here to the introduction to his *Weltgeschichte des jüdischen Volkes* (Berlin 1925–29, 10 vols.), in which he distils both his own ideas and his critique of those of his predecessors. I have used the English translation of this text: S. Dubnov, *History of the Jews, From the Beginning to Early Christianity*, trans. from the 4th Russian edn. by Moshe Spiegel, revised edn. vols. 1 and 2, South Brunswick, N.J. and London 1967.

both the 'theological' and 'spiritualistic' conceptions, the latter for reducing Jewish history to persecution and the striving for intellectual creativity. With good reason, Dubnov maintains that 'the Jewish people in all times and in all countries has had a history of its own, not only spiritually, but socially as well'. This fruitful point of view leads him to uncover interesting insights and to reject those theses based on a pure idealism that has been abandoned by the development of historiography in other domains. For example, in the 'sects' of Judaism during the Hellenistic and Roman epochs (Pharisees, Sadducees, Essenians, and so on), he sees not so much groupings crystallized around theological schisms as political-religious parties upholding divergent options on political and social problems, these divergences *also* being expressed ideologically in conflicting theological theses. This is a point of view adopted by historians in other domains, the generalization of which in Jewish studies has been prevented by ideology on the one hand and by the 'provincialism' of extra-European studies on the other.[3]

But despite all his merits—and even though he assures us that he does not mean 'to evaluate historical events in a nationalist spirit', arguing that it seems to him possible to recognize the Jewish people as the creator of its own destiny while lamenting 'those moments when cultural insulation was increased, frequently out of necessity, for the sake of self-defence, to sorry extremes'—Dubnov falls back into idealism with his conception of the 'Jewish nation' as a 'living organism' subject to the laws of evolution. He maintains that during 'the periods both of its own statehood and of the Diaspora, the history of Jewry is a vivid expression of nationalism, not merely of a religious group among other nations.' This nationalist organicism soon plunges him into many a distortion similar to those his sociological approach had helped him to avoid.

It is most assuredly a great advance to hold that the Jewish people in Antiquity, whether independent, 'protected', or dispersed, did not live solely by contemplating the monotheistic idea; and that the

---

[3]Compare the rather confused discussion of Marcel Simon, *Les Sectes juives au temps de Jésus*, Paris 1960, pp. 5 ff. On the lag in the development of oriental studies, see Claude Cahen, 'L'Histoire économique et sociale de l'Orient musulman médiéval', *Studia Islamica*, Paris, no. 3, 1955, pp. 93–115.

Jewish communities of the medieval or modern diaspora were neither purely subjects of intellectual life nor purely objects of persecution.[4] Equally assuredly, we must acknowledge, with Dubnov, that these various entities manifested the general tendency of social groups to preserve their own existence over time, and also, let us add, to defend their interests and aspirations, to defend or extend whatever advantages they enjoyed. But this applies to the groupings themselves, and not to some mythical organism that allegedly welds them into a continuous trans-historical entity. If the historical continuity of these various formations is obvious, if some of them arise out of the remnants of others that wither and die, it does not follow that their perpetuation is necessary—or, to put it another way, that these entities are but manifestations, incarnations, of a trans-historical reality, the 'eternal Jewish people' seeking to assert itself in different forms down through the centuries, and driven, like living organisms, by an intrinsic need to grow and mature (and perhaps die?). As Salo W. Baron, another great historian who viewed the Jews synthetically, clearly understood, the positivist Dubnov thereby ranges himself with the idealist historians he is criticizing. The primacy that he, like Ahad Ha-am, another positivist, ascribes to this internal factor—this 'sort of autonomous national will that is said to have been the motor force shaping the destinies of the people, and which, in the supreme interest of national self-preservation, is said to have accomplished the necessary efforts of adaptation required in the various regions and epochs'—turns his doctrine into a mere variant of the humanist conception of Jewish historians of the nineteenth century. In this conception (held by Graetz, for instance), the 'spirit of Judaism' takes the place of God as the decisive factor, and Jewish history is said to consist in 'the gradual progression of the national or religious Jewish spirit in its various vicissitudes and varied adjustments to various milieux'.[5]

But S.W. Baron, so lucid about Dubnov, also falls into nationalist idealism himself. His 'socio-religious' approach, in which religion

---

[4]Although in practice Dubnov did not go far beyond this stage, as we are told by his successor in the synthesis of Jewish history, Salo W. Baron, 'Emphases in Jewish History', *Jewish Social Studies*, New York, vol. 1, no. 1, January 1939, pp. 15–38; see p. 28.
[5]S.W. Baron, 'Emphases', pp. 26 ff.

occupies an exceptional place among social factors only because of the exceptional situation of the Jews in the diaspora, also represents a great advance. No one can deny that religious ideology did play an exceptional role in the scattered communities, among which it was the principal bond. But the search for a unifying factor in Jewish history also leads S.W. Baron to postulate the necessity of the con-catenation of successive incarnations of Judaism, and to seek its secret in the particular character of the Jewish religion—a historical religion according to his definition.[6] Consequently, it is not just that Jewish religion is thrown into relief, which would be legitimate, but it is postulated as an independent factor, detached from the real life of the communities and the Jewish national formations to which Baron nevertheless accords such close attention.

All these interpretations of Jewish history, idealist to varying degrees, are ideological. By that I mean that they are inspired by the desire to demonstrate (or at least to suggest) what they postulate, and that what they postulate corresponds to exigencies that are not scien-tific but instead pragmatic and vital for the consciousness of an in-dividual or a group. We then have people or groups who *need* to found their existence on the notion of the necessary permanence of Jewry as a community, whether religious or temporal. In either case, it seems to me, socio-historical vision is distorted. But from a strictly ideological point of view, concepts of this type can very well corres-pond to several different ideologies. It may be a simultaneously religious and nationalist ideology, in which the universal God is specially concerned with the survival of the chosen people (a concept already criticized by the pagans Celsus and Julian 'the Apostate'), or it may be a secular nationalist ideology that recognizes the Jewish nation as the sole supreme value. There may also be universalist ideologies, religious or secular. In a religious outlook, the election of Israel can be strictly subordinated to a divine plan directed for the good of humanity. In the corresponding secular ver-sion, although idolatry of the ethnic group is eschewed, the idea that the strictly Jewish entity could be dissolved in any form is repu-diated. One is then drawn to seek and to define a substratum of per-

---

[6]See in particular the first chapter of the second edition of his great work, *A Social and Religious History of the Jews*, New York 1952, vol. 1.

manent values bound up with the existence of the various Jewish entities of the past, and to proclaim, for the past and the future alike, the necessity of this bond between a given collection of values and a minimum Jewish grouping. It then supposedly follows that humanity as a whole has an interest in the perpetuation of this Jewish grouping, so that the worship of these values may also be maintained.

However severe one may be with idealist and religious socio-historic reconstructions, it is obvious that clear distinctions must be made among the various ideologies with which they are associated. No universalist 'materialist' can view with an identical regard religious or secular nationalist ideologies on the one hand and those that ascribe primacy to the service of humanity on the other.[7]

As against these idealist views of Jewish history there stand the conceptions which Marxist tradition, along with Léon, calls 'materialist'. Before examining whether this appellation is justified in all respects, let us first try to define their basic inspiration.

As far as socio-historical study is concerned, those who adopt these concepts begin with a basic methodological stance. They are unwilling to accord any scientific privileges to the various Jewish entities of the past and present. The Jews have indeed constituted specific groups and categories, perhaps even exceptional ones in the sense that a set of laws and conjunctures gave rise to types of formations and evolution not encountered elsewhere. But they are not exceptional in the sense that the general laws that govern the history of human groups do not apply to them.

Methodologically, then, we must refrain from postulating the action of any historical dynamic that is not founded on some substratum of forces the operation of which can be analysed as a function of factors that are also at work elsewhere, throughout the history of human societies.

Now, here as elsewhere—and this is another methodological premiss, that of Marxist sociology, derived from generalizations about historical experience as well as reflexive deductions—no substratum of empirical forces can be discovered to account for the action of any 'spirit', or immutable 'essence' characteristic of a people

---

[7]Although the willingness of certain of their adherents to accommodate nationalist propensities (often unconsciously) can sometimes be disquieting.

or civilization regardless of the situations in which they find themselves. There is no such thing as an independent 'Western spirit' or 'Chinese spirit', although a set of relatively constant empirical factors may at least bring about some degree of permanence of the ideal phenomena that accompany them. In the case of the Jewish entities down through history, however, far fewer consistent empirical factors can be detected. It is therefore hard to see what substratum of empirical forces could be the basis of any so-called spirit of Judaism identical over time, independent of differences in period, locale, and social structure, acting similarly on the various groups of Jews of very different nature. The influence of the Jewish religion on the destiny of the Jews is certain, of course. But the Jewish religion, like others, has changed in the course of time, often expressing different content in identical formulations, as S.W. Baron himself has shown.[8] It is also true, of course, that certain characteristics have indeed remained unchanged through history. But it is incumbent upon those who affirm that this is so to demonstrate it, and also to uncover the effects of these characteristics, as well as their scope and mechanism. It does not seem to me that they have shown that certain unvarying features of the Jewish religion (which is the only constant element of Jewish history)—whether its historic character or something else—have been able to produce a tendency to conserve Jewish existence in extremely diversified forms, to replace one formation with another ceaselessly through their effect alone. Still less can we consider this the result of a 'spirit of Judaism' situated somewhere between heaven and earth, acting through unknown and intangible mechanisms, and escaping any serious influence of the usual factors of human history.

Marx's statement that Judaism survived not despite history but through it[9] is not a mystical or philosophical axiom of untestable origin. It is simply a methodological requisite of any scientific history. Jewish history must be explained by the usual historical factors, as even religious minds can admit if they accept the idea, asserted for millennia by the great universalist religions, that God

---

[8]For example, in the article cited above, 'Emphases in Jewish History', pp. 31 ff.
[9]'On the Jewish Question', in Karl Marx, *Early Writings*, trans. by Rodney Livingstone and Gregor Benton, Harmondsworth 1975.

acts through secondary causes. However that may be, even though here as elsewhere complete explanations can be expected only asymptotically, through the permanent, continuous, and cooperative efforts of historians and sociologists, and although one cannot hope to do more than narrow the margins of uncertainties and illuminate obscure areas little by little, at least it can be affirmed that there is nothing in Jewish history that imperiously compels recourse to the effects of any mystical forces standing outside the usual mechanisms of the social history of humanity.

Thus, neither reality, nor the concrete life of Jewish groups, nor the psychologies of individual Jews can be explained as the translation into the real world of uncaused ideal phenomena. Granted, these ideal phenomena exist, and they are not at all epiphenomena. They have had extremely important effects. But in no way can they be considered to lack causes, to be unaffected by reality, and therefore immutable. They can always be analysed, and their dynamic interpreted as a consequence of their past, their state at an earlier phase, on the one hand and of the particular current situation of the group that is their living support on the other.

The study of the socio-historic mechanisms that have acted on Jewish history, when conducted along this non-idealistic line, does not necessarily entail a vulgar conception of Marxism that postulates economic factors as the sole significant ones, as Léon, it seems to me, sometimes has a tendency to believe, and as the term 'materialism' might suggest (and has in fact suggested) to many. The concrete situations I have just now mentioned are not defined in exclusively economic terms, nor can they be reduced to economic conditions. To begin with, it would be appropriate to define just what is meant by 'economic'. This term is sometimes given an excessively narrow definition that would justify the criticism often levelled against the approach in question. Nonetheless, Marx never meant to preach an exclusive economism. Economic activity, in the broad sense, has its role to play in the dynamic of history—and a very important role it most certainly is. Marx defined and emphasized this role, habitually neglected in his time, no more.

There was in Antiquity a Jewish group of a national type, characterized, among other features, by a national religion, as was the rule at the time. The Hebrew, and subsequently the Jewish, nation[10] conformed to the normal tendencies of national groupings in the social, economic, political, and cultural conditions of the time. Naturally, it also had particular features of its own. The evolution of its religion as a function of the history of the nation lent this ideology a unique character. The Hebrew and Jewish prophetic tradition, a phenomenon that was common at the time, went through a very specific evolution, and the victory of the Jewish nation over neighbouring nations both afforded that tradition free rein and assured the preservation of the documents in which it was expressed.[11] The national god Yahveh finally came to be conceived as the god of the universe, the one god excluding the very existence of the other national gods.

The intense Jewish emigration of Antiquity, too, must be explained by factors that were also at work everywhere, economic in the first place. The Jewish nation was divided into a diaspora composed of multiple local groups and a Palestinian Jewish 'establishment' (*yishuv* in Hebrew). The latter, as Léon explains very well, was not at all annihilated by the destruction of the Jewish state by Pompei in 63

---

[10]This term seems justified in the case of the Jewish people of Antiquity and in other similar cases prior to the advent of capitalism. Marxist tradition, even when anti-Stalinist, has had too strong a tendency to pride itself on the so-called scientific definition of the concept 'nation' given by Stalin in his article of 1913, which is actually a scholastic definition that does not concord with all the facts. But of course the entire question of a 'definition' is itself scholastic, and we are free to adopt whichever one we want, including Stalin's, which would exclude the ancient Jewish people from the designation. Except that the important point is that we find in this and other similar formations many features that later appear in nations of the capitalist type. I have discussed this question elsewhere. See in particular 'Sur la théorie marxiste de la nation', *Voies Nouvelles*, no. 2, May 1958, pp. 25-30; 'Le Marxisme et la Nation', *L'Homme et la Société*, no. 7, January-March 1968, pp. 131-149, and 'Nation and Ideology' [in the present volume].

[11]The existence of that which has perished is forgotten. This is a natural tendency that is reinforced by ideology. The admiration quite legitimately aroused by certain parts of the Old Testament—a slanted anthology of ancient Hebrew literature—must not induce us to forget that Israel's neighbouring peoples also wrote, also produced literary works; and there is no reason to believe that this lost literature was inferior to that of Israel. The Bible sometimes alludes to their sages. Likewise, we tend to forget that there was an entire prophetic current opposed to the one that eventually triumphed, whose literary efforts were not preserved. These 'false prophets', villified by the 'true' ones (although it could easily have gone the other way), were probably quite interesting.

BC, nor by the repression of the later Jewish revolts of AD 66–70 and 132–135 by Titus and Hadrian—whatever may be said by the arguments peddled (albeit for different reasons) by Christian churches and Jewish nationalists, whether religious or secular. Rather, the erosion of the importance of the Palestinian 'establishment'—notably because of an intense process of assimilation—reduced it little by little to the status of one group of communities among the others, embedded, like the others, among non-Jewish populations.

Many of these Jewish communities scattered around the world disappeared, melting away through assimilation into the societies within which they were located after adopting the religion, or one of the dominant religions, of those societies (this was the only way to do it in those days). Others shrank in number and withered through the individual assimilation (that is, the conversion) of many of their members to these religions. Nevertheless, a significant number of these communities throughout the world remained, preserving the religion of their ancestors, often converting fresh proselytes to it, maintaining cultural features linked to the religion (while as a whole adopting the ambient culture), and conserving links among one another, despite the considerable differences separating them. How can we account for this persistence if we reject both the religious explanation that it was God's will and the nationalist-idealist claim (far more irrational, in its own way) that mysterious factors imbued these multifarious groups with a national will to live?

To account for this fact, Léon takes up the theory of the people-class suggested by Marx and formulated in sharper terms by Max Weber: the Jews formed a sort of Indian caste perpetuating itself even in a world without castes. This explanation has some merit, especially for the Christian world of the West, from the time of the Crusades onwards (at least within certain limits, which I will come to later). But Léon does not see that at a stroke he has leapt over a thousand years (at least) during which this factor was not operative.

Features essentially characteristic of Europe after the Crusades have often been unduly and unconsciously transposed to the past. They have also been transposed, equally unduly, to other cultural spheres. Even in the diaspora, the Jews of Antiquity were not especially engaged in commerce. Léon was misled on this point by historians who had used the inadequate documentation of the time and were influenced by this tendency to transpose subsequent conditions backward in time. An author very familiar with the history of the Egyptian Jews writes that in Egypt under the Roman Empire they were 'beggars, sorcerers, peddlers, artisans, and traders of all kinds, dealers in antiques, and usurers, bankers, farmers, tenants, workingmen, and sailors, in short, they did everything from which they could hope to derive a livelihood'.[12] And S.W. Baron notes that this portrait 'also fits, with minor modifications, other countries of the dispersion'.[13] Flavius Josephus was able to write at the end of the first century after Christ: 'As for ourselves, therefore, we neither inhabit a maritime country, nor do we delight in merchandise,...and having a fruitful country for our habitation, we take pains in cultivating that only'.[14] In his beautiful thesis, B. Blumenkranz has shown on the basis of very nearly exhaustive documentation that before the eleventh century, Jews in Western Europe lived without segregation in the midst of the European population, having more or less the same professional occupations as the middle layers of the latter. The remarkable works of S.D. Goitein have shown that in the Muslim world as well, the Jews were distinguished from the Muslim or Christian populations only by their religion and the cultural features directly linked to it.

Before the modern epoch, however, societies of the national type —those that prefigured modern nations, extending beyond the

---

[12]L. Fuchs, *Die Juden Aegyptens*, p. 49; cited by S.W. Baron, *Social and Religious History*, vol. 1, p. 260. Compare what is said by the foremost expert on the Jews of Egypt in Antiquity: 'Current opinion among scholars, based on the literary sources, is that the principal occupation of the Egyptian Jews was commerce and money-lending. The papyri do not confirm this. They inform us that the social conditions of the Egyptian Jews were as varied as could be, and that their participation in agriculture, livestock raising, the military profession, and administration was in no way inferior to their activities as merchants and money-lenders'. (V. Tcherikover, 'The Jews in Egypt in the Hellenistic-Roman Age in the Light of the Papyri', *Revue de l'Histoire juive en Egypte*, Cairo, no. 1, 1947, pp. 111–142, see p. 116.) He adds: 'There are almost no examples of Jewish merchants in the papyri, and this probably corresponds to the real state of affairs' (p. 121). Banking 'still attracted but few Jews', states S.W. Baron (*Social and Religious History*, vol. 1, p. 261, with references).
[13]*Social and Religious History*, vol. 1, p. 260.
[14]*Contra Apion*, I, 12, Josephus, *Complete Works*, trans. by William Whiston, London 1963, p. 610.

earlier tribal structure, whatever they may be called[15]—were characterized by extreme internal partitioning, which seems to me related quite simply to the insufficient force of the unifying factors. The mercantile economy, large-scale international trade, and the relative power of state structures had finally succeeded in piercing the barriers between tribes or village communities, in imposing unification on a more or less broad scale. But the state still commanded limited means of action. Sub-administration, as it would be called today, was the rule and not the exception. This impelled leaders to administrate through the intermediary of multifarious bodies, sorts of sub-states that were also quasi-states. The pre-nation was a conglomerate of largely autonomous communities, which administered themselves and from which minimal allegiance to the state was demanded. The essential symbol of this allegiance was taxes, to which the sovereign bodies quite naturally assigned top priority. In many cases a military contribution was also required. Public order had to be respected. Apart from that, these communities lived their own lives. For their members, they represented the general society to which they owed their allegiance most of all, of which they felt themselves an integral part, and at the level of which they conceived their interests and aspirations, as is the rule in the structures that predate the age of modern individualism, in which people feel linked (at most) only to the state that dominates and controls them from above.

It is thus to the advantage of these communities to encourage this tendency towards preserving their own existence, which characterizes social groups in any event. There was indeed a hierarchical social stratification, kinds of pre-classes,[16] just as there were kinds of prenations. But common action and consciousness on their part collided with the force of the community structures. They therefore broke loose only on great occasions, notably in Christian Europe, where

---

[15]'Nationality' (Russian: 'narodnost'), 'ethnic group', 'people', etc.; cf. my articles on the Marxist theory of the nation cited in note 10 above.

[16]Cf. my article 'Dynamique interne ou dynamique globale: l'exemple des pays musulmans', *Cahiers internationaux de sociologie*, no 42, 1967, pp. 27–47. [Likewise, my article 'Histoire économique et histoire des classes sociales dans le monde musulman', in *Studies in the Economic History of the Middle East*, Michael Cook ed., London 1970, pp. 139–155.]

powerful institutions consolidated the hierarchy in question.

The Jews organized and administered themselves as Jews, presented themselves to society as forming a Jewish group in the midst of others. They tended to remain Jews so long as no powerful forces compelled them to cease to be. The size of the communities varied as a function of all sorts of factors, but strong pressure was never lastingly and simultaneously exerted to uproot this set of communities completely in all the countries in which the Jews lived (that is, throughout nearly the whole known world). There is nothing astonishing in this, given the multiplicity of independent state structures enveloping the Jewish communities and their very feeble resources compared with those that exist today, the terrorist aspect of government intervention compensating only in part for its lack of continuity, its sporadic character. The so-called miracle of Jewish survival at which Christian theologians and Jewish nationalists alike have marvelled, albeit in different tones, may be reduced to this.

In the Muslim East, where medieval conditions have largely persisted to the present day, sects or religious communities have subsisted for centuries and millennia, even though few of their adherents show any great interest in the doctrines that gave rise to them so long ago. The Druzes, for example—members of a sect formed in the eleventh century and theoretically possessing a very scholarly doctrine derived in part from neo-Platonist philosophy—are no more than Syrian or Lebanese peasants who are aware that their customs are different from those of others and who tend to react as a unit, much like a little nation or sub-nation, however much they have been encompassed within many different successive states. They have fiercely defended their identity, their particularism, their group interests, and they continue to do so to a large extent, despite the fact that they share most of the cultural features of their neighbours of the other religious communities, speak the same Arabic language, and belong to the Arab ethnic group according to all the usual criteria—and this despite the recent strength of the ideology of Arab nationalism, which exerts pressure towards unification.

Likewise, the great ideologies of the past—religious and not nationalist—have reacted against this tendency towards the persistence of particularism. These ideologies acted to guarantee state unity. The Hellenistic monarchies and the Roman Empire, strong and unitary states that resemble modern nations in some respects, did not impose a single ideology on their subjects, but allowed a certain degree of pluralism. Their requisites were minimal. They never envisaged the suppression of the Jewish *ethnos*. The conflicts of these states with Israel occurred solely because of what seemed an excess of particularism among this people, an inclination towards separatism that raised concern about their loyalty to the state. Yahvism, the religion of Israel, had evolved from a national cult increasingly aiming at intra-national exclusivism towards an exclusive universalist cult. Yahveh had first been imposed as the sole god of Israel. Considered stronger, more potent, than the gods of the other nations, he was in the process of being dubbed the only existing one. Many Yahvists scorned other gods,[17] going so far as to consider them non-existent. The Yahvist school had codified in extreme detail the particular rites that were to distinguish the true Israelite, faithful servant of Yahveh, from other peoples. In the atmosphere of the Hellenistic world and culture, many Jews[18] sought to adapt the national religion to the general ideas of the ambient civilization. The Epicurean Antiochus Epiphanes supported this assimilationist faction in the interest of the unity of his state, and not at all out of zeal for the gods of paganism. Hence the revolt of the intransigent Yahvists, initially a civil war among Jews, which led to the victory of extremist nationalism in Israel (even then).[19] But the new state of Israel had to find a *modus vivendi* with the powers of the region, which for their part sacrificed the assimilationists and accepted the particularities of the Jewish religion and cult in exchange for political reconciliation with the now-sobered extremists. After the Hellenists, the Romans learned that it was better to accept these particularities and treated them with great respect, often exempting Jews from common law out of regard for their particular conceptions.

---

[17]Despite countervailing tendencies in the Hellenistic and Roman periods. It is striking to note, for example, that in the Septuagint, the Alexandrian translation of the Bible, the passage of Exodus (22:27) in which it is forbidden to curse the *elohim* (that is: perhaps, the judges), was rendered by the equivocal sense of this word, 'You shall not curse the gods'. This translation was used by Philon and Josephus to prove that the Jews respected the gods of other nations.

[18]Daniel 9, 27. Cf.E. Bickermann, *Der Gott der Makkabäer*, Schocken, Berlin 1937, p. 136, who enhances the sense by translating *rabbim* as 'most'.

[19]See the demonstration of E. Bickermann in the admirable work just cited.

The famous wars of 66–70 and 132–35 were not at all attempts by the Romans to destroy the specific Jewish *ethnos*. They consisted in repression against rebels who were striving for political independence by employing popular exasperation at the acts of tactless and rapacious Roman functionaries. As elsewhere in the Roman Empire, the partisans of independence were naturally recruited most of all among the most disadvantaged, among the poor and among those who, for one reason or another, felt their interests and aspirations trampled upon by the Roman regime. Whatever Léon may say, then, I believe that they may be considered essentially national insurrections, despite the mixture of social motivations that always emerge in national movements. One indication of this is that social layers and individuals thoroughly hostile to the revolt were nonetheless compelled to participate in it. Following the exactions of Gessius Florus, which provoked the Jews, and given the passivity of the central government (represented by Nero) when presented with Jewish complaints, and the usual cycle of protests of varying violence and acts of repression of varying atrocity, the party of those whom Josephus called the seditious (*stasiastai*), revolutionaries (*neoteridzontes*), and warmongers (*hoi kinountes ton polemon*) carried the day against the party of those, including himself, whom he called the powerful (*dunatoi*), the princes of the priests (*arkhiereis*), and the peaceful among the population.[20] 'They won to their cause the last partisans of the Romans, by force of persuasion' (Josephus, *The Jewish War*, II, xx, 2),[21] at least in Jerusalem, and the symbol of the sacred union was the election of leaders cleverly chosen from the latter party, among them Josephus himself. Once the choice was made and the die cast, many reacted (though more sincerely) much as

---

[20]Cf. F.-M. Abel, *Histoire de la Palestine depuis la conquête d'Alexandre jusqu'à l'invasion arabe*, Gabalda, Collection Études bibliques, Paris 1952, vol. 1, p. 483. [On this whole question, one may now read with great profit the scholarly and intelligent introduction of Pierre Vidal-Naquet, entitled 'Du bon usage de la trahison', to Flavius Josephus, *La Guerre des Juifs*, translated from the Greek by Pierre Savinel, Paris 1977, pp. 7–115, further developed in the Italian edition, *Il Buon Uso del Tradimento*, Rome 1980.]

[21]The quotation below from Flavius Josephus, *The Antiquities of the Jews*, is from the translation by William Whiston (see note 14 above). Those from *The War of the Jews* are from the translation by G.A. Williamson, Harmondsworth, first published 1959, in the Penguin Classics series.

Josephus himself claims to have done once installed in his post as governor of Galilee: 'for he saw the inevitable end awaiting the Jews and knew that their one safety lay in a change of heart. He himself, he felt sure, would be pardoned if he went over to the Romans, but he would rather have died over and over again than betray his motherland (*tên patrida*) and flout the trust reposed in him in order to make himself at home with those he had been sent to fight' (ibid., III, vii, 2, p. 182). The course of events, the Roman victories, and the long siege of Jerusalem aggravated internal tensions and assured the victory of intransigent extremists over those who were suspected, not without reason, of harbouring conciliatory tendencies. Hence also the struggles among the various extremist parties—grouplets whose numbers were swelled by circumstance—and the predominance among the rebels of the most revolutionary trends, hostile to the rich and powerful.

The religious element in this war is obvious. It is even more visible in the revolt of 132–35, in which Rabbi 'Aqiba played a great role of ideological inspiration. The nationalists were able to base themselves on the few vexations that narrow-minded, corrupt, or provocative prosecutors like.Gessius Florus had introduced against Jewish religious customs; they were also able to capitalize on the messianic current of thought. But it was quite clear that the principal motivation was the struggle against political oppression. Many very religious-minded people held that their faith was perfectly compatible with submission to Rome, provided the necessary protests were issued when Roman functionaries interfered with the religious customs of their people.

Léon correctly invokes similar uprisings around the same time in other Roman provinces. In these cases, as in Palestine, social demands enhanced the enthusiasm of disadvantaged layers in their participation in the national revolt. He could also have mentioned the example of the Gauls, contemporary with and closer to the Jewish case in some respects. In 69, taking advantage of the turmoil that both preceded and followed the fall of Nero, the Batavian prince Julius Civilis aroused his people—Germans in immediate contact with the Gauls—by appealing against the vexations suffered at the hands of Roman officers. He was careful to envelop his call to revolt in a religious atmosphere. He convoked the notables to a sacred grove (*sacrum in nemus*) on the pretext of a banquet (itself doubtless religious). His speech, enumerating the cruelties suffered, was followed by solemn oaths in which those in attendance pledged themselves 'by barbarian ritual and traditional curses' (*barbaro ritu et patriis exsecrationibus*) (Tacitus, *Histories*, IV, 14–15; trans. by Kenneth Wellesley, Harmondsworth 1964). The rebels were inflamed by the predictions of the Germanic prophetess Veleda (ibid., IV, 61–65), and after their initial victory, they appeared to the Germans and Gauls as 'liberators' (*libertatis auctores*) (ibid., IV, 17). The Gauls were attracted by the appeals of Civilis, especially when it was learned at the beginning of the year 70 that the Capitol had been burned during the struggle in Rome between the partisans of Vespasian and Vitellius. In Gaul as in Jerusalem, memories of past glory were intermingled with a messianism faced toward the future. The burning of the temple with which the fortune of Rome was associated reminded them that they had once taken the City itself, and seemed to them a sign of the wrath of the gods (*signum caelestis irae datum*). 'Now, however', says Tacitus, 'fate had ordained this fire as a sign of...the passing of world dominion to the nations north of the Alps. Such at any rate was the message proclaimed by the idle superstition of Druidism' (*Histories*, IV, 54). All this, backed up by quite realistic considerations about the difficult situation of the Romans (which proved, however, to be fallacious), convinced the Gauls, the Trevires Julius Classicus and Julius Tutor, to rise up, along with the Lingon Julius Sabinus. They proclaimed an Empire of the Gauls (*Imperium Galliarum*). But it is here that the difference from the Palestinian development arises. About the time that Titus was entering Jerusalem (September 70), delegates of the Gallic *cités* were holding a congress in Reims to decide whether to seek 'independence or peace' (*libertas an pax placeret*) (ibid., IV, 67). Speakers were heard defending both sides of the question. Julius Auspex, from Reims, made a speech in favour of submission and peace, which closely recalls the one delivered, in vain, by the Jewish King Herod Agrippa in Jerusalem four years earlier (Josephus, *The Jewish War*, II, xvi, 4, pp. 144–150). The themes were the same: the power of the Romans, the weakness and divisions of the subjugated nation, the transitory and remediable character of the vexations committed by the regime's functionaries. But the Gauls—who

Agrippa, among others, says 'submit to being the milch cow of Rome and receiving from her hands what they themselves have produced...not from effeminacy or radical inferiority, for they fought for eighty years to save their liberty'—chose peace.

In Judea, although the party of peace was defeated, it nevertheless remained strong. The uprising did not at all command the unanimous support of the Jewish nation. Let me simply quote S.W. Baron, who sums up the facts this way: 'As it was, the very large Syrian-Jewish population seems to have kept aloof during all three uprisings [against Antiochus Epiphanes, and against Rome in 66-70 and 132-35]. ...Perhaps even more disastrous were the inner dissensions in the rebellious regions themselves. During the Great War [of 66-70], not only Palestine's Greek municipalities but even such preponderantly Jewish cities as Sepphoris and Tiberias actively opposed the revolutionary armies. Not even in Judea did unanimity prevail. The small group of early Christians left Jerusalem at the outset,...and declared in favour of neutrality. The really influential leaders of the people, whether Sadducees or Pharisees, were sharply opposed to a war with Rome....Roman oppression was purely political and fiscal. It was not even directed against the Palestinian people as a political entity....To oppose such a political force by another, a rebel army, would, the Pharisees felt, transfer the battle to the domain of statehood and armed forces in which the Romans were so much superior. Under the pressure of patriotic zealots, Rabban Johanan ben Zakkai and other Pharisaic leaders joined halfheartedly for a time a campaign which, even if successful, would have involved sanctioning a principle inimical to their own.'[22] It should be recalled that the Talmud hails the defeatism of Johanan ben Zakkai. His words in support of peace, spoken in the besieged city and reported to Vespasian by Roman spies, earned him the benevolence of the Roman general when his disciples brought him outside the walls in a coffin. Vespasian granted his request for the foundation of the Yabneh academy, in which he would later teach the Torah.[23] All subsequent Judaism was to emerge from this school of Yabneh. It was because of this defeatist attitude that Johanan can

---

[22]S.W. Baron, *A Social and Religious History of the Jews*, vol. 2, pp. 99-101.
[23]*Aboth de Rabbi Nathan*, version I, IV, 11b-12a. I quote from the English translation

be considered, as S.W. Baron says, 'the rebuilder of national life'.[24]

It seems clear that in Judea, as in Gaul and many other places, what was at issue was what we would call a national liberation struggle (*polemon huper tês eleutherias*, says Agrippa). But the Romans, although they wanted submission, did not seek to level all particularisms. They were content simply to combat customs they considered outrageous (not without inconsistency) according to their conception of 'civilization' (which was, of course, ethnocentric).

For instance, they were against the human sacrifices practised by some Gauls (although gladiatorial combat seemed to them quite normal), and circumcision, which they considered the equivalent of castration. At the extreme, the emperor Hadrian (117–138), who sought to extend unification by bringing together the ethnic groups subjugated by the empire and by eliminating customs contrary to the spirit of Hellenistic civilization, forbade circumcision (a measure that also applied to the Arabs and the Egyptian priests) and wanted, like Antiochus Epiphanes, to build a temple to Zeus Olympios (or Jupiter Capitolin), whom the Jews refused to acknowledge as their God, for reasons he was unable to understand. Once again, extremist Jews—despite pious conciliators—seized the opportunity to announce the imminent arrival of the Messiah and the deliverance or redemption (*ge'oullah*), the freedom (*herouth*) of Israel, in the parlance of the revolution. But although he repressed this revolt harshly and took even more severe measures to nip any fresh attempt in the bud, Hadrian—who had begun his reign by removing the statue of Trajan, considered shocking by the Jews, from its position at the Temple—did not reduce the rights of the Jews as citizens in any way and did not revoke their exemption from compulsory practice of the imperial cult, an extraordinary privilege. His successor, Antoninus, abolished both the prohibition of circumcision (except for men of non-Jewish origin) and the other measures taken during the repression.[25]

---

in *A Rabbinic Anthology*, by C.G. Montefiore and H. Loewe, London 1938, p. 266, text no. 680. [In the article cited in note 20 above, P. Vidal-Naquet makes some very pertinent comments on these points.]

[24]S.W. Baron, *Social and Religious History*, vol. 2, p. 277.

[25]Cf. F.-M. Abel, *Histoire de la Palestine* vol. 2, pp. 62–65 and 83–109; S.W. Baron,

The extension of Roman citizenship to the majority of the subjects of the Empire also applied to the Jews, whose monotheistic scruples were even taken into consideration in the oath permitting accession to public functions.[26]

Pagan ideology allowed considerable pluralism. Nevertheless, economic and social conditions were encouraging unification. In the Roman Empire free competition among cults was permitted to a certain extent, just like free competition among commodities. People of Roman stock could worship Egyptian gods, for example. Cultural particularism among the ethnic groups could take refuge in the persistent worship of local gods. An appearance of ideological unity was assured by the simple expedient of identifying the indigenous gods with those of the Roman pantheon. Sometimes this fusion was real, while in other cases an ancient divinity was simply worshipped with an additional, Roman name. The provinces also preserved greater or lesser originality, depending on such factors as geographical unity, the strength of cultural traditions, and the degree of intermingling of the populations. The economic and cultural preponderance of the eastern part of the empire was apparent here too. 'It is here', wrote Franz Cumont, 'that the principal centres of production and export were found.' Thus, 'not only were the gods of Egypt and Asia never supplanted like those of Gaul or Spain, but they soon crossed the seas and finally attracted worshippers in all the Latin provinces...and it could be argued that theocrasy (the mixture and fusion of gods) was a necessary consequence of the mixture of races, that the gods of the Levant followed the great commercial and social streams, and that their establishment in the West was the natural consequence of the emigration that drew the excess of inhabitants of the Asian cities and countryside to the less densely peopled lands.'[27]

The process of pluralist unification, if we may use the term, favoured the eastern cults, not only because of the cultural superiority of the Orient, but also, and probably mainly, because many of them (precisely the ones that spread) had assumed a new character as mystery religions, both universalist and individualist, offering their

[26]S.W. Baron, *Social and Religious History*, vol. 2, pp. 108–110.
[27]F. Cumont, *Les Religions orientales dans le paganisme romain*, 4th edn, Paris 1929, pp. 19–21.

adherents paths to personal salvation irrespective of tribal or local links to the ethnic group or the native soil. Judaism itself acquired this character, and as such gained the adherence of a considerable number of converts. This religious individualism was obviously related to the social individualism fostered by political, social, and economic conditions.

The Jewish *ethnos* retained its specificity through the convergence of a number of different factors. It embodied the conjunction of a very well defined *ethnos* and a religion of universalist salvation. Yahveh, the national god, had such particular characteristics that he resisted any assimilation to other gods. The attempt of Antiochus Epiphanes to identify him with Zeus Olympios, although well received by many assimilationist Jews, had failed. For Hellenists, in any event, it was simply a matter of giving a name to a god who was reputed not to have one.[28] As E. Bickermann has shown, the failure was the result essentially of the struggle of intransigent Jews against those (moderately) assimilationist Jews who had accepted this *denominatio*. As we have seen, Hadrian's attempt also failed, after encountering opposition that was more nationalist than religious in substance. In any event, Yahveh, with his distinctive, even if negative, features, remained the god of Israel, and of Israel alone. The only way to join his cult was to be adopted by his people, to become a member of that people. Half-conversions of sympathizers of Judaism were accepted for a whole period. But as satellites of the religion, they remained outside the Jewish *ethnos*. The crux of the history of early Christianity was precisely the question of how to weld adherents who refused to enter the Jewish *ethnos* into what was essentially a Jewish institution, the early Church. This was the subject of the whole debate between the Apostles and Paul, the echoes of which have come down to us in the *Acts of the Apostles* and the *Galatian Epistle*.

The Roman Empire, a pre-nation of impressive dimensions, unified in part by a close-knit network of economically interdependent units, fostered the fusion of certain ethnic groups and certain cults as well, but not the disappearance of universalist religions or sects. The ethnic groups of the western part of the empire were fused,

---

[28.]Cf. E. Bickermann, *Der Gott der Makkabäer*, pp. 92 ff.

and they lost, along with their languages (Iberian, Gallic, and so on), the cultural features that distinguished them from one another, thus becoming mere regions of the Latin world, of *Romania*. Geographical factors, relative isolation, and the memory of a glorious past permitted at most a certain degree of regionalist consciousness which, once historical conditions were propitious—after economic impoverishment, the dislocation of commercial links, and the barbarian invasions—would later permit a slow rebirth of national (or pre-national, if you will) identity, along with linguistic differentiation. The ethnic groups of the east, while retaining their popular languages (Greek, Coptic, Armenian, and so on), sometimes fused among one another, as in Anatolia or Syria-Phoenicia, but they preserved a set of specific cultural features more sharply, albeit in the framework of new entities. Because of its powerful geographical unity, Egypt retained a national identity of its own, as indeed it has generally done throughout its history. The Jews were protected against any fusion by the close-knit tissue of particular practices imposed by strict Yahvism on the first 'Zionists', who had returned to Judea from Babylon at the end of the sixth century before Christ. One could very well seek accommodation with the ambient world, agree even to respect the gods of neighbouring peoples, as Alexandrian Judaism did, and adapt as much as possible to Hellenistic civilization, as was done for a whole period symbolized by the frescoes of the synagogue of Doura Europos (in the Damascus museum), in which Moses is depicted in the unexpected features of a pedagogue bearing the thin Greek-style ringed beard. But those who abandoned the distinctive practices of the *ethnos* immediately stood outside it. Before the accommodations of the third century, this was necessary in order to accede to certain public functions.

A good example of this is Tiberius Julius Alexander,[29] nephew of the illustrious Jewish philosopher Philo of Alexandria and son of a

---

[29]On this point, see essentially E. Schürer, *Geschichte des jüdischen Volkes im Zeitalter Jesu Christi*, third and fourth edns, Hinrichs, Leipzig, 1901–11, vol. 1, p. 568, n. 9; J. Schwartz, 'Note sur la famille de Philon d'Alexandrie', in *Mélanges Isidore Lévy, Annuaire de l'Institut de philologie et d'histoires orientales et slaves*, Brussels, vol. 13, 1953, pp. 591–602; J. Danielou, *Philon d'Alexandrie*, Paris 1958, pp. 12 ff; H.G. Pflaum, *Les Carrières procuratoriennes équestres sous le Haut-Empire romain*, Paris 1961, vol. 1, pp. 46–49; S.W. Baron *Social and Religious History*, vol. 2, p. 369, n. 5; V. Burr, *Tiberius Julius Alexander*, Bonn 1955.

very rich *alabarque* (tax collector) of that city, related to the family of the Herods. His father had financed nine doors of Herod's magnificent temple in Jerusalem, which was then under construction. He himself, a distinguished intellectual (his famous uncle thought it necessary to devote an entire treatise to refuting the theses his nephew had propounded in a conference on the intelligence of animals), 'did not continue in the religion of his country', according to Josephus (*Antiquities of the Jews*, xx, v, 2, p. 418), who reproaches him only gently, saying that his father 'prevailed over him out of his piety towards God'. He pursued a career in the Roman administration, and was procurator of Judea towards 45–48. The Jewish historian notes (*The Jewish War*, ii, xi, 6, p. 131) that he, like his predecessor, the pagan Cuspius Fadus, 'left native customs severely alone and kept the nation at peace.' His Jewish origin was judged worthy of mention by neither Suetonius (*Vespasian*, sect. 6) nor Tacitus, who calls him only 'distinguished Roman knight' (*illustris eques romanus*) and 'of Egyptian nation', meaning 'birth' (*ejusdem* [i.e. Aegyptiorum] *nationis*). (*Annales*, vx, 28; *Histories*, i, 11.) Named prefect (or governor) of Egypt, he repressed a Jewish riot in Alexandria and was the first to nominate Vespasian as emperor. Under Titus, he was second in command of the army that besieged Jerusalem. Apart from the one reservation signalled above, Josephus spares no praise of his intelligence, military experience, loyalty, and 'magnificent fidelity' to the Flavian dynasty (*The Jewish War*, v, i, 45–46). It is quite possible that it was his son or grandson of the same name who was a member in 118–119 of the sacerdotal college of the Arvales Brothers, one of the most ancient congregations of Roman paganism.[30]

Thus could one abandon the Jewish *ethnos*. But although it was forbidden to join it without having been born to it, no one was under any pressure to leave it, or to abandon the universalist religion linked to it. The repressive measures against the extremist nationalists, advocates of political independence for Palestine, or against the Jews of the provinces who from time to time had bloody clashes with the other ethnic groups of the same area (contemporary Jewish nationalist literature incorrectly calls these pogroms, and sees them as

---

[30]E. Schürer, *Geschichte*, p. 568, n. 9.

manifestations of eternal anti-Semitism), were police operations that did not overturn this principle. Vespasian and Titus refused to assume the title *Judaicus*, or 'conqueror of the Jews', as the emperors had taken the titles *Germanicus*, 'conqueror of the Germans', or *Africanus*, 'conqueror of the Africans'. They were supposed to have conquered not the Jewish people, but a faction of Jewish extremists gone astray in Judea. It was Judea that had been mastered (*Judea capta* or *devicta*, it says on Flavian coins), not all the Jews, among whom these sovereigns counted very many supporters, and even, in the case of Titus, a tenderly beloved friend, Berenice. If he did not marry her but left her, *invitus invitam*, it was for fear not of specifically 'anti-Semitic', but of Roman traditionalist reactions, such as those Anthony had suffered for his liaison with the Egyptian Cleopatra.

In truth, then, there is no reason why Judaism should have disappeared during this epoch. It persisted, an ethnic nucleus surrounded by a nebula of sympathetic proselytes attracted by its universalist aspects. This fringe, often hesitant and sometimes eventually rebuffed, could, and often did, reinforce the Jewish *ethnos* with fresh infusions of blood despite the sanctions they could incur. Relations between the two forms and tendencies of Judaism were uneasy and laden with contradictions, as is shown, in one extreme case, by the Greco-Syrians of Damascus, who in the year 66 massacred the Jews of Damascus without letting on to their wives, nearly all of whom had embraced Judaism (*The Jewish War*, II, xx, 2). The success of Christianity was due in large part to the fact that it resolved this contradiction, presenting to the Roman world a form of Judaism that could be accepted by all, freed of ethnic implications and the encumbering obligations of ritual. Let it be noted in passing that Léon's formulations about early Christianity are debatable. Its popular and, as he puts it, 'anti-plutocratic' character is certain. But in essence it was not a social revolutionary movement, but a religious one drawing its strength from rather contradictory social, ideological, and cultural factors, prominent among which was certainly the reaction of frustration on the part of the poor and oppressed of Judea and Galilee. Still less is Léon's comparison between triumphant Christianity and fascism acceptable. In the final analysis, a comparison with Stalinism would be more apt, but here again many reservations are in order.

To return, however, to the Jewish *ethnos*, it thus continued to exist, an endlessly dispersed diaspora with its two stable territorial bases in Palestine and Babylonia, from which emanated, significantly, the Mishnah and the two Talmuds, drafted in the regions of greatest Jewish concentration, where the problems of agricultural and artisanal life as much as those of urban and commercial life had to be treated from the standpoint of religious jurisprudence. The Babylonian base flourished under the rule of the Sassanid Persian Empire, which was relatively tolerant. The Palestinian base (now centred in Galilee) withered very slowly under the rule of the Roman Empire. In no way did the emperors persecute the Jews, even favouring them as the Christian threat mounted,[31] but they were careful to avoid any possible resurgence of their dangerous nationalism. On the other hand, bad experiences with wavering proselytes, and the necessities of a new organization based no longer on the aristocracy and the priests but on clerks contributed to turning the Jewish community back on itself. The general trend of the eastern nationalities drifted towards de-Hellenization—at least superficially, for many of the Hellenistic elements that had been absorbed were retained, here as elsewhere, whatever some may say.

The victory of Christianity in the Roman Empire changed the living conditions of Judaism somewhat. The Jews had to deal with a state ideology of totalitarian bent pressing for ideological unification. During the initial period following the triumph of the church, its cadres manifested fanatical intolerance, mobilizing the Christian masses to demand that reluctant emperors take energetic measures against their rivals, until victory seemed definitively won and consolidated. We know how quickly paganism vanished from the Christian empire. Why didn't Judaism disappear too?

For this period, too, any explanation based on the functional specialization of the Jews must be rejected. At the conclusion of an exhaustive investigation of the condition of the Jews in the Latin world before the Crusades, B. Blumenkranz sums up the results on this point as follows: 'The Jews were subject to the same laws as the Christians, and nothing else distinguished them either. Speaking the

---

[31]Cf. M. Simon, *Verus Israel*, Paris 1948, pp. 135 ff.

same language, dressing in the same manner, engaging in the same professions, they intermingled in the same houses, just as they all came together under arms to defend the common homeland.'[32] In the course of his work, he explains: 'Apart from public functions... there was no activity from which the Jews were formally excluded.' The restrictions mentioned were religiously based, in general not applied, and were far from reducing the Jews to any specialization whatever. Thus the attempt to prohibit Christians from consulting Jewish doctors, and the prohibition on trade in liturgical objects. 'No document of our period, whether legal or practical, charges the Jews with usury; [moreover], at that time there was very simply not yet any commerce in money on a large enough scale to make it a problem of public order.' In addition, while 'there was no lack of attempts to deny Jews the right to own land, on the whole they remained without success.'[33] Those are the decisive points.

The only thing that distinguished the Jews from the Christians in the West at that time was religion. It was at this level that the effort at ideological unification could take root. The Christian people, it seems, were free of special resentment against the Jews. The few rare incidents that have come down to us seem due to factors other than the ethnic-religious cleavage, or else amount to the usual minor conflicts that result from any sort of differentiation. Sometimes the provocation came from the Jews. Sometimes the Christian crowd took the side of the Jews, as in Paris in 582, when a Jew named Priscus was killed during a brawl by a Jew recently converted to Christianity. One of the murderer's companions was lynched, and the murderer himself barely escaped the same fate.[34]

But the regime was a Christian regime. Why did it not apply a determined policy of ideological unification, which would have reinforced it? Here we must consider (apart from the persistence of the tradition of Roman law, particularly strong among the first Christian emperors) the pluralistic features of this type of pre-modern state, of which I spoke earlier. Blumenkranz goes into more specific and precise details about the Frankish states (which differed from

[32]B. Blumenkranz, *Juifs et Chrétiens dans le monde occidental* (430–1006), Paris-The Hague 1960, p. 375.
[33]Ibid., pp. 344–49.
[34]Gregory of Tours, *Historia Francorum*, VI, 17, cf. B. Blumenkranz, pp. 378 ff.

Spain). Ideological flexibility was requisite: 'The states that arose here on the ruins of the Roman Empire included a multitude of peoples and small tribes who retained their own characteristics in many respects.' There were the Roman citizens and the Barbarians; 'among the Barbarians, many ethnic groups', for example the Alamans, Burgondes, Saliens Franks, and Ripuaires Franks in Gaul. 'Although Spain was able to strive more easily for the unification of laws and institutions, everywhere else the principle of national law, of personal law, took root and was maintained. In this multiplicity of statutes, Jewish particularism was much less striking than it was in Spain, where unity of faith was meant to crown the unification imposed, if not attained, in all other domains. The particularism of the Jews was therefore protected by the principle of the multiplicity of law itself.'[35]

In sum, the Christian state acted towards the Jewish minority as the Soviet Marxist state did towards its defeated ideological competitors: the Christian Churches and the various religious communities. The Stalinist constitution of 1936 guaranteed 'freedom to practise religious worship and freedom of anti-religious propaganda' to all citizens (Article 124). In both cases, the victorious ideological movement, as a result of a combination of wisdom and lack of resources, renounced any attempt to impose itself by constraint, but accorded itself the privilege of means by which to expand, forcing the vanquished into passivity and hoping that this would lead to their withering away gradually and peacefully.

If a different attitude was taken towards pagans, whose 'freedom to worship' was smashed by the Christian state after a brief transitional phase of tolerance, it was perhaps in part because of the schism in ideology itself, which ranged Judaism and Christianity on the same side, mother and daughter religions, both monotheistic and universalist at least in principle. But it may well have been mainly because the organization of pagan practices necessarily had the character of a public cult. In the struggle between Christianity (the 'preponderant belief', as the pagans bitterly called it[36]) and declining

---

[35]B. Blumenkranz, pp. 374 ff.
[36]Cf. P. de Labriolle, *La Réaction païenne, étude sur la polémique antichrétienne du Ier au VIe siècle*, Paris 1942, p. 483, n. 2. On the scope and limits of the first anti-

paganism during the fourth and fifth centuries, at stake was the ideology that would be adopted by state and municipal institutions, the practices these institutions would finance, the public holidays that would be celebrated, the divinities to which the authorities would pledge their allegiance. No problem of this sort existed as far as Judaism was concerned, for this was a cult reserved for a particular ethnic group, whose members, if it came to that, could always be forbidden the right to proselytize beyond the limits of their *ethnos*, and which, after the third century, could not possibly have aspired to control the state. In the view of history that the Church came to adopt, the triple division between pagans, Jews, and Christians was reduced in law to a dichotomy between Hellenes and the Hellenized. The Gentiles, in a word, were called upon to convert to Christianity, a religion that had adapted Jewish principles to their own customs, whereas Judaism still survived, at least temporarily, as an olive tree onto which had been grafted the wild pagan shoots that prospered at the expense of the natural branches, to put it in the imagery of Saint Paul (Romans, 11:16 ff.).

This toleration of Judaism as a defeated and subordinate ideological movement, but one whose right to exist was affirmed, was taken even further by Islam. Muhammad, the founder of Islam, at first believed that he was bringing the Arabs a revelation substantially identical to that with which the Jews and Christians had been favoured. Astonished at the reserved (to say the least) reception he got from the Jews when he entered into direct contact with them in Medina, he found himself compelled to defend his own version of monotheism and the authenticity of his revelation, which nevertheless drew much of its authority from this essential concord with the earlier monotheistic revelations. Despite his political conflicts with the Jews of Arabia, he did not retreat from his fundamental conception, proclaiming only that the written texts produced by the adepts of these prior revelations, whenever they appeared to run counter to his own message, had been distorted, the promise of the advent of that message maliciously deleted. Conversion to Islam was

---

Jewish measures of the Christian empire, see the precise and detailed article by E. Demougeot, 'L'Empéreur Honorius et la politique antijuive', in *Hommages à Léon Hermann*, Latamus, Brussels-Berchem 1960, pp. 277–91.

demanded only of Arabs. Despite their errors, Jews and Christians were still thought to harbour a substantially correct faith, valid for them. In the countries conquered by the Arab Muslims during the seventh century (where Jews and Christians, along with Mazdeans in Iran, formed the majority of the population), no attempt whatever was made to convert them; they were simply subjected to Arab political authority, the official ideology of which was Islam, and they were asked to pay a special tax, at first rather a moderate one. After the Abbasid revolution of 750, which abolished Arab ethnic privilege, social factors brought about their gradual conversion to the predominant doctrine, although strong minorities attached to their traditional faith have remained to this day.

Long distance trade and the regional specialization of agricultural and craft production developed enormously in the Muslim Empire and the states that arose from its fragmentation (which nevertheless preserved close links). The Jews, like the other elements of the population, participated in this development, and many of them became merchants. As the leading specialist in this matter has noted: the 'bourgeois revolution' of the Muslim Empire during the eighth and ninth centuries 'certainly expedited the process by which the Jews were transformed from a people engaged mainly in manual trades into one whose most characteristic occupation was commerce....In Muslim times they again found themselves confronted by a highly mercantile civilization [after similar developments in Babylonia in the sixth century before Christ, and then again in the Hellenistic world—M.R.], but responded to the challenge so completely that they became themselves a nation of businessmen.' Significantly, the author also notes: 'This transformation by no means went on unopposed. An early Jewish writer of the Karaite sect [Karaitism was a Jewish 'heresy'—M.R.] stigmatized the devotion to the business profession as un-Jewish and as an aping of the Gentiles—meaning the Arabs or the Muslims in general.'[37]

Nevertheless, this still did not entail a functional specialization, for there were many non-Jewish merchants and many Jews who were not merchants. There is evidence of a very wide range of professions

---

[37]S.D.Goitein, *Jews and Arabs, Their Contacts Through the Ages*, New York 1964, pp. 105 ff.

among the Jews. Nor can there be any talk of specialization in money-lending, despite the facilities afforded them for this sort of trade by their membership (like the Christians and others) of a non-Muslim community that was unimpeded by the Muslim prohibition of loans with interest (a highly theoretical prohibition in any event).[38] It is true that during the High Middle Ages, essentially from the seventh to ninth centuries, trade between the Muslim and Christian worlds was a specialty of the Jews, because of the facilities they enjoyed as a result of their ubiquity, their education in an age of illiteracy, and the fact that they were only half-citizens in the existing empires (Frankish, Byzantine, and Muslim), and thus entitled to certain rights while escaping many of the restrictions imposed on others. Nevertheless, even during the ninth century, when their role in this trade reached its apogee (they were then rid of their Syrian and Greek competitors, while the new intermediaries, Italians and Scandinavians, were not yet in full flight), only a tiny minority of Jews participated in it, and as I have just said, their exclusive hold on it was only partial and quite temporary.[39]

Once again, the persistence of the Jewish entity, both in the Latin West prior to the Crusades and in the Muslim world down to the present day, results simply from the pluralistic character of these societies, from the inadequacy of the forces of unification, from the lack of genuine efforts on the part of the preponderant ideology within the state to extend totalitarianism as far as the destruction of rival theologies. In these conditions, the normal tendency of communities to perpetuate themselves and to defend the interests and aspirations of their members at the level of the community triumphed.

What, then, was the nature of the Jewish entity within these societies? Was it a religion, an ethnic group, a pre-nation? The question cannot be answered in black and white terms, however painful

---

[38]In all three of these religions, various casuistic devices enable the religious prohibition of loans with interest to be circumvented more easily when one's partner is not a coreligionist. [I have dealt with this problem at length in my book *Islam and Capitalism*, Harmondsworth 1977.]

[39]This whole argumentation is justified, for example, in an article by one of the experts best informed about this problem, R.S. Lopez, 'L'Importanza del mondo islamico nella vita economica europea', in *L'Occidente e l'Islam nell'alto Medioevo*, Centro italiano di studi sull'alto Medioevo, Spoleto 1965, vol. 1, pp. 433–460.

this may be to scholastic minds accustomed to plugging facts into well-defined categories and to pasting clear and sharp labels on them.

Beyond the epoch during which the conditions of production and reproduction prevented the formation of aggregate units larger than the clan or tribe, groupings of local units arose in certain conditions, when the components felt they shared a common origin and had some common institutions, a common language (with various different dialects), and a more or less common culture, within which figured a common religion (and therefore ideology). This sort of formation may be called an ethnic group. Neither the existing political states nor the spheres in which a dense network of economic relations assured a certain degree of unity necessarily coincided with the frontiers of these ethnic groups.

The Jews were united by their membership of a common religion, and also by their feeling that they shared a common origin. In societies of this type, this implied certain common cultural features, particularly in their dietary and culinary practices and in literary or historical traditions. Under Islam in particular, at certain times of crisis, regulations were enacted requiring the wearing of distinctive articles in order not to allow members of the defeated ideologies to pass themselves off as true believers, as 'preponderants'. But on the whole, the Jews shared the culture of the peoples among whom they lived; they spoke and wrote their language, retaining Hebrew solely as a liturgical language. Their ideological unity forged certain bonds of solidarity among them which transcended the political, ethnic, and cultural frontiers in which their many communities were geographically enveloped. The best short-hand formula to designate this ensemble thus seems to me to be: a religion having certain characteristics of an ethnic group.

Other religious groupings found themselves in rather similar situations, but most were less universally scattered, and in itself that facilitated local pressures towards the total annihilation of the group. Manichaeanism was quite widely dispersed, but it lacked any common liturgical language, and since it recruited among various ethnic groups, there was no consciousness of common origin. A universalist religion without ethnic characteristics, and split into various currents as well, the many branches of Manichaeanism, from China to

Languedoc, eventually yielded to the pressure of the 'preponderants' of each milieu. Those ethnic groups lacking any religious peculiarity —for example the pagan Syrians, or the Christians of Gaul, rather numerous during the Merovingian epoch—were also eventually assimilated. The conjunction in Judaism of religious and ethnic particularism assured its survival within pluralist societies in which unifying forces were weak.

The sole example of a lasting and energetic attempt at unification is eloquent. It occured in Visigoth Spain after the conversion of the dominant Goths from Arianism to Catholicism in 587. The reasons for the effort seem clear. By adopting Catholicism, the religion of the majority of the (Hispano-Roman) people, the Goth kings sought to achieve the unification of their subjects in all domains: religious, juridical, and political. Under Arian rule the Jews had been subject to the common law of the Christian Empire (though from the point of view of dogma the Arians were just as opposed to the Jews as the other Christians[40]), and therefore tolerated on certain conditions as a defeated ideological movement, as has been noted above. They constituted a rich, relatively powerful, numerous and long-established element of the population. All the more reason to draw them into the unification process, into the consciously undertaken formation of the Hispanic nation. The only conceivable way to do this under Christian ideological domination was to convert them to Christianity. Hence the laws that at first sought to encourage conversion in a roundabout manner, and later, in the face of resistance and the problems thus generated, and despite the theoretical opposition of the Church to these practices, the decision to compel them to convert. Following a pattern often repeated elsewhere, the laws in question quite naturally aroused discontent among the Jews, and stimulated opposition to the state; this opposition then served in turn as an argument for intensifying the anti-Jewish measures. It should be added that the news from the Orient about Jewish uprisings in the Byzantine Empire and the collusion of the Jews with the Persian enemies of the Empire, and later the obsession with the Muslim advance then sweeping across North Africa, did nothing to soothe the

---

[40]Cf. M. Meslin, *Les Ariens d'Occident (335–430)*, Paris 1967, pp. 365 ff., for example.

fears and mistrust of the Goth sovereigns. Their behaviour led to a logical conclusion: the complicity of the Spanish Jews with the Arab invaders.

It was, writes B. Blumenkranz, 'that rare occasion when the civil and the religious power combined their respective efforts in a significant territorial ensemble',[41] despite some reluctance on the part of the Church. But the attempt failed. The causes of this failure were multiple. Among them were most probably the still-insufficient resources of action commanded by the state at the time, the relatively brief duration of the experiment, and the unstable conditions of the Visigoth central power. A great role was probably also played by the fact that this experiment in unification unfolded in a milieu still imbued with the earlier pluralist conceptions. In Spain itself, Jews resisting the royal measures enjoyed complicity among the general population and the clergy alike. Compulsory conversion was repugnant to Christian ideology, as was forcefully argued by the scholar and influential prelate Isidor of Seville. Even though the Church proved complacent in practice, accepting the definitive character of the forced baptisms it had condemned, this led to half-measures that undermined the effectiveness of the entire enterprise, to the regret of later kings, who partially revoked the edicts of their predecessors. The laws in question were not applied in Septimania (the region of Narbonne), a dependency of the kingdom. Many recalcitrant Jews sought exile in Gaul, whence some returned when things had calmed down; others left for North Africa or Italy. It seems that in his own states the pope tolerated the return to Judaism of those converted by force.

That all this was less a matter of the conquest of souls than of political and social unification is quite clear from the measures taken—a phenomenon unprecedented in Christendom, and one that would recur only in Spain itself eight centuries later, under slightly different circumstances. The Jews who had converted to Christianity were increasingly suspected of secretly harbouring their particularisms. Increasingly vexatious measures were taken in a futile struggle to verify the authenticity of their assimilation. The term 'Jew' came to be applied to newly converted Christians of Jewish

---

[41]B. Blumenkranz, p. 105.

descent, and they were treated with suspicion, discriminatory measures being taken against them without even bothering to inquire into whether or not their profession of Christian faith was genuine. Jewish practices were often continued. It is significant that Jews were allowed to marry only (long-standing) Christians. In short, it was an attempt at assimilation by constraint, the objectives of which went beyond the limits of strict religious conversion; and it was conducted with inadequate means and in an atmosphere of ideological and cultural reticence towards such methods. There is no reason for astonishment at its failure.[42]

The Visigoth attitude came to the fore again—very partially, and far less systematically, but over a much wider territory—at the time of the Crusades. These were ideological wars. By the force of circumstance, the Jews were excluded from the Christian ideological unity that had been brought about, albeit fleetingly. Since the logic of ideology always tends towards a Manichaean classification of events and people, it was natural that these non-Christians were seen as accomplices of the anti-Christians against whom war was being waged, the Muslims. Nevertheless, despite persecutions, confiscation of property, expulsions, and massacres, it was not until the age of the Spanish Inquisition that things were generally carried to the extreme extent of the Visigoth laws. Once again, there was no lasting, persistent, systematic, and generalized effort to eliminate the Jewish entity. Those who were persecuted too severely in one country or were expelled from it were able to find refuge elsewhere,[43] albeit sometimes outside Christendom, in the relatively more hospitable Muslim world.

To this negative reason for the survival of Judaism during and after the epoch of the Crusades a positive cause must also be added: the functional specialization that the Jews were coming to acquire. It is during this epoch that, within certain limits, there is validity to the theory of the people-class implicit in the minds of Europeans of the

---

[42]On this Visigoth experience, see especially B. Blumenkranz, p. 105 ff.; S.W. Baron, *Social and Religious History*, vol. 3, pp. 33–46; *Historia de España*, directed by Ramón Menéndez Pidal, vol. 3: *España visigoda*, Madrid 1940, pp. xxv ff., xliii ff. (on the ideal of unification—*una fides, unum regnum*—and on Hispanic nationalism at the time), and pp. 177 ff.

[43]Cf. S.W. Baron, *Social and Religious History*, vol. 4, p. 148.

nineteenth and twentieth centuries, made explicit in a few pages of Marx, formulated in various ways by Max Weber[44] and Abram Léon, endorsed, with nuances here and there, by Marxist tradition, and exaggerated by anti-Semites to consequences both delirious from an intellectual point of view and indescribably savage in practice.

The process had been described many times, with greater or lesser breadth and depth of knowledge of the facts depending on the author, and most learnedly, on the whole, in a rich chapter of Salo W. Baron's great history of the Jews. Between the sixth and twelfth centuries, 'the Jewish occupational stratification underwent a radical change. A people theretofore still largely deriving its livelihood from farming and handicrafts was being transformed into a predominantly mercantile population with a strong emphasis on the money trade. The climactic stage of that evolution was not to be reached until the later Middle Ages and, even then, was to be limited only to a few areas north of the Alps and the Loire. But the basic trends became fully manifest long before 1200. They operated most strongly under

---

[44]More precisely, Max Weber considered the Jews a 'pariah people' (*ein Pariavolk*) in the manner of the pariahs of India: a 'guest-people' (*Gastvolk*) ritually separated from the social surroundings, either formally or *de facto*. But he immediately mentioned several differences from the pariah castes of India. From a structural point of view, the most important of these is that the Jews were a pariah people within an ambient society that had no castes. (M. Weber, *Gesammelte Aufsätze zur Religionssoziologie*, vol. 3, *Das antike Judentum*, Tübingen 1921, pp. 2–6.) But this is precisely a capital difference. There is no doubt that there are instances of concord with the phenomenon of castes. But in Antiquity the Jews were a nation like others, and emigrated and were dispersed like others. Except that the accumulation of the ritual rules through which the founders of Yahvism had sought to maintain its specificity and rigorous attachment to the national god made them both a structured ritual group (*ritualistischer Verband*) (ibid., p. 352) and what I call an ideological movement. This, however, is not sufficient to constitute a caste. The caste's difference from 'certain ethnic groups and sects' membership of which is hereditary—among other things, the fact that the society as a whole is not divided into such groups—is well noted by E.B. Harper, *Structure and Change in Indian Society*, edited by M. Singer and B.S. Cohn, Wenner-Gren Foundation for Anthropological Research, New York 1968, p. 52, cf. p. 74. On the Jews of India, who *did become* a caste within Indian society, see S. Strizower, 'Jews as an Indian Caste', *The Jewish Journal of Sociology*, vol. 1, April 1959, pp. 43–57; reproduced in *Religion, Culture, and Society*, L. Schneider, ed., New York 1964, pp. 220–232. [It should be noted that as early as 1914 the Marxist theorist Karl Kautsky characterized the Jews of the Middle Ages and of modern times as a 'hereditary town-dwelling caste' in his excellent article 'Rasse und Judentum', *Die Neue Zeit*, 30 October 1914; cf. M. Massara, *Il marxismo e la questione ebraica*, Milan 1972, pp. 113 ff. and 441 ff.]

Western Christendom, and were constantly reinforced by the gradual transfer of the Jewish people's centre of gravity from East to West, as well as by the slow infiltration of Western concepts and institutions into the Muslim areas.'[45]

A range of causes *tended*—with very important exceptions—to make the Jews abandon landed property. In the West, the increasingly crystallized feudal system found it difficult to integrate the Jews, for it was not easy to ask them to swear a Christian oath and it was distasteful to recognize them as suzerains of the common people, and still less of Christian nobles (although it did happen). On the other hand, no important factor ran counter to their continued participation in industrial and craft activities. International trade, notably between East and West (in which the Jews, as we have already seen, played an important although never exclusive role), saw sharpened and better-organized competition from non-Jews, especially from the twelfth century, when the corporations were formed in the West and the Italian mercantile republics acquired decisive economic and political importance.

The process of accelerated urbanization through which the Muslim world was then passing encouraged many Jews to embark on careers in banking and the liberal professions, although these were by no means their exclusive preserve. In 'antiquity and, in its continuation, under Byzantine domination, Jews never constituted an important segment of the banking profession. By legalizing a modest rate of interest, the later Roman and Byzantine Empires obviated the necessity of legal evasions and prevented the creation of special ethnic or religious groups dedicated to this commercial branch.'[46] The religious laws against 'usury', very broadly interpreted in the Muslim East and in Christian Europe alike, on the contrary helped to encourage the Jews in this specialization. In the Muslim East, the opportunities available to Muslims for getting around the law and the presence of the Christians, another subjugated minority, effectively impeded this evolution, repugnant to the entire orientation of the medieval Muslim world, towards a dynamic economy with a

---

[45]S.W. Baron, *Social and Religious History*, vol. 4, pp. 150 ff.
[46] Ibid., p. 198.

highly developed 'capitalist' sector.[47]

If there were Jewish bankers—not necessarily restricted to issuing interest-bearing loans—there were also Christian and Muslim bankers, and all the professions (especially the urban ones) had representatives among the Jews. The high proportion of merchants of all varieties merely reflects a general urban phenomenon. In the Latin West, on the other hand, 'powerful forces increasingly drove Jews into moneylending as their major occupation....From the outset, Jews arriving in more advanced lands possessed more cash than their Christian competitors.'[48] Compensation paid for land confiscations augmented their initial capital. Very slowly, the ecclesiastical prohibitions finally had their effects, preventing the clergy, for example, initially the most important group of moneylenders, from continuing this activity. The Jews were able to engage in it openly, although sometimes only as figureheads for unscrupulous Christians. The kings above all—the protectors of the Jews, who were considered their serfs and therefore placed outside feudal protection—had every interest in encouraging the Jews to specialize in this commerce, which they were thus able to control. After allowing the Jews to enrich themselves, they could then despoil them, by confiscation or by more subtle methods, with much greater ease than they could their potential Christian rivals. Nevertheless, 'it was not until the thirteenth century that moneylending became the preeminent occupation of Jews in France, and still later in Germany'.[49] In Spain it was never a preponderant activity for them. 'We must bear in mind, however, that Jews never became the sole, and frequently were not even the main, suppliers of credit. The Church may have been increasingly successful in eliminating moneylending by the clergy, but it never seriously hampered such transactions among merchants. Foreigners, in particular, were generally less subject to the pressures of public opinion and threats of anathemas...' They often became lenders. 'Afterwards, foreigners from Mediterranean countries who were frequently called by such names as Lombards and Cahorsins (often, like the term "Jews",

---

[47]Cf. Maxime Rodinson, *Islam and Capitalism*, especially pp. 12 ff. and 28 ff.
[48]S.W. Baron, *Social and Religious History*, vol. 4, pp. 202–3.
[49]Ibid., p. 205.

these designations were used in a generally pejorative vein) took over a major share in English and French banking. Even if employed in the service of the Papacy,...they were no more popular with their debtors. Ultimately, they, like their Jewish competitors, suffered from street attacks and formal expulsions. In fact, they were usually expelled before the Jews.'[50]

The theory of the Jews as a people-class thus has some validity from the lower Middle Ages onwards in Western Europe. Once again —and this bears repeating—this does not mean that the Jews were the only ones to engage in money-lending, nor that all Jews were moneylenders. In fact, there were serious class divisions within the Jewish communities. But it is fair to say that throughout a region of particular importance in the world, these communities revolved around those of their members who practised this profession, and that poor Jews shared in the profits of the bankers through mendicancy, patronage, and so on.

It is also quite true that the advances of the capitalist sector and then of the capitalist economy in Western Europe made the Jews less useful, and that, this being the case, it was easier for unifying ideological trends that implied the persecution and then the expulsion of these heterogeneous communities to gain ground. Especially since the violent popular hatred aroused by the initial consequences of capitalist development could easily be diverted against this minority, which seemed its most trenchant symbolic support and against whom the ideological arsenal of Christendom offered so many keen weapons. The Jews truly appeared as the scapegoat, the classic image of the genuine anti-Semitism that Jewish nationalists have sought unfairly to impute to all conflicts involving Jews throughout space and time.

But here again, the Jews were not eliminated. The specialization of the Jews, shared by some Christians but in numbers still insufficient for the development of the new economy, continued to make them useful, and enabled them to find specific spheres of activity wherever conditions were favourable. The sovereigns of Renaissance Italy— the popes in the first place—already affected by an initial wave of secularism that reawakened the tolerant traditions of the Roman

---

[50]Ibid., p. 207.

Empire, freely allowed the Jews to participate in all aspects of common life. The many German principalities, endebted first by wars and then by the necessity of sustaining a life luxurious enough to meet the need for prestige of their princes, had recourse to the financial capacities the Jews had acquired. Further east, when Poland sought to enter the sphere of the capitalist economy, it called upon Jewish merchants.

The necessity for ideological pluralism was felt ever more strongly in Western Europe after the Reformation. It was first tried in the Netherlands, where there was a multiplicity of sects and a high level of commercial development. What began as religious tolerance gradually grew into tolerance of indifference to matters of religion. The eighteenth century was to see blows against the Catholic church as the ideological mainstay of the old social order that the rising bourgeoisie was striving to bring down. The Jews benefitted from all these developments, which tended to guarantee the free development of their religious community.

It is true that in another sense secularization was tending to whittle down this community. Indeed, the modern state, founded on the basis of the rise of the capitalist bourgeoisie and, at the outset, of centralized monarchies, was tending to abolish the pluralism of the earlier societies, to suppress all particular community legal systems, along with any autonomy of a quasi-state type, any state within the state. The multiplicity of sects in the countries of refuge, like the Netherlands, and in the new countries peopled with immigrants, like the United States; the conciliatory liberalism that had arisen after the religious wars in England; the yearning for authoritarian centralization, as in France, and for the overthrow of any Roman tutelage, as in Austria, were all leading, in conjunction with the philosophy of the Enlightenment, to a tendency to consider all subjects or citizens of a state as members of a national community having the same status as all others. Membership of a church, religion, or sect was becoming a mere choice that would lead to adherence to a free association at most. By tradition, there were still state religions, but the status entailed few privileges. Religions were losing what state or quasi-state character they may have had.

This rule was applied to Judaism too, although with greater delay and reluctance than for the various Christian churches. The oath, in general sworn according to a Christian formula, was an obstacle to full citizenship, notably in the Anglo-Saxon countries. In France the principal obstacle was the particularist ethnic characteristics the Jews had acquired (notably in Alsace) as a result of their long marginal existence. But in the end all this was overcome.

The decay of Jewish community autonomy made integration into the ambient society much easier. The development of the capitalist economy, with its unifying power in the framework of new nations, tended to efface the particularisms of the Jews and their possible functional specializations, although the final after-effects were slow to disappear. In Western Europe and America religion became their only remaining specific feature, along with, of course, the ritual practices it entailed, which affected many an aspect of their behaviour. But the perpetuation of these practices and modes of behaviour was no longer protected by the Jewish community, which was no longer any more than a free association. To leave it no longer required abjuration or excommunication, as was still the case for the 'renegade' Spinoza in the seventeenth century, although even then it was already somewhat symbolic. Since they lived in a society that increasingly treated them as equal, and since they were adopting its values and customs, many Jews were coming to find intolerable the tyranny of ritual practices that seemed increasingly cumbersome, archaic, and antiquated. As in the Hellenistic society of Antiquity and during the Muslim Middle Ages, they were impatient at being kept from full participation in the common civilization by a particularism linked to previous conditions. Some kept the faith of their ancestors as one religious 'opinion' among others, while rejecting the rites or trying to adapt them to the practices current in the wider society.[51] Others questioned even this 'opinion' and adopted either another religion or, in the new atmosphere, one of the secular ideologies then on the rise.

---

[51]An example would be the efforts to bring Christmas and the celebration of the Chanukah festival closer together in the United States (cf. Will Herberg, *Protestant, Catholic, Jew, An Essay in American Religious Sociology*, Garden City, N.Y. 1955.) Likewise, under Muslim civilization, the efforts of the son of the great Maimonides, head of the Jewish community in Egypt, to 'Islamicize' Jewish rites (S.D. Goitein, *Jews and Arabs*, pp. 182 ff.; for other adaptations, see pp. 178 ff.). For the Hellenistic epoch, see S.W. Baron, *Social and Religious History*, vol. 1, pp. 165 ff., vol. 2, pp. 3 ff.

This time Judaism was on the road to complete liquidation. In Western Europe and America it was preserved by the constant influx of Jews from countries of Eastern Europe or the Muslim world, in which medieval conditions had persisted: the autonomy and particularism of their communities, the visible sign of which was the preservation of special dialects or even languages (like Yiddish, a Germanic dialect spoken in Slavic countries), accompanied, in the latter case, by an entire Yiddish literary culture. But it was not long before the new arrivals followed the evolution charted by their previously established co-religionists before them.[52] Moreover, the countries from which they had come, which were themselves entering the sphere of Western capitalism, the destroyer of particularisms, were showing signs of advancing down the same road. One could predict, with the 'Stalinist' Marxist Otto Heller, 'the end of Judaism'[53] as a particular mode of life. Some men and women of Jewish descent preserved a certain faith among others. Others, on the contrary, were melting into the wider society like many of their forebears in the past, preserving varying degrees of sentimental attachment to a particular tradition that did have its glories. For many, even this descent was finally forgotten. It is hard to see any reason to consider this trend catastrophic.

Judaism was preserved by anti-Semitism and by modern political Zionism, which was a consequence of it. It seems to me that on the whole Léon is right about the factors that were at the root of these tendencies. In this already too long introduction I will not dwell on subtle differences with some of his assertions, which seem to me somewhat too abrupt. It will suffice to note—with a perspicacity that is all too facile after the quarter of a century of developments since his death—that (unfortunately) he underestimated the intensity of the feeling of identification that would lead many Jews to a nationalist attitude as inconsistent as it is pernicious. In any case, this feeling was terribly reinforced by the savagery of Hitlerite persecu-

---

[52]This process is particularly striking in the history of the British Jews. See Maurice Freedman, ed., *A Minority in Britain, Social Studies of the Anglo-Jewish Community*, London 1955.

[53]O. Heller, *Der Untergang des Judentums*, 2nd edn, Verlag für Literatur und Politik, Vienna-Berlin 1933. Compare the more cautious conclusions of George Friedmann, *Fin du peuple juif?*, Paris 1965.

tion, by the demented massacre of which the Jews were the principal victims. Just as the pole of attraction formed by the new Hasmonaean state in Palestine partially arrested the process of Hellenization in the diaspora during the second century before Christ,[54] so the creation of the state of Israel in 1948 encouraged sentiments of solidarity among Jews everywhere, which contributed to reinforcing or reconstituting a particularism that had been crumbling and, moreover, most often lacked any cultural, social, or even religious base. I do not believe that this is anything to be happy about.

The present situation of the Jews, apparently triumphant in Israel and at the apogee of their prestige in the capitalist world, is more tragic under this glory than it often was under humiliation. Zionism achieved its principal objective, the creation of a Jewish state in Palestine, by exploiting a situation brought about by European and American imperialist powers, and by relying directly on one or another of these powers on various occasions. As Léon among others pointed out, this has not at all resolved the 'Jewish problem', but has even aggravated it seriously. As many people had predicted, Jews and non-Jews alike, not only revolutionaries and Marxists, but also bourgeois liberals, it has in the first place created an intractable problem in the relations between the Jewish colony of Palestine and the Arab people whose elementary right to be master in its own territory was violated by this colony. The Palestinian protest was soon supported by the entire Arab world. It could not have been otherwise during a period of rising Arab nationalism. The cycle of protests and reaction thus set in motion has already given rise to several wars and innumerable minor military operations, riots, clashes, and attacks, both individual and collective. It is readily predictable that this process will continue, and there is every reason to expect one or several tragedies of the first order in Palestine.

As was inevitable, the Palestinian problem, created by Zionism and compounded by its local triumph, has spread hatred of the Jews into the Arab countries, where anti-Semitism was previously virtually unknown. The Zionists have very actively aided this with their in-

---

[54]Cf. *Corpus papyrorum judaicarum*, vol. 1, V.A. Tcherikover, ed., in collaboration with A. Fuks, Cambridge, Mass. 1957, pp. 46 ff.

cessant propaganda designed to persuade people that Zionism, Judaism, and Jewishness are equivalent concepts. The Palestinian problem has contributed to strengthening the most reactionary forces in the Arab countries, who are quite content, like their colleagues everywhere, to accord national questions priority over social progress. Even socialist elements were constrained to devote a great part of their efforts to the struggle against the state of Israel, which in the eyes of their masses seemed, not without considerable justification, to be the incarnation of a world imperialist advance. Zionist success in Palestine has afforded the imperialist powers myriad opportunities to peddle their support and weaponry in the Middle East. In Israel itself, the reactions of the Arabs have enabled the most chauvinist and retrograde orientations to gain ground, through a blackmail based on national unity similar to that which is used in the Arab countries. An important part of the world Jewish population, the Israeli Jewish colony, thus finds itself committed to a dead-end course, driven to a policy of preventive aggression abroad and discriminatory legislation at home, the entire situation encouraging a racist and chauvinist mentality that impels society down the road of social regression.

This immense mess could not be limited to Palestine, nor even to the Arab world. It was inevitable that under the conditions of sharpened sensitivity among Jews everywhere after the great Hitlerite massacre, many of them, unaware of the circumstances of the Palestinian tragedy or deliberately trying to ignore them, would feel elementary solidarity whenever vicissitudes in Palestine led to a set-back for the Jews there, or more often (up to now) to the prediction of a set-back, which prediction Zionist propaganda (and Arab propaganda as well, though for different reasons) took care to present as virtually certain and as inevitably assuming tragic dimensions.

Thus, while religious Judaism was turning back to the impasses of ethnocentric religiosity, which it had never completely abandoned, the Jews of the entire world were lured far from the universalist horizons towards which so many of them had turned in the previous period. Solidarity with Israel entailed many dangerous implications in terms of options in international politics. But above all it gravely risked recreating a quasi-national entity that had been on the road to liquidation for several centuries. Constant moral and physical blackmail is exercised against Jews who refuse to consider themselves members of a distinct community to which they owe allegiance. It is demanded of them that they support choices made on Palestinian soil by bodies over which they have no control and as the consequence of previous choices which the majority of the Jews of the time had refused to endorse, or had even ardently combatted.[55]

The entire action and thought of the international socialist movement—and of what Mannheim has called liberal-humanitarian ideology as well, though often inconsistently—had been directed towards overcoming national antagonisms. The class struggle was accorded priority not because struggles between classes were held to be an ideal, but because it was thought that they could lead to the abolition of classes, and thus to a just, rational, and harmonious society. It was thought that any oppressed national collective should be defended and liberated. But nationalist ideology, which ascribed primordial value to the nation, had to be combatted, struggles between free and independent nations had to be abolished, for it was indeed hard to see how these sterile conflicts, with their cyclical defeats and setbacks, futile massacres and periods of tranquillity during which preparations for further massacres were made, could lead to harmonious coexistence—unless nationalist ideology itself was abandoned and society devoted itself to resolving the problems of social organization.

If struggles between nations set off a dynamic that many Jews rejected, correctly regarding them as pernicious, then struggles between quasi-nations within existing nations threatened to be even worse. In some rare cases, progressive movements of social reorganization can proceed concurrently with national struggles. This is far more difficult when it is a question of nation-like groups within a single nation. The quasi-national allegiance then quickly gains primacy over fidelity to a social layer or class around which the struggle for a new form of society can be mobilized. This is easily

---

[55][According to W. Rabi, to demand control over actions taken in our name is to betray cowardice. A thug's morality! Were the French (or Germans!) who refused to support the military adventures embarked upon by their governments cowards, then? My country, right or wrong! Those who invoke memories of the great massacre so often—and so often for contestable causes—should at least remember that the German translation of that lovely slogan was inscribed on the gate at Buchenwald.]

seen in the United States, for example, where for all sorts of historical and sociological reasons different nationality-like groups have preserved some coherence within the wider American nation—first of all, though not exclusively, the black quasi-nation. The recreation by Zionism and its consequences of the Jewish quasi-nation brings grist to the mill of this retrograde process and threatens to accelerate it. The hostility now arising between blacks and Jews in the United States could be a mere foretaste of even more dangerous phenomena. The perils of this prospect must be taken seriously.

The Jews might allow themselves to be drawn by this evolution into taking positions against the ideals and aspirations of the Third World, which by the very force of circumstance are shared by the Arabs. All readers, I believe, can well imagine the fatal repercussions of such an eventuality. In the interests of brevity, I will forgo their enumeration.

In the Communist countries as well, Zionism has provided the ruling layers (or classes) with an excellent pretext for abandoning their ideological principles, capitulating to the anti-Semitism of the masses, and even worse, making use of it for purposes that can only be called reactionary. Under Stalin, the deformed application of a nationalities policy that was based on just principles led to the preservation of the Jewish entity in the USSR instead of encouraging its assimilation. The capitulation of the regimes to popular anti-Semitism, which sharpened the rancour and despair of the Jews, turned them towards an incomparably idealized Israel, partly out of ignorance and partly out of a need for fabulous escapism from the sad reality. Zionism has contributed to reviving this nostalgia, to turning hopes outward, to increasing the distrust of the authorities, to offering justification for their fears, to supplying arguments for their hypocritically discriminatory measures. It was more or less the same, with some local variations, in the People's Democracies.

In the increasingly serious struggles now under way both within each group of countries (capitalist world, socialist world, and Third World) and between these categories, the Jews are driven by the process set in motion by Zionism towards options that are reactionary in the full sense of the word. All of us, Jews and non-Jews alike, must do all we can to arrest this evolution, the consequences of which could be terrible.

There is no use proclaiming that the 'Jewish problem' would be resolved in an ideal society and in conditions of complete harmony among nations. For the moment, any system of social or national oppression and exploitation in whatever form can only aggravate it, making use of even the vestiges of Jewish specificity. It is now clear to everyone that oppressive systems can arise on foundations other than that of a capitalist economy, a prospect unappealing to those beloved of illusions, but fully in conformity with the implicit or explicit underpinnings of Marxist sociology, even if Marx, out of ideological ardour, sometimes forgot it.

Logically, the 'Jewish problem', the relations of tension between Jews and others, can be fully 'resolved' in only one of two ways, leaving aside the radical solution worked out by Adolf Hitler: either through the withering away of specifically Jewish characteristics, leading to total assimilation and to the disappearance of Jewish specificity itself, or through the establishment of a perfectly harmonious society. The first perspective now seems far off. The second, to say the least, is not right around the corner. But in any case, it seems clear that any struggle for a more rational and more just society brings us closer to this ideal. It may at least be asked of the Jews that they not place themselves on the wrong side, that they not impede this struggle.

In the pre-1945 situation in which Léon lived, when the struggle against fascism had priority, Jews of all categories, opinions, and ideals were placed in the progressive camp by Hitlerite ideology, whether they liked it or not. To place oneself there today no longer requires mere passive observation of the savage enmity of the most brutal reactionaries, but an act of lucidity and positive will. It is imperative to do it.

In the abstract, an ingathering of Jews having retained some ethnic or quasi-ethnic specificity into a community of a national type in the broadest sense could have been conceivable—quite apart from the faithful of the Jewish religion, for whom affiliation to a religious-type formation is a right. But the Zionist option brought about this ingathering under the worst possible conditions. Its consequences led almost inevitably to placing it in a reactionary context. And as I have already argued, any artificial conservation of specific features that were tending to disappear itself encourages alignment with options of this sort.

In the present conditions of exacerbated struggle between the hungry masses of the Third World and the capitalist imperialist powers, of pressure by the masses of the Communist world for democratic socialism, and of international and intranational tensions in the capitalist world,[56] it is imperative to prevent the 'Jewish problem' from being used to aid the manoeuvres of the most reactionary forces. The struggle against them is everyone's business. The fight to turn the Jewish masses away from them is more particularly the business of Jews. That this is difficult makes it all the more necessary. It requires, as I said earlier, lucidity and courage. Abram Léon gives us an example of both of these.

These pages, in which I have tried to complement certain points of Léon's analysis, seem to me to confirm it, on the basis of incontestable historical facts. Unintelligent pedants may dwell on this or that lacuna or error of detail, this or that schematization in his book. In the terrible conditions of the Belgian resistance to the German occupation, while under the additional handicaps of being a Jew (he, too, in the Hitlerite and Zionist sense of the word[57]) and belonging to the Trotskyist movement, he was able to gather very ample documentation and, most important, to delineate the general outlines of the 'Jewish question' in a substantially correct manner. That itself is no small achievement, and none of his critics, however erudite they are and however useful their own works may have been, has had Léon's courage in rejecting explicitly and openly an entire structure of pernicious and absurd theories. This passivity in the face of nationalist delirium on the part of the best specialists in Jewish history (and often their complicity with it) has had serious consequences in the past. There is every reason to fear that in the future these consequences will be even worse.

Léon may have been wrong on this or that point, sometimes led astray in his particular hypotheses. But he was right about the essential thing, the capital thing. Judaism is explained by history and not

---

[56][This was written in 1968. Today I would make this rapid portrait of current struggles somewhat more balanced. But there is no sense in doing that here. The consequences I drew then still seem valid to me.]

[57]See above, p. 13.

outside it. It merits no special scientific or moral privilege. There was no divine or extra-rational necessity for the survival of the Jewish people or the Jewish religion as such. The only moral necessity is to demand respect for the legitimate collective rights of a religious or secular community when it exists, but not to maintain it, recreate it, or reinforce it when impersonal social factors (and not brutal constraint, force and persecution) cause it to wither. If Judaism or the Jewish people have been the bearers of some particular values that are laudable, beautiful, and still useful, then these must be defended because of their intrinsic validity, without regard to the people or ideology that has adopted them. The Jews are men and women whose individual right to existence must be defended, just like anyone else's, against anti-Semitic barbarism. Any structure that some of them have been led to create must be judged on its own merits and demerits.

Group idolatory has always had pernicious consequences, both scientifically and morally. The greatest glory of ancient Israel was to have produced men, the great prophets, who were able to abandon it, for the first time in history. Léon was part of their lineage in spirit far more than in blood. We must rally to the beacon he bequeathed us, lest we be led down the path of social regression.

4
Nation and Ideology

The following essay appeared in the Encyclopaedia Universalis *(vol. 11, Paris 1971) as the third of several articles under the entry 'Nation'. Although it does not deal especially with the Jews, past or present, it does treat more general matters of obvious concern to any interpretation of Jewish history and contemporary politics alike. Contrary to the claims of its advocates, nationalism has not been a universal feature of human thought throughout history. On the other hand, as I pointed out in the previous essay (see note 10), there has also been some tendency to treat nationalist ideology as an unprecedented phenomenon peculiar to the era of the rise of capitalism. While there is doubtless a kernel of truth in that view, there is equally no doubt that ideological forms of group identification, some of which bear a close resemblance to modern nationalism in many respects, are very ancient indeed. Despite its laconic style (probably inevitable in an encyclopaedia article), I hope that the following piece offers some useful observations on the nature of nationalist ideology and its relation to other forms of human self-identification.*

'People', 'ethnic group', 'nationality', and 'nation' are different terms designating various types of aggregate formations whose scope goes beyond and transcends that of the primary aggregate groups: clans, tribes, cities and villages, city-states, provinces. All of them suggest the rise of bonds of solidarity that unite these ethnic, territorial, or simultaneously ethnic and territorial, groups. There is no agreement about the different types of formation to which these labels should be applied. The important point is to understand that there is an infinite gradation of forms, and the criteria of differentiation are multiple.

Any group of this type will have, at a minimum, a vague consciousness of itself, an implicit ideology that corresponds to its perception of reality and responds (more or less well) to the exigencies of its conditions. Intellectuals, albeit sometimes of a very primitive sort, develop more or less elaborate theories, and thus make these basic ideological elements explicit, warping them somewhat in the process. At the very least, the ethnic-national group is defined, set off from others. The cultural features and institutions that constitute, or are supposed to constitute, its specificity are thus welded to its identity. All its manifestations of unity are thereby justified and legitimated.

All these various ideologies, however much or little explicit and theorized, may be called ethnic-national ideologies. The more specific term 'nationalism' has generally been applied either to the ideology of the nation-state in its contemporary form or to the most highly theoretical, most aggressive (and also most detached from any other reference-point) versions of this ideology produced by the various ethnic-national groups.

1. Ethnic-National Ideologies and Formations

Ethnic-national ideologies vary first of all, of course, according to the sort of group to which they correspond.

Unorganized ethnic groups are unstructured, or ill-structured, sets of practically independent units like tribes or city-states. Examples would be the tribes of Gaul, the Germanic, Israelite, or Arab tribes, the Sumerian, Greek, or Mayan city-states, the Egyptian nomes of the pre-dynastic age. These units, the members of which speak the same language and have many cultural features in common, acknowledge a kinship system on the pattern of the clan or family. There are often institutions that serve to manifest this very relative unity, at least at certain intervals. Examples are amphictyonies, pilgrimages to a common sanctuary, fairs or common markets, sport or literary competitions like the Olympic Games or the pre-Islamic Arab market of 'Okaz.

Ethnic-national states emerge when a state structure is formed encompassing a given ethnic group or significant part of it. Political unity may then level internal differentiations to a certain extent, depending on the strength of the state and the degree of integration permitted by economic and geographic conditions. Ethnic-national ideology is then reinforced and becomes state ideology. This is what happened in Pharaonic Egypt, in the ancient kingdoms of Israel, and in the great Chinese kingdoms. Several states may be formed within the same ethnic group, in which case ethnic ideology largely retains the same character as in the previous instance.

Empires are state units within which one ethnic group (in general already grouped into an ethnic-national state, or at least arranged into tribes or federated city-states, as in the case of the Aztecs) dominates others. These are powerful formations which develop an ideology of their own separate from or standing above the ethnic ideologies. If, as sometimes happens, the various ethnic groups tend to fuse within it, then the case of the ethnic-national state re-emerges.

Universalist religious communities likewise normally encompass several ethnic groups in whole or in part. Here again, religious ideology constitutes a serious competitor of ethnic-national ideology.

The dislocation of empires creates ethnic-national *territorial states* corresponding either to fractions of ethnic groups or to more than one ethnic group. In Europe during the latter part of the Middle Ages powerful monarchies in France and England, supported by rich, influential, and dynamic bourgeoisies, created *national* states (or *nation-states*) that encompassed the greater part of an ethnic group whose internal units were almost completely obliterated by the sweep of economic integration. Likewise, the adaptation of the great universalist religious communities to the variety of local conditions and states, sometimes going as far as ideological schism, divides them into *national churches* whose ideology may combine with that of the national state, especially when the latter sets itself in opposition to the universalist community (as in the case of Gallicanism).

In the framework of ethnic-national states, empires, or nation-states, *ethnic groups* or *quasi-nations* may subsist or arise, in subordinate positions; depending on the circumstances, they are unified to a greater or lesser extent, more or less integrated into the state, and more or less sensitive to the integrating ideology of the state. They thus constitute ideological minorities of an ethnic-national character, sometimes attached to a religious community (Parsees in India, Jews, etc.), sometimes more or less specialized in some particular social function (smiths, pariahs, etc.) and assuming the character of castes (blacks in the United States). They may sometimes be reduced to the point of disappearance through fusion, or on the contrary they may become consolidated to the point of demanding secession. Even dependent minority religious communities devoid of any ethnic character of their own, however, may nevertheless often approximate this type of grouping (the various Christian churches of the Middle East, for instance).

During the nineteenth and twentieth centuries, the world-wide predominance of the nation-state (at least as the sort of grouping universally acknowledged as superior), combined with the correlative decay of religious communities as an acceptable kind of supra-functional grouping, has led to the formation of a *society of nations*. The latter reproduces, at a higher level, the universe of co-existing ethnic groups that prevailed not long ago. The proliferation of international links leads to supra-national aspirations, to the formation of supra-national communities, leagues of nations, federation projects, sometimes to attempts to create empires, like the German National Socialist empire. On the other hand, the formation of a *universalist ideological community*, the Communist world, which at a certain point approximated (at the least) the imperial type, reproduces the past dynamic of the constitution and dislocation of empires and churches, with ideological schisms, the consolidation of nation-states not fully integrated into the empire, and aspirations for the formation of nation-states on the part of politically integrated ethnic groups or nationalities. The complexity of these various formations demonstrates that a *plurality of possible frameworks* may exist for the same individual or the same group. One may belong simultaneously to two formations, to two different levels.

2. Orientations and Structure
of Ethnic-National Ideologies

Orientations Depending on Conditions

An ethnic-national ideology can be understood only as an over-arching orientation that leaves its mark on all elements of the structure of that ideology. In sum, this orientation constitutes the relationship between the situation in which the group finds itself and the aspirations of its members, depending on the possibilities, real or imagined, of satisfying these aspirations.

Normally, ethnic-national ideologies are *ideologies of affirmation* that simply lend an ideological form to consciousness of relative unity. From this angle, they represent 'ideological' ideologies in the strict sense, according to the classification proposed by Karl Mannheim—in other words, they simply transcend the real situation of the group, embellishing, mystifying, and mythifying it, without genuinely seeking to realize the ideal thus portrayed. But the affirmation slackens or is intensified depending on the circumstances, essentially as a function of internal tensions between groups, as well as threats or attractions from outside.

Powerful tension between internal groups can lead in practice to disdain for the ethnic-national unit, and more rarely to a challenge to it at the level of theory. It is more facile to denounce the enemy groups as betraying the ideal behaviour of the ethnic group.

Sharp and lasting conflicts between neighbouring ethnic groups can lead to *ideologies of competition or combat*, to mobilizing ideologies. Apologetic myths and others disparaging the opposed ethnic group then proliferate. The gods of both sides are drafted into service, and simultaneously exalted or disparaged. As one example among thousands, let us cite Virgil's verses assimilating Octavius's campaign against Anthony and Cleopatra to a struggle between the Roman and Egyptian ethnic groups:

omnigenumque deum monstra et latrator Anubis
contra Neptunem et Venerem contraque Minervam
tela tenent.

'Barking Anubis, a whole progeny of grotesque
Deities are embattled against Neptune and Minerva
And Venus.'

Aeneid, VIII, 698–700 (trans. by C. Day Lewis).

If an ethnic group normally unified (or at least federated) by a state embarks on an imperialist policy, dominates or strives to dominate other ethnic groups, an *ideology of domination* arises. The reign of this dominant ethnic group is identified with cosmic order, its mores and institutions with the realization of the human ideal itself. Those who resist are denounced as rebels against universal order and are consigned to the category of the sub-human, the bestial, and associated with the disorder of the elements at the time of primeval chaos, with the precultural unreasoning vagaries of pure nature. Once again, these are 'ideological' ideologies in Mannheim's sense.

Ideologies of resistance are formed in opposition to these efforts at domination, and if the domination is an accomplished fact, these may become intensely mobilizing *ideologies of revolt*. Insistence is then placed on ethnic loyalty, on fidelity to the national values and gods, against the putative or real dominators, and above all against any forces within the ethnic group itself that opt for 'collaboration'. Beyond that, an entire ideology of national independence, of liberty, denounces oppression and tyranny in themselves, as well as the cruelty and dissolute morals that are assumed to be intrinsic to the dominating ethnic group, and the luxury they draw from their pillage. Sometimes this ideology may even go beyond the ethnic horizon. An appeal for solidarity from other threatened ethnic groups is then issued, and an underlying unity may even be postulated. The Celts and Germans against the Romans, for example. Now it is a matter of what Mannheim calls 'utopian' ideologies, which transcend the real situation of the group and trace the portrait of an ideal situation which the people are called upon to realize through action.

If repeated experience persuades people that revolt or resistance is futile, then *ideologies of resignation, submission*, or even *renunciation* may arise. Submission is often extolled in encomiums to the conquering nation, to its virtues, its 'mission', the benefits of the tranquillity it establishes, and the values of the civilization it fosters within its empire. If cultural and legal conditions permit, assimilation or integration into this nation is preached. Moreover, demographic, financial, or other considerations may induce the conquerors, for their part, to encourage such assimilation, to open their ranks to their subjects, as the Romans did, for instance, in the celebrated edict of Caracalla (in 212). Hence the apologia for Roman assimilation by the Gaul Rutilius Namatianus in the fifth century:

> *Fecisti patriam diversis gentibus unam*
> ....
> *Urbem fecisti quod prius orbis erat.*

'From different peoples you have formed a single fatherland..., what was a world you have made a single state' (*Itinerarium*, i, 63, 66).

Alongside these ideologies of submission, and in similar circumstances, *ideologies of renunciation* of the national problem itself may arise: adherence to universalist philosophies or religions.

Levels of Organization and Production of Ideologies

Ethnic-national ideologies are organized and made explicit at various levels.

This may occur at the level of the entire society, of the ethnic-national group as a whole. If the latter seeks only to continue to exist and is not subject to dangerous threats, then it will generate conservative 'ideological' ideologies that aggrandize the real situation, or at best paint a portrait of gradual progress. 'Utopian' projects can arise only among poorly integrated groups, or they may grow out of the domain of social struggle, which lies beyond the subject of this article. If, on the contrary, the group is threatened or decides to threaten others, then 'utopian' ideologies of conquest and domination emanate from it.

Ethnic-national ideologies can be the product of *specialized groups* or *classes*, like intellectuals, military officers, or productive workers. To the extent that their ideologies are not adopted by the broader society, these groups constitute a class apart. Soldiers, for example, may produce ideologies of domination in the context of a peaceful society, or workers pacific ideologies in the context of a conquering society (but the opposite can happen too).

The ideologies in question can be produced or adopted by *ideological movements* structured into organizations to varying extents. A social or religious movement, for example, may adopt a project of an ethnic-national type by integrating it into the ideological synthesis that motivates it (like early Islam). It can also be a movement essentially devoted to the national cause, and therefore a nationalist movement. We may then be dealing with broad informal movements attracting masses through many competing organizations or even outside them, or a movement may also be composed of a single, well-defined organization, a party.

Theories, whether elaborate or not, are the work of intellectuals. The latter quite naturally express not only the point of view of the functional group they represent, but also that of the *class* to which they belong. Nevertheless, two points must not be overlooked. On the one hand, the material, basis, and point of departure of their theories is the sentiment, the implicit ideology, engendered by the general situation of the ethnic group of which they are a part. On the other hand, the theory has a mobilizing function and therefore must respond to the sentiments of the masses of the ethnic group as a whole. These theories therefore cannot be reduced purely and simply to the utilitarian myths of one class of the nation from which they issue, as Marxists too often tend to assume. They succeed only to the extent that they go beyond a narrow class horizon. But the class aspect in which they are garbed cannot be denied either.

Representations

Ideology is a biased representation of the world oriented towards social action. From it are drawn prescriptions of behaviour and action, whether individual or collective. An ideology may leave out of its domain a part of the universe for which objective representations are necessary, determined solely by the necessities of technical action and the possibilities of comprehension of reality, but it often tends to penetrate even this domain. The material for this is drawn for the most part from the objective world, the various elements of the latter being assigned positive or negative labels depending on the general orientation of the ideology and the organizational form that governs its formation. Moreover, extrapolation is the rule, whether it be generalization of real qualities of beings, their multiplication through the proliferation of abstract or supernatural beings, or the projection of the present into the past or future. There is a constant process of myth-making.

The principal actor in the cosmic drama is the ethnic-national group itself, sometimes transposed or incarnated in a human chief or an 'ethnarch' divinity (to use the term and theory of the Emperor Julian). The group is sharply set off from the outside world, and its relations to other groups defined. This is expressed in myths that are most often genealogical, myths of origin. The relations recognized by the ethnic-national units—and sometimes also the bonds of hostility or alliance, sympathy or antipathy, with neighbouring groups—are transposed into kinship ties. These myths may also be linked to cosmic myths situating the history of the group within a broader history of the universe, and rendering the group sacred by associating super-human wills with it, thus creating a 'sacred history'. Various groups are ascribed a set of features, a personality, a 'character' of the sort that would normally be attributed to an individual. These features may correspond in part to observations of real facts. But they are 'essentialist'. They generalize to the entire group traits that may be valid only for some of its members. They eternalize them and ascribe to the members of the group an eternal 'propensity', an immutable essence that they cannot, and never will be able to, shake off.

These judgements are also apologetic. They exalt the group from which they emanate, and identify its norms with those of the human species in its 'normal', 'healthy', or 'superior' form. The other groups, especially those that are adversaries, are on the contrary disparaged, belittled, and 'diabolized'. Their origin is traced back to sordid incidents (like Moab and Ammon, enemy cousins of Israel whose origin is accounted for by the incest committed by Lot's daughters, or the current mythology of the American Black Muslims on the origin of whites). Their disagreeable, abnormal, and ultimately even sub-human characteristics are also said to be linked to an essence that they cannot shed.

The competition, conflicts, and struggles of the group with any others tend to be described as an eternal combat between good and evil. Everything is absorbed into this outlook, and becomes either good or bad; the domain of the neutral tends to contract. In addition, as J. Gabel has convincingly noted, ideological consciousness tends to blur the coordinates of space and time. The successes of the group, and its past glory, are linked to its essence, just as the failures and misdeeds of adversary groups are to theirs. Present national consciousness is projected back into the past. Deviations from the present norm, the differing loyalties of yesteryear, and tendencies towards other forms of association are seen as deviations or monstrosities. All of history is reconstructed as a function of a single project: the constitution of the ethnic-national group as it exists today.

At a certain stage, the need is felt to summon up justifications of this representation of the world in the framework of a system of thought broader than the mere ascription of the qualities of the group to the will of its 'ethnarch' god-protector. Secular theories then take shape, like Aristotle's explaining Hellenic superiority by geographical determinism. (*Politics*, vi, 7, 1327b.) Much more recently, appeals have been made to the scientific advances of the nineteenth century in linguistics or anthropology. This has produced racist theories that amount to apologies for a particular nation or set of ethnic-national groups (the Whites, the Anglo-Saxons, etc.).

The ideological representations comprise not only myths defining the group and its essence, but also others that delineate the ideal situations that are to serve as its model. These are situated in a mythical time at either the dawn or the end of history. In either case, a situation is portrayed in which the group—a free people, strong and happy—lives in harmony and peace, respected or even served by the other groups, if not identified with humanity as a whole. All tensions, internal or external, are liquidated. If what is involved is an 'ideological' myth in the strict sense, a conservative myth of affirmation, then all are called upon to strive, in their daily behaviour, to approximate this ideal model, generally situated in the past. If this sort of myth has taken on a 'utopian' coloration, then the model is projected into the future, to be realized through political action under the leadership of the authorities of the ethnic-national group, and all are called upon to participate.

In organized movements, myths and representations generally take the form of dogmas, of 'theses' to which assent is required on pain of expulsion and accusation of treason.

Rites, Practices, and Organizations

Rites and practices, when related to myths, mark the unity and identity of the ethnic-national formation and celebrate its superiority or its rejection of the superiority of others. They define, proclaim, and inculcate a system of values that structures the group morally, and calls for devotion to it. Examples are religious festivals and common sacrifices to the ethnarch god, commemorations of real or imagined events that are said to mark the foundation and life of the group, public prayers and fasts, national pilgrimages. The individual's membership of the group is marked not only by public rites, but by private ones as well. Israelite circumcision is the most extrême example of this type, but the various rites of passage in which the collectivity intervenes (like national funerals) should also be noted.

The organizations or movements that diffuse ethnic-national ideologies naturally have their own initiation ceremonies, manifestations of unity, and so on. They develop organizational structures of varying degrees of ramification, with general staffs that lay down programmes, strategies, and tactics, and with theorists, rank-and-file members, statutes defining the rules of functioning, and so on.

In the ethnic-national ideologies of affirmation, the practices required are often simply those technical and social activities that are indispensable to the life of society. It is asked only that they be performed with the greatest of care, with maximum effectiveness and self-denial, with enthusiasm and desire to serve the group. Examples are voluntary supplementary labour of the Stakhanovite type, education of the masses, aid to the poor, military service, and even commercial trade, as in Venice. Sometimes special organizations, orders,

and associations are set up for this purpose. In the 'utopian' ideologies these activities are accompanied by political activism. When
they are carried out by specialized organizations or movements, this
activism can acquire an exclusivist character, the tasks of combat or
propaganda being performed at the expense of normal social activities.

Symbols

The manifestations of unity cannot be everlasting. Hence the particular importance of those symbols which, at any given time, mark
membership of the ethnic-national group: tattoos, scarring, body
painting or mutilation, national costumes, flags and emblems, types
of houses and village plans, types of writing, and finally, language.
Organizations and states exert pressure for the widespread adoption
of these signs of identity, which mark the group off from others. The
integration of heterogeneous groups is one of the objectives sought
(and often achieved) in this manner.

Norms and Sanctions

Adherence to ideological representations and dogmas, participation
in practices and rites, fidelity to organizations, and respect for symbols are moral norms imposed by sanctions if necessary. Failure to
observe them is stigmatized under the name 'treason'. Disavowal by
the group, internalized as a feeling of guilt, is often sufficient sanc-
tion to obtain at least an apparent observation. But sanctions are
often stipulated in laws and customs not only for acts of hostility
against the group but also for patent lack of respect for the norms in
question.

3. Ethnic-National Ideologies
and Other Ideologies

At the beginnings of history, when the human world appears as a universe of juxtaposed ethnic groups, ethnic-national ideology is frequently dominant. Only the bare outlines of ideologies erected on other foundations appear, in specialized cultural groups or associations based on age or sex, for example. But there is lively competition with the ideologies of other, more narrow aggregate groups: tribes, cities, villages, and so on. Frequently these latter prevail, leading to struggles that will be called fratricidal by the people of future centuries imbued with ethnic-national ideology, and to alliances with foreigners that will be called treason. The polemics intersect. The oldest war song conserved by the Israelite tribes of the North (that of Deborah, directed against the foreign chief Sisera) praises the participating tribes, reproaches neutrals, and curses a city whose abstention was particularly grievous (Judges 5). Those Gallic tribes initially allied with the Romans, even the faithful Eduens, eventually rallied to the call for ethnic solidarity issued by Vercingétorix. After a disaster suffered by the Spanish in 1520, the senate of the allied city of Tlaxcala deliberated on whether it would not be appropriate to abandon Cortes and rally to Tenochtitlán (Mexico), a traditional enemy but an ethnic relation.

In multi-ethnic empires, state ideologies are mingled with myths in which the sovereign, the dynasty, or the imperial order is linked to the cosmic order. Tension often arises between these and the ethnic-national ideologies of the various ethnic groups encompassed by the empire, the ideologies of domination of the ruling ethnic group, and the ideologies of resistance or submission among the subjugated ethnic groups.

Tensions likewise emerge between universalist ideology and ethnic-national ideologies when different ethnic-national groups are encompassed, even if only in part, in universalist ideological communities (religious in the past, secular today), whether or not these communities are identified with a state. Nevertheless, compromises can be arrived at between them, though not without damage to the intellectual coherence of the various ideologies, and also not without conflict. One has only to think of the conduct of the national Catholic churches during the First World War, each declaring itself guided by God and risking potential conflict with their theoretically common chief, the pope. Even the judges of Joan of Arc sought to embarrass her by playing upon this conflict, asking, 'Does God hate the English?'

In a given territory, the universalist churches assume an ethnic-national coloration, sometimes creating a hierarchy of their own, which permits a more elaborate conciliation between the universalist and ethnic-national ideologies. In the East, the Russian, Georgian, Armenian, Syrian, and Coptic national churches constitute developments of this order. In its initial stages Islam, in principle a universalist religion, supplied an ideological framework for the ethnic-national sentiments of the Arabs. Buddhism takes a form like this in Tibet. Mazdaism was a religion of universalist inclination that nevertheless congealed into a sort of ethnic-national Iranian church, even when the Iranian Mazdeans dominated other peoples and communities.

This process runs especially deep when an ideological schism occurs along ethnic-national lines: among the Hussite Czechs, for example, and in Communist China today.

There are many cases in which a state ideology or universalist ideology presses ethnic-national ideologies nearly to the point of disappearance. The latter may survive only among intellectuals, the members of a particular class, or may disappear even among them, especially since a process of fusion, assimilation, or integration may destroy the old groups in favour of new ones lacking an ideological tradition. But the foundations for the development of ethnic-national ideologies remain.

The ideologies of functional groups, and above all of classes, often possess such strength that they are able to compete with ethnic-national ideologies (as was, in fact, the case for the ideologies of the city-states). Classes often prefer the defeat of their own ethnic group or state to a victory that would favour their opponents in the struggle for power. They then justify their actions by invoking the higher good of their group, which they say would suffer internally from a victory over an external foe. There are many examples of this, from the Peloponnesian War to the Second World War. This attitude is theorized by the indifference, in principle, of universalist ideologies, whether religious or secular, to national allegiance. But their universalism may sometimes mask a covert ethnic-national ideology. Class ideology is sometimes confused with a humanist or humanitarian universalist ideology that accords priority among values to the good of humanity in general. The supreme good of the class is identified with the good of humanity, as it was once identified with the good of the group. We have seen many vicissitudes of these universalist ideologies.

The greatest enemy of ethnic-national ideology is individualism, practical or theoretical. But the latter develops only in particular social circumstances.

4. Ethnic-National Ideologies and the World

The Essential Tasks of Ethnic-National Ideologies

Ethnic-national ideologies have a role to play in the essential tasks that are incumbent upon any society. As soon as economic, demographic, geographic, and other conditions make possible a formation of broader scope than the tribe, city, etc., an indispensable mechanism of integration is furnished by these ideologies. At the same time, since any social formation requires some image, some self-consciousness, they provide the ethnic-national group with a functional and operational image adapted to the vital exigencies of this formation.

The modes of integration furnished by ideology have been enumerated as follows by E. Lemberg: delimitation from outsiders; affirmation of superiority, especially if the group began in a situation of inferiority; resistance (sometimes offensive) to pressure from outside, to a real or imaginary threat; internal moral structuring through the definition and imposition of a set of values proclaimed as superior to all others; deployment of measures designed to assure the unity and purity of the ethnic-national formation; calls for self-sacrifice, for devotion to it. We may detect here the three principles that Alain Touraine has defined as indispensable to a 'complete social movement': the principle of identity; the principle of opposition (to a given adversary); and the principle of totality, namely reference to higher values, to great ideals theoretically acknowledged by all, to a philosophy or theology claiming to account for the universe as a whole.

These definitions enable us to criticize both those who consider ethnic-national ideologies as super-structural epiphenomena that can be eliminated, through reductionism, from the tableau of essential social phenomena (like dogmatic Marxists, who tend to reduce them to class ideologies) and those who regard them as unconditional and fundamental features whose effectiveness is always and everywhere superior to any other. In particular, the delimitations of ethnic-national formations are contingent, a matter of conjuncture. No more than preferential propensities can be invoked in favour of any particular delimitation. France could as well have been formed without Brittany or Franche-Comté but with Belgium or Switzerland, for example. Hence the conflicts that may break out between ethnic-national ideologies that are delimited differently. The supremacy of ethnic-national ideologies over other group ideologies is also a matter of circumstance, situation, and conjuncture.

When real links, in particular economic ones, between the various infra-ethnic units were relatively lax, ethnic-national ideology was also relatively feeble, exposed to many highly effective competitors, which have been listed above. When the rise of integrated national markets within the framework of ethnic-national states created greater unity, ethnic-national ideology became a powerful force. The bourgeoisie, which participated in this integration in a very special way, became its most ardent defender, though often rivalled in this by the reigning dynasty. With the aid of the latter, the bourgeoisie fought the often cosmopolitan aristocracy, which was wedded to different values, and the religion that was tied to the aristocratic order and tempted by the universalism and individualism of the quest for salvation. The bourgeoisie's demand for a powerful state guaranteeing individual liberty went beyond dynastic legitimation inasmuch as the monarchy was organically tempted by despotism. Hence the appeal, initially confused, to the concept of the sovereign will of the people (which could best be defined within the framework of ethnic-national formations), expressed by the invocation of parliaments or general estates. It was thus easy to mobilize the confused sentiments of identity, implicit or latent, of all the members of these formations, and to solicit the allegiance of the lower classes. It was within this perspective that the bourgeoisie created the nation-state.

The Ideology of the Nation-State

This ideology very soon falls under the totalitarian and imperialist temptations often expressed in the term 'nationalism'. Around 1300, for example, Pierre Dubois, a jurist in the service of Philippe le Bel, called for the abolition of papal and ecclesiastical power and for French hegemony over the Christian world. The model also very soon exercises an irresistible attraction. As early as the fourteenth century, intellectuals belonging tó ethnic groups that had bourgeois states (though divided ones) dreamed of powerful and united nation-states—like the Italians Petrarch and, later, Machiavelli, stimulated by memories of Roman glory. As long ago as 1342, Marsilius of Padua was already putting forward a radical theory of the autonomous secular state, the necessary prelude to a nationalist ideological theory of the national state.

The supremacy of ethnic-national ideology, which can henceforth be termed nationalist, was assured by its theorization at the end of the eighteenth century, in connection with the evolution of economic and social conditions and with political circumstances. Christian universalist ideology was losing its grip and the state ideologies their power of attraction as a result of their connection with a social order that had become dysfunctional. Doctrines of the supremacy of the will of the people found welcome reinforcement in their appeal to the profound forces of the popular psyche, so intimately related to the cultural specificities that seemed to delimit both the ethnic-national formations and their linguistic frontiers (language being the most evident of the signs). Hence the infatuation with the Middle Ages, when this popular culture had flourished spontaneously. The rationalist universalism of the Age of Enlightenment, with its philosophy of the monarchical state as a utilitarian structural framework, was denounced as abstract, as evincing ignorance of and contempt for profound popular dynamism.

The doctrines of the state as an organic totality demanding the adherence of individuals were drawn together by Rousseau, and more explicitly by Fichte, linked to moral activism and the Kantian ideal of the autonomous determination of the I. Herder (*Auch eine Philosophie des Geschichte*, 1774; *Ideen zur Philosophie der Geschichte der Menschheit*, 1784–1791) made them an apology for national diversity. This was in part a German reaction against French cultural imperialism, which lay concealed behind their universalism. Herder held that nations are characterized by the original languages in which their real experience is crystallized. It is the vocation of each nation to form a state, which alone can enable it to escape assimilation. The various nationalisms thus lead to a general doctrine of nationalism.

The popularity of this nationalist doctrine has been immense. It served to assure the victory of the bourgeoisie in central, southern, and eastern Europe, as well as in Latin America, enabling them to legitimate their power and mobilize the masses of their respective peoples behind them. Later it rendered the same service to the colonial elites, which were thereby able to rid themselves of European domination. Here as elsewhere, the controversy between the advocates of the adoption of a European ideological option grafted onto a different reality and those of spontaneous growth based on local conditions is futile. The European ideological model was adopted because it responded to the exigencies of the circumstances of the Third World in the twentieth century.

Nationalist doctrine was able to be theorized into a conservative ideology, invoking that same fidelity to ethnic-national traditions which, in other circumstances, serves to lead revolt against foreign domination. As we know, it was thus able to become a rampart against revolutionary currents, notably in Europe. In particular it permitted the fervour born of internal tensions and problems to be diverted towards imperialist expansion. The same process may be observed in the Third World with the contradictions born of the revolutionary use of the same sort of ideology. It will continue.

National conflicts have been legitimated in part through polemics about the definition of the national group, such as that of Renan against the German theoreticians.

The strength of nationalist ideologies in central and eastern Europe compelled the theorists of Marxist universalism to attempt to integrate this factor into their ideologies (Otto Bauer, Karl Renner, Stalin), into their ethical system of rights and duties, and into their strategy (Lenin).

Theorists of (or for) the Third World, moreover, have had a tendency, during a phase that may perhaps be temporary, to invest their nationalism with a framework that extends beyond that of the nation-state, to all the black African peoples, for example. These conceptions nevertheless constitute an ethnic-national ideology, since the factor of unity is sought in a supposed community of origin.

The supremacy of ethnic-national ideology thus seems assured for the time being, given the perhaps temporary decline of Marxist universalist ideology, which had been its only serious rival. It has even borrowed the methods of Marxism, as well as some of its doctrines (like that of capitalist imperialism) and a part of its legitimation, through the classic syncretistic procedure of identifying national aims with the humanist aims it had put forward. The concept of imperialism—in the form of a specific and exclusive characteristic of the European-American capitalist world, opposing the progress and liberty of all humanity—has done great service in this perspective. This supremacy has its theorists and apologists who, going beyond the classical Marxist perspective of the limited and conditional justification of national demands, are developing the idea that the essential quest for identity is the principal mainspring of history, that there is a permanent 'basic principle' (which is the transmutation of the romantic *Volksgeist*), that a healthy 'nationalitarianism' is profoundly legitimate as opposed to a perverse nationalism or 'ethnism' that demands that the world be divided in accordance with the frontiers of ethnic-national groups, however minuscule, and even when their specific character has been effaced by history. These theories correspond to a particular situation, and are its ideological development.

The theorist of ideologies can only note the capital role played by ethnic-national ideologies during various phases of history, the contingent character of their emergence and of their more or less affirmed supremacy, and their virtues and their vices, not the least of which is to lead to a view of a world in which hostility between groups becomes eternal, with contempt for the interests, aspirations, and even the very lives of foreign groups.

5
What Is Zionism?

This sketch was requested of me by the Encyclopaedia Universalis, *in which it appeared in 1972, under the entry 'Zionism' (vol. 24, pp. 1061-65). Because of the great passion aroused by the subject, the entry was divided into three separate articles: a Zionist exposition by the French philosopher Robert Misrahi (subtitled 'Creation and Defence of a New Jewish State'); a text (with the subtitle 'An Enterprise of Colonization') by an Arab, the Syrian philosopher Sadiq J. al-Azam, also the author, incidentally, of a famous attack on religious ideology that caused him serious trouble in Lebanon; and the following piece, subtitled 'Theoretical Sketch of an Ideology'. It was republished (with some minor corrections) under the title 'Sketch of Zionist Ideology' in the review* Raison présente, *no. 34 (April-June 1975, pp. 13-23). An earlier English version appeared in U. Davis, A. Mack, N. Yural-Davis, (eds.),* Israel and the Palestinians, *London 1975.*

The word 'Zionism' was coined at the end of the nineteenth century to designate a collection of various movements whose common element was their plan to create a spiritual, territorial, or state centre, generally to be located in Palestine, for all the Jews of the world. The success of political Zionism, with its state ambition, assured the priority, even the exclusivity, of this sense of the word. Once its aim was attained, Zionism, an ideological movement of a political type, encountered new problems that have imposed a new definition. Anti-Zionist ideologues, too, have often used the term 'Zionism' in a lax fashion.

For some, Zionism is the product of a permanent national aspiration on the part of all Jews, and for that very reason legitimate and benevolent. For others, it represents an essential betrayal of universalist values, whether those of the Jewish religion, liberal humanism, or proletarian internationalism. For yet others (and sometimes for the same people), it is above all a malevolent product either of the noxious essence of the Jews or of imperialist capitalism.

Here I will deal primarily with those ideologies that aim at gathering the Jews together, first within the general framework of efforts to ingather or establish a state centre for dispersed minorities held in inferior social positions, and then with respect to the various Jewish conceptions which, in the course of history, have favoured Palestine as the site of such a centre. The actual implementation of the former efforts in the case of the Jews will be explained as a result of the possibilities open to a realistic project of this type in the economic, political, and ideological conditions of the late nineteenth century, a time when this project was also aided by the situation of the Jews in Europe. I will deal briefly with the consequences of this project in Arab Palestine, first for the Arabs, especially the Palestinians, and then for the Jewish community and the orientation of Zionism itself. Only then can the elements of an ethical assessment and criticism be defined.

1. Sources of the Ideology of Ingathering in Palestine

'Zionisms', or Centripetal Tendencies of a Dispersed Group

As a general rule, a group that is held in an inferior position may generate separatist tendencies, alongside demands for equality and the desire for integration, especially, although not exclusively, if it is dissimilar to the ambient society. If such a group is dispersed, the separatist tendency sometimes aspires to the creation of a more or less autonomous centre in some particular territory, a centre endowed with the independence of decision-making conferred by a state structure. We may thus speak of 'Zionisms', in the plural. A symbolic example is the myth of the Amazons, which expresses a tendency of this type for the female sex, at least to the extent that it was thought conceivable. 'Colonies' in the ancient sense of the word, to take another example, were ingatherings of expatriates who were sometimes recruited especially from dissatisfied groups in the metropolis. Some tribal migrations have had a similar character. Likewise the Puritan, and later the socialist, colonies established in America.

The formulation of a state project of this kind requires conditions such as a minimum of shared consciousness of identity and regular interchange among local groups (conditions that do not pertain, for example, among the Gypsies).

The tendency in this direction becomes stronger the more the set of people in question is frustrated, harassed, and persecuted. The state project is especially likely to arise among dispersed groups that present more or less the character of an ethnic group and among whom the model of an ethnic state exists, either in their own history or in the example of others. The ideology of modern nationalism, which in general upholds national values as supreme, strongly encourages such an orientation. The situation of American blacks has given rise to several projects of this kind among them, one of which was realized, Liberia. A minority religious community confined to inferior social positions may formulate identical aspirations, all the more strongly if they exhibit certain common ethnic and cultural features. This was the case among the Muslims of India—hence the creation of Pakistan.

Any new state created in this way will necessarily encounter the same problems: relations with the diaspora that remains outside the state (which may include opponents of the state project, active or passive); the relationship of the people of this diaspora to the states in which they live; the maintenance within the new state of the special character afforded it by its founders (in the Greek myth, this was the problem posed for the Amazons by their male children); relations with the indigenous inhabitants when the territory that has been occupied is not empty.

Among the Jews there were projects of ingathering elsewhere than in Palestine. Herzl himself was for a time attracted by Argentina and by Kenya. For some time the USSR encouraged a Yiddish-speaking Jewish entity in Birobidzhan, which is still officially the 'Jewish autonomous territory'. Judaism was the religion of states in Yemen (in the fifth and sixth centuries) and in southern Russia (the Khazar state, eighth to eleventh centuries).

Palestino-Centric Trends in Jewish History

In ancient times, the attachment of the Israelite or Hebrew ethnic group to its country, Palestine, was quite natural, barely theorized at first. But the internal evolution of the ethnic religion in the kingdom of Judea led, in the seventh century before Christ, to the proclamation of the cult of the ethnarch god Yahveh in the Temple of Jerusalem as the sole legitimate one; this led to the mounting consecration of that city.

The loss of independence of the Hebrew kingdoms of Israel (721 BC) and Judea (587 BC), and the consequent massive deportations to Mesopotamia aroused aspirations of return—of political restoration and restoration of the legitimate cult through the reconstruction of the Temple of Jerusalem—especially among the deportees, who swelled an already numerous emigration. These aspirations were expressed in a religious ideology that emphasized the eternal rights of the people of Israel to Palestinian land, guaranteed by the promises of Yahveh, and prophesied the reconstruction of a new Jerusalem (poetically called 'Zion') in which the Jews (meaning the Judeans), having returned to their homeland, would restore the cult of Yahveh. The ethnic god having acquired universal power through the prophetic movement, all the nations would flock to the holy city, which would become the theatre of the eschatological judgement and of the banquet of joy offered all humanity.

This ideology was later to inspire all subsequent tendencies of more or less similar orientation, notably because of the authority of the texts in which it was expressed, which soon became holy (for the Christians as well, later on: hence the thesis of a 'Zionism of God', the title of a recent book by a Protestant pastor). At the end of the sixth century before Christ, a group of 'Zionist' deportees returned to Palestine with the permission of the Persian kings, rebuilt the Temple, and reconstituted a community faithful to Judaism, a community that was at first autonomous under foreign suzerainty, then independent (from 142 to 63 BC), and finally withered very slowly under the Roman Empire, after the repression of the revolts of the years 70 (marked by the definitive destruction of the Temple) and 135 (from which date the Jews were forbidden access to Jerusalem).

A very numerous diaspora persisted and grew in size. As long as the Temple existed, many Jews acted (though very sporadically) on the biblical recommendation of a pilgrimage to Jerusalem three times a year. As in any emigration, the vicissitudes of the Palestinian metropolis—struggles, revolts, glories, misfortunes—were followed with interest, so long as it was the centre of a significant Jewish community (and the seat, until AD 425, of the patriarch, theoretically the spiritual head of all the Jews). In addition, it was held to be holy, as the abode of the ancestors and the theatre of the sacred history of the people of Israel, where many a theophany of Yahveh was located.

The dispersed Jewish communities (religious communities preserving many features of an ethnic group or people) lived under varying conditions depending on time and place, but none that inspired complete satisfaction, for they were almost always subordinate minorities. Their ideological orientations were thus complex and variable. The 'utopia' of an eschatological restoration of Israel in Palestine (a country generally designated in Hebrew under the name *Eretz Yisrael*, the 'land of Israel') never disappeared. But it engendered only very limited projects in reality: pilgrimage; individual settlement in Palestine to lead a pious life while patiently awaiting the Messiah, who would restore all; at most maintenance or reestablishment of a significant Palestinian community, itself lacking any political project, but capable of providing a spiritual centre for all Jews.

The more prosperous and free, or even endowed with authority, any Jewish community of the diaspora became, the more Palestino-centrism or Palestinotropy waned, although without ever disappearing entirely given the eschatological myth and the special charisma of Palestine guaranteed by the sacred texts. From the second to the seventh century after Christ, for instance, the Babylonian community—prosperous, enjoying great intellectual and spiritual prestige, living quite peacefully under the authority of an 'exilarch' supposedly descended from David, and recognized and honoured by the Persian regime—competed with Palestine. Judah ben Ezekiel

(220–99), a leader of the Babylonian school, declared it a sin to emigrate from Mesopotamia to Palestine before the end of time.

Misery and persecution, on the contrary, tended to encourage Palestino-centrism. Given the weakness of the Jews and the political situation in Palestine, however, people made do with the fervent but passive hope of eschatological restoration, and with the limited projects and actions listed above. Sometimes a false messiah would proclaim that the end of time had come and would lead a small group to Palestine. Theological developments idealized Palestine to the utmost and elaborated a theology of exile (*galut*). Metaphysical flourishes, like that of the very influential cabalist school of Isaac Luria (1534–72), deprived exile and ingathering alike of any concrete reality, turning them both into cosmic situations.

More realistic Palestino-centric projects arose beginning in the sixteenth century under the combined influence of the massive expulsion of Iberian Jews, the massacre of the Jews of Eastern Europe (1648–58), the mounting secularization of European thought, the speculation of Protestant Christians about the end of time and the role of the Jews according to the Bible, and the great tolerance, and later the decline, of the Ottoman Empire. The Spanish rabbi Berab (1474–1546) unsuccessfully proposed the restoration of a supreme religious authority in Palestine. The Jewish banker Joseph Nasi, who enjoyed the favour of the Ottoman court, managed to obtain a small district around Tiberias, where towards 1565 he settled some refugees by developing a textile industry from which they drew their livelihood. In the seventeenth century, Shabbatai Zevi, having proclaimed himself the Messiah, tried to inveigle the Jews into an immediate departure for Palestine to await eschatological restoration. But there was no definite political project, whatever the fears of the Ottoman government may have been.

2. The Actualization of the Ideology: Zionism

From Pre-Zionism to Zionism

Aspirations for ingathering—while they existed among the Jews at least in a latent state, along with others, some linked to Palestino-centric tendencies and some not—had not paved the way for any realistic political project. The flourishing of colonial projects in Christian Europe beginning in the sixteenth century, combined with the factors already mentioned, gave rise to a welter of plans (primarily among Christians) designed to gather the Jews together either in Palestine or in the Americas, in the interest of some power, or even some individual (the Maurice de Saxe plan, for example). The oldest may have been the project of Issac de La Peyrère, who in 1642 proposed the colonization of Palestine by converted Jews (like himself), under French aegis. [Some people acted on this idea in 1799, but with no notion of conversion, on the occasion of Bonaparte's expedition to Syria.]

Secular nationalism appeared among the Jews only after 1840, under the influence of the rise of nationalist ideology in Europe. Two rabbis, Yehouda Alkalay (1798–1878) and Zebi Hirsch Kalischer (1795–1874), reinterpreted Jewish eschatology in this sense, while in 1862 Moses Hess (1812–1875), an assimilated socialist Jew, also elaborated a Palestinian project, along resolutely irreligious lines. This trend, which received virtually no support among the Jews, came on top of the plans of the Christian states to divide up the Ottoman Empire, the Protestant missionary effort to convert the Jews, the Jewish or Judeophilic philanthropical schemes, and the millenarian speculations; the result was a proliferation of Palestinian projects. These began to receive the support of a Jewish base of some significance only as a result of the rise of anti-Semitism after 1881, the generalization of the concept of the non-European world as a space available for colonization, and the decline of the Ottoman regime. It was then that the most harassed, most persecuted, and least assimilated Jewish masses—those of Eastern Europe, already driven to a fairly massive emigration—became receptive to such projects, which nevertheless remained a minority option: very few of the emigrants headed for Palestine. It was Theodore Herzl—coming after less convincing ideological efforts (Pinsker, etc.), and in competition with projects based on purely religious aspirations (the departure of groups ready to await the Millennium in Palestine), secular aspirations to improve the lot of the Jews (agricultural colonies on various sites), or the establishment of a Jewish spiritual or intellectual centre in Palestine—who finally drafted, in a form that could mobilize, the charter of a secularized Jewish nationalism focused (primarily, but not exclusively) on Palestine.

The Social Causes of Zionism

Leftist tendencies, whether Zionist or anti-Zionist, have generally sought, in accordance with Marxist dogmatism, to legitimate their options by situating their struggle within the framework of a class struggle. The left Zionists emphasize the strength of the Jewish proletarian element and of socialist ideology in the Zionist movement, and suggest that in certain conditions Israel could contribute to the world anti-imperialist movement. Anti-Zionists of the left (and sometimes even of the right) emphasize the bourgeois and capitalist leadership of the movement in the past and its imperialist connections in the present. The common view is of class-based general staffs drafting their plans and mobilizing their troops in order to defend or promote their own interests.

Although this view of things must be rejected, it is true that these contrasting ideological theses contain elements of fact (though welded into dubious syntheses) that are partially valid for rational sociological analysis. The Zionist movements, divided into many currents, channelled and organized various trends that had real roots in the Jewish population, primarily in Europe and America.

This was a highly varied human group: religious Jews, irreligious Jews who nevertheless wanted to retain some link with their Jewish identity, assimilated Jews interested neither in Judaism nor in Jewishness but nevertheless regarded as Jews by others. Apart from ancestry, all they had in common was precisely this estimation by others. Dispersed, the Jews belonged (unevenly) to various social layers, and to different ones in different places; some were more, some less integrated; sometimes they shared a culture peculiar to the Jews in certain countries (Yiddish-speakers in Eastern Europe); and they were divided by many ideological currents.

Zionism pressed them to choose between projects of integration (or at most of local cultural autonomy), which entailed the adoption of the aspirations and tasks proposed in the various nations, and a separatist nationalist project based on those vestiges of a common history still remaining in their own consciousness and in that of their surroundings. Various factors, both individual and collective and quite diverse, encouraged one choice or the other. Many families were divided in this respect. But any reaction of rejection of the ambient milieu fostered the separatist option.

It is nevertheless quite true that membership of a given class could tend to make people lean towards one or another of the available options. Eli Lobel has proposed a subtle analysis of the fluctuating attitudes of various Jewish layers towards Zionism. Here there is insufficient space to summarize it adequately or to add further nuance.

Very schematically, we may say that the movement recruited its rank-and-file troops from the poor and persecuted Jews of Eastern Europe, at least those of them who, while still responsive to the community structures, were inclined towards emigration to Palestine either by religious sentiments or by the sequels of the Palestino-centrist trends described above. The leadership tended to be provided by middle-class intellectuals who sought financial support from the Jewish big bourgeosie in the West, only too happy to divert from Western Europe and America a wave of lower-class immigrants whose alien ethnic characteristics and revolutionary tendencies endangered their own chances of assimilation.

Zionism, therefore, cannot be considered simply the product of a particular class of Jews. It is true that in order to achieve its ends the movement as a whole sought and obtained the support of various European and American imperialist powers (first Britain, then the United States), and that it also obtained the greater part of its financial support from the most affluent layers of Jews, especially in the United States, who themselves refrained from emigrating to Palestine. It is also true that the excommunication of Zionism by the Communist International drove many Jewish proletarians away for a long time. The tragedy of the situation of the Jews in Europe after 1934, and especially after 1939, on the contrary won it the support of many Jews of all social layers and all ideological tendencies who had long remained reticent.

3. The Realization of the Zionist Project and Its Consequences

Relations With the Arabs

Initially, Zionism paid very little attention to the fact that the territory it was claiming was occupied by another population, the Arabs. This was understandable at a time when colonization seemed a natural and laudable phenomenon. Nevertheless, some political Zionists, a great authority of spiritual Zionism like Ahad Ha-'am, and many anti-Zionist Jews warned against the problems raised by this fact.

The question became primordial during the period of the British mandate (from the end of the First World War until 1948). The leadership of the Zionist movement shelved the old project of an exclusively Jewish state as an immediate tactical objective, while maintaining it as an ultimate ideal and goal. Tendencies emerged among left Zionists and idealists like Judah Leon Magnes and Martin Buber to retreat to the ideal of a binational Jewish-Arab state in Palestine. Some negotiated with Arab notables. Nevertheless, most Jews found it difficult to renounce freedom of Jewish immigration to Palestine (and they were less and less inclined to renounce it in face of the rise of Nazi anti-Semitism), a point equally difficult to accept for the Arabs, since this immigration, if unchecked, threatened to turn the Jewish minority into a majority and thus to lead to an alienation of the territory.

After the formation of the state of Israel in 1948, the idea of a binational state (in the sense of a state in which Jewish predominance would not be constitutionally guaranteed) was in practice abandoned by the Jewish side. On the Arab side, from about 1967 onwards the Palestinians raised the idea of a democratic secular state in which Jews and Arabs would be citizens enjoying equality before the law. Most Israelis and their friends, noting the absence from this plan of any effective guarantees for the collective interests of each ethnic-national group, have been suspicious of its sincerity. Moreover, the Palestinian and Arab organizations refuse (at least publicly) to acknowledge the existence of a new Israeli nation. They consider the Jews of Palestine as members of a religious community (hence the insistence on secularism in their programme), on the model of the many Middle Eastern communities that coexist within the same state. The exclusively Arab character of Palestine is not in question. Any solution of this kind therefore implies the Arabization of the Western Jews now living in Israel. This is rejected by the immense majority of Israelis, who are committed to a Jewish state of Hebrew language and culture, even by Arabic-speaking Israeli Jews (very numerous now), who are tending, on the contrary, to be Hebraized. Some of those most favourably disposed to Arab grievances (who are not very numerous in any event) would at most resign themselves to a genuine binational state in which the two ethnic-national elements would conserve political structures of their own, with guarantees for the defence of the collective aspirations and interests of both sides. But Israeli military successes and the absence of any plan of this kind on the Arab side scarcely encourage the development of such an attitude.

Zionist Ideology After the Triumph of Zionism

Political Zionism attained its goal, the creation of a Jewish state in Palestine. This state can now be defended with the usual means of state structures: diplomacy and war. From this some have logically concluded that Zionism, in the strict sense of the word, no longer has any reason for being. Friends of Israel should be called 'pro-Israeli', whether they are Jews or not. David Ben Gurion himself seemed favourably disposed to this thesis. Israeli youth shows little interest in classical Zionist ideology. Some Israeli nationalists may even want to dispose of it and to sever their special ties with those Jews who have chosen to remain in the diaspora, whether or not this attitude is accompanied by the recognition of a legitimate Palestinian nationalism, as it is by the non-conformist member of the Knesset Uri Avneri, who argues for a binational federation.

Nevertheless, a powerful Zionist movement does persist, divided into many ideological currents, especially on the social level. It is a secular Jewish nationalism, although based on a definition of 'Jew' that can admit no criterion but religious affiliation, present or ancestral. It nevertheless continues to insist that Jewry has had a national vocation down through the ages. It strives to reconcile this diagnosis with the desire of most Jews to remain members of other national communities (normally patriotic and possibly even nationalist). Even among very many Jews who reject such nationalism in its theoretical form, it still militates against trends toward assimilation, cultivates all vestiges of special identity, preaches active solidarity with Israel, seeks to mobilize the resources and energies of the Jews in its favour, and indeed makes this a duty, just as it upholds the (highly theoretical) duty of *aliya*, or the emigration of every Jew to Israel. In fact, this is a subject of discussion and dissension, American Jews in particular refusing to acknowledge this individual duty. Their attitude is therefore not easily distinguished from a systematic pro-Israelism scarcely discernible from that of non-Jews.

There is much confusion about all these concepts. In general, anti-Zionist opinion, especially among the Arabs, refuses to distinguish among Israeli patriotism or nationalism, a pro-Israeli attitude, recognition of the legitimate existence of a state of Israel, observation that a new Israeli nation has been formed, and the traditional Palestino-centric attitude of religious Jews. All this is thrown together in the concept of 'Zionism'. In a more polemical vein, some have gone so far as to characterize as Zionism any defence of the individual rights of Jews, any sympathy for the Jews, or any criticism of the Arab position. Pro-Israeli and genuinely Zionist opinion, on the other hand, also tends to confound these various attitudes, so as to extend to the most contested of them the good name enjoyed by the others.

Consequences of Zionist Success for the 'Jewish Problem'

The Zionist attitude also relies on the success of the movement in its apologia, pointing to its beneficial consequences for the circumstances of the Jews as a whole.

Some of these are undeniable. Israeli economic and military successes have tended to eliminate the traditional image of the Jew as a sickly person incapable of physical effort or constructive vigour and thus cast into either a disembodied intellectualism or sneaky, shady, and malodorous activities. The improvement of their image has tended to liquidate certain anxieties, certain complexes of Jews. More concretely, the state of Israel offers a secure refuge for persecuted and harassed Jews (except in the event of a more pronounced concretization of Arab enmity).

Nevertheless, these are not the only consequences. Once a certain threshold was reached, the Zionist movement, created by a handful of Jews and mobilizing only a minority of them, compelled all Jews to take some attitude to that movement. The creation of the state of Israel has compelled them, *nolens volens*, to take part in problems of Middle Eastern international politics that normally would have been of little interest to them. The dangers the Jews of Palestine have faced, or believe to have faced, have in large part oriented them towards a feeling of solidarity that the Zionist and Israeli authorities have sought to extend and use. From the outset, Zionist propaganda had in any case presented the Zionist option as a duty, as the natural outcome of tendencies latent in all Jews. On many occasions, Israel proclaims itself their representative. The set of Jews has thus tended to appear to others as a grouping of a national type, which seemed to confirm the traditional denunciation of them by anti-Semites.

This has had serious disadvantages, first of all for the Jews of the Arab countries, formerly one Arabic-speaking religious community among others, despised and harassed in the most backward countries, but not suffering grave problems, for example, in the countries of the Arab East. It was inevitable that in the atmosphere of the Israeli-Arab struggle they would be suspected of complicity with the enemy, and most of them have had to leave their countries. It likewise gave rise to suspicion of Jewish citizens in the Communist states, which had taken a vigorous position in favour of the Arabs. Some politicians have used these new suspicions, along with the inveterate remnants of popular anti-Semitism, for internal political purposes, and in Poland they led to a real recrudescence of organized anti-Semitism.

Quite apart from these cases, in the countries in which the 'Jewish problem' was on the road to liquidation, Jewish identity has been kept alive for many Jews who did not at all desire it: those who believed that a more or less shared ancestry, cultural vestiges that were often very slender and in the process of withering away, and above all a common position as target of anti-Semitic attacks and object of the seductive efforts of Zionism (the former at least declining and the latter often rejected) did not justify membership of a specific community of an ethnic-national type. The consequences of the success of Israel thus strongly impeded efforts at assimilation, which had been on the road to overall success.

Even for the small number of Jews in these countries who were attached only to religious Judaism and sought assimilation on all other levels, this situation led to their communitarian or existential opinion assuming a national coloration, especially since the success of Israel revivified all the ethnic elements of the traditional Jewish religion, turning it away from the universalist tendencies that had also endured since the time of the prophets. Religious Judaism, long opposed to Zionism, rallied to it little by little.

Elements of an Ethical Judgement

All these elements of fact will not suffice to ground an ethical judgement, which inevitably also implies reference to some chosen values. Zionism is a very special case of nationalism. If a critique of a purely nationalist type is disarmed before it, a universalist critique, on the contrary, is better-founded intellectually. By definition, such a critique cannot limit itself to weighing the advantages and disadvantages of Zionism for the Jews. It would primarily emphasize, apart from the general consequences of defining the Jews as a nation, the considerable wrong done to the Arab world by the project implemented by political Zionism centred on Palestine: the alienation of an Arab territory, a cycle of consequences leading to the subordination and expulsion of a very significant portion of the Palestinian population (it is hard to see how the Zionist project could have succeeded otherwise) and to a national struggle that diverts much of the energy and resources of the Arab world from more constructive tasks, a development that seems to have been inevitable in an epoch of exacerbated nationalisms and of violent struggle against all varieties of colonial enterprise.

Criticism of the methods of Zionism is inoperative and insufficient in itself. Objective analysis can only dismiss both the intemperate idealization of the movement by Zionists and their sympathizers and the no less frenzied 'diabolization' in which their opponents have often indulged. Divided into many divergent branches, the Zionist movement has the normal characteristics of any ideological movement of this type. In particular, they are often reminiscent of those of Communism. The Zionist organizations have employed the usual methods, certain groups and individuals seeking to attain their ends with more scruples than others. Cases of both self-sacrifice and personal exploitation of the ideology can be found, as well as instances of brutality and humanity, examples of totalitarianism based entirely on efficacy and others in which human factors have been taken into account.

Naturally, any universalist critique of nationalism in general also targets Zionism, for in it we find all the unpleasant features of nationalism, beginning with contempt for the rights of others, in a manner declared and cynical by some and masked by others, often transfigured by ideology and thus rendered unconscious among many, disguised in their own eyes by secondary moral justifications.

6
Dialogue With the Palestinians

I thought it would be useful to include in this volume the bulk of the text of an interview I gave in 1972 to a friend who worked in the PLO offices in Beirut: an Arabic translation of it was published in one of the journals of this organization, Shu'uun Falastiniyah *(Palestinian Affairs).*

The reason I think it useful is that it may enable open-minded readers, both Jews and non-Jews not completely blinded by Judeo-centric ideological polarization, to get a feel for the state of mind that prevails among Arab, and especially Palestinian, intellectuals, among men and women who are also open-minded. This state of mind, moreover, is not limited to intellectuals. It must be added at this point that membership of the Palestine Liberation Organization, and of its official bodies in particular, in no way rules out open-mindedness, whatever Mr Begin and those who follow him may say. Judeo-centrists, of course, for whom the smallest challenge to the eternal right of Zionist Jews to Palestinian land is sacrilegious, will neither notice nor discover anything new here, and will see it as no more than a dialogue between two anti-Semites, one of whom happens to be Jewish. Perhaps, however, some may be struck by the absence of 'racial' hatred and by the effort to understand displayed by a member of the people despoiled in the name of that 'eternal right', a personal victim of this much admired Zionist movement.

Perhaps some of those blinded in this way might finally come to understand that these victims of the realization of the Zionist project are also people, and that if they complain about Jewish actions, Jewish words, Jewish theories, or even Jews in general, this does not mean that they belong in the same category as the pogromists of

Kishinev or the SS officers of Auschwitz, who can be answered only with physical struggle.

Coincidentally, perhaps some particularly clear-minded Zionists may be able to contemplate the notion that anti-Zionism is not 'the anti-Semitism of fools', as is proclaimed by many 'left Zionists'. If they attain this level of comprehension, they will be able to conclude that anti-Zionists are not necessarily anti-Semites or fools. They may then understand that you can talk about Israeli realities to people who have been crushed by these realities only in carefully weighed terms that may seem equivocal to people like Rabi in Europe.

I have made some cuts in the text of the interview, since in it I was obliged to go into certain detailed explanations required for a Palestinian and Arab audience but much less so for a French, European, or North American one. In any event, in some cases remarks similar to those I have deleted appear elsewhere in this volume. Word of honour, I am not trying to hide anything. The deleted passages contained no call to murder.

The person who conducted the interview is Daud Talhami, a Palestinian engineer who has long worked in France. Before 1967, we spoke from the same platform. I dare to call him a friend, even though I do not agree with all his points of view and all his attitudes. He, too, is a man committed, and this has some of the consequences I discussed earlier in my self-criticism. But Zionists are ill-placed to reproach a member of a people despoiled (by them) for having committed himself to a movement struggling against that despoilation. To the interview, I have appended some of the observations he had printed in that issue of Shu'uun Falastiniyah, *intended for Palestinian and Arab readers who may have been shocked by some of my statements. These may in turn be shocking to others for diametrically opposite reasons. But it would be salutary to think about them, to understand the depth of the chasm that Daud Talhami and I were trying to narrow a bit, without insulting or being suspicious of each other. I hold this to be a necessary effort, even though there are those who advise me to keep silent and to take an interest in the Bororos instead.*

The interview appeared in the Ayyar (May) 1972 issue of Shu'uun Falastiniyah *(no. 9), pp. 85–94. It seems that at least a portion of it was reprinted in the magazine* Usbu' al-'Arabi *(The Arab Week), of*

Beirut. Extracts were translated into Hebrew and published by Shimon Balas in the 12 July 1972 issue of the journal 'Al Hamishmar (of Mapam). I have added a few explanatory notes between brackets.

A somewhat similar interview was given to Ibrahim Suss (before he rose to a high post in the PLO apparatus) and published in English in the Journal of Palestinian Studies, *vol. 4, no. 3, spring 1975, pp. 23–45.*

An Encounter With Maxime Rodinson

by Daud Talhami

Maxime Rodinson was born in Paris in 1915. He is a sociologist, orientalist, director of studies at the École pratique des hautes études (Sorbonne). ... He has ... applied himself to the study of oriental questions in general and of the Palestinian question in particular. ... The journal *Shu'uun Falastiniyah* addressed certain questions to him, which he naturally dealt with in the light of historial circumstances according to his interpretation. His answers were clear, and we have decided to publish them faithfully, as they were, in spite of the contradictions that readers will find between their own convictions and the positions of Mr Rodinson, because we are convinced of the necessity of keeping informed of all points of view expressed about our problems, in order to nurture a constant dialogue during this difficult phase of the long struggle of our people on the road of liberation, as well as to deepen our understanding of the enemy camp and, more generally, of the Jewish question and its connection to Zionism and Israel. After the questions and answers, we will add some remarks about the positions of Mr Rodinson and about some points that figure in his answers.

Q. What is your position on Marxism, Judaism, and Zionism?

Answer. I'll start with Judaism, because it's the easiest. Judaism is a religion, and since I am an atheist—in spite of my respect for all religions, Judaism as well as the others, neither more nor less—I have no special connection to it. Nevertheless, perhaps because my ancestors believed in this religion, I feel emotionally concerned with anything that has to do with the Jews in general, especially since there are people who continue to consider me a 'Jew' regardless of my position on the religion. That was also the situation of my parents, who were killed by the Nazis, although from their childhood they had had no connection with any strictly Jewish organization.

As far as Zionism is concerned, it is my duty to make my position on it clear, for exactly the same reasons. In general, my parents and I were hostile to Zionism—that is, we didn't want to belong to a purely Jewish state. I consider myself French, and the French people is the only one to whose service I consider it my obligation to dedicate myself in any special way. My language is French, my culture is essentially French. I can sing in French, for example, whereas I don't know any Hebrew or Yiddish songs. So I am hostile to Zionism, but I sometimes wonder whether my hostility to the idea that impelled certain Jews to try to build a state of their own would be absolute in itself. Last year I was invited to a congress near Chicago organized by Americans of Arab origin. There I listened to a man of the Muslim religion, by the name of Faruqi, who said in his speech that he was fundamentally opposed to Zionism, even apart from the problem of the conquest of Palestine by the Jews, and that his hostility would be unchanged if the Jewish state had been established on the moon. Later I mentioned that for my part, I personally would not be opposed to the idea of a Jewish state on the moon (which aroused laughter from the audience), although I would feel some reluctance, since it seemed to me that the establishment of a Jewish state, even on the moon, would affect my situation as a citizen of Jewish origin in French society. Nevertheless, I would be prepared to accept this new situation if Zionism had a real solution to the problems faced by a certain number of Jews.

But Zionism established this Jewish state—and this is my main objection to it—at the expense of the Arabs in general and the Palestinians in particular. This point aside, everything else is secondary and is open to discussion. For example, if a group of people who engage in minority sexual practices [and who consider themselves harassed by the majority] decided to set up a state of their own on a deserted island in the Pacific Ocean, the validity of that option could be discussed.[1]

Finally, as for Marxism, I was a member of the Communist Party for many years; I later left it, and I now consider myself an independent Marxist. Indeed, certain of the sociological laws discovered by Marx seem to me to have some scientific validity today. Ideologically, the values that Marxism has upheld—at least in theory, although not always in practice—are values which, it seems to me, one ought to uphold. Indeed, service to humanity (and therefore internationalism) seems to me more worthy of support than service to one people at the expense of others. The same goes for religious conceptions; my doubts about them make it impossible for me to regard them as potential replacements for the humanist ideal.

Q. In your articles and conferences ..., you have defined your analysis and positions on the Palestinian problem. Is it possible for you to sum up this position for our readers in the light of the most recent developments in the Arab region and in Israel itself?

A. That's a vast subject. Let me stick to the main outlines. ... Generally, my positions on the basis of the conflict have not changed: I still consider the state of Israel a colonial phenomenon, for as I have always reiterated, Palestine in 1890 was an Arab country just as much as France was French. It was then that Herzl came along, the founder of the movement that called for the creation of a Jewish state in Palestine. There were only two ways to attain this goal: either through subjugation of the inhabitants and domination over them, or through their expulsion. No other method was possible, and this is what finally happened in reality. I have sometimes been told that to acknowledge the colonial nature of Israel is to imply the necessity of de-colonization in accordance with the logic of the liberation movements of people today. I have already responded to this. ... I have said that the termination of the colonial situation is a formula that could have several different meanings. In general, the colonial situa-

---

[1][An apparently incongruous remark that may make me look like a sex maniac. But most Arabs, conditioned by the traditional multi-confessional structure of their societies, consider religious affiliation a criterion absolutely valueless in the formation of a state—hence the outrageous character of the Zionist claim in and of itself. The example of Pakistan makes them ill at ease (the Professor Faruqi quoted above quite logically condemned the formation of that country on the same level as Israel). My intention was to suggest that no criterion was outrageous in and of itself. For more on this point, see the section on 'Zionisms' in the previous essay, pp. 131–33.]

tion ends when all relations of domination, oppression, and exploitation end. In the case of a settler-colonialism, this does not require that the new inhabitants be expelled and return to their place of origin. Nor that they in turn be placed under the domination of the original inhabitants. There are, then, several ways to bring the colonial situation to an end ... and since I am a peaceful man by nature, I prefer methods that would require the fewest sacrifices of human life, among the oppressors and the oppressed alike. Indeed, the oppressor is not an oppressor absolutely and for all time. People are drawn by circumstances or ideologies to engage in the practice of oppression, and all the peoples of the world have gone through stages in which they have inflicted oppression on others and have suffered it themselves in turn.

In short, I believe that in themselves the demands of the Palestinian people are just and equitable. This people was driven from their land by the action of the Zionist movement, and it is quite natural that they should rebel against this fate. This is what I always tried to demonstrate in my public talks before 1967, when French public opinion was completely unaware of the roots of the Arab revolt. The French believed that the Arab refusal to recognize the existence of Israel originated in religious or racial fanaticism, or some similar wicked instincts. At that time, I would repeat continually that the Palestinian or Arab reaction was not at all extraordinary, and that if other peoples had suffered the same fate, their reaction would have been no different. Today, as well, I still repeat that the principal demands of the Palestinian people—and here I am not talking about the particular forms in which they are expressed, in other words, the strategy and tactics, but about the demands themselves—cannot disappear or be invalidated, so long as a single Palestinian remains on earth.

Q. What is your view of the analyses and slogans of the organizations of the Palestinian resistance, especially as concerns the Jewish question and the fate of the Jewish community in Palestine?

A. It is here that there may be opposition between our points of view. In particular, when I look at the programmes that have been put forward by the various Palestinian organizations, I must say that I find them inadequate. In no way do I desire to enter into discussion and conflict with the representatives of the Palestinian people on this subject. I believe that the Palestinian people, through harsh experience and more secure paths, will come to determine what their struggle requires; in the meantime, I will try to comment on the points I consider insufficient and unconvincing.

First of all, it must be acknowledged that the present slogans are an advance on those that prevailed before 1967. But nevertheless, they are not the best. ... In the first place, there is confusion ... which in general is related to factors like the exigencies of mass mobilization and the specific Middle Eastern concept of a religious community, which in my view does not fit the Israeli situation.

I recently re-read some statements by Palestinian leaders that illustrate what I mean. In its issue of last September, the Cuban review *Tricontinental* published an interview with Yassir Arafat in which he said: 'We used to say that there were two nationalities in Israel, the Arab nationality and the Israeli nationality. In reality, there are three: the Arab nationality, the oriental Jewish nationality, and the western Jewish nationality.' Right now I do not want to comment on the question of oriental and western Jews. I just want to note what Arafat says later in answer to another question in the same interview: 'The solution to this problem has been put forward by the Palestinian revolution, whose goal is to build a Palestinian state in which Jews, Muslims, and Christians would be able to live peacefully, in equality and freedom.'[2] I have also read a statement by Yusif Sayegh, who says that the Jews (the Jews of Israel, that is) 'have formed a community in our country by exterminating our society; whereas it is our aim to return our community to its homeland without exterminating their community. Our ambition is that the two communities should compete through emulation on the basis of harmonious coexistence.'[3]

It seems to me that there is a contradiction in these positions. It shows up clearly in Yassir Arafat's statement. He starts by saying that there are two nationalities in Palestine, and then he speaks of the coexistence of Muslims, Christians, and Jews. Now, these last three terms designate religious and not national or ethnic communities. It

[2] 'Palestine: la révolution du peuple', interview with Yassir Arafat, by Osvaldo Ortega, *Tricontinental*, French edition, Havana, vol. 6, no. 66, September 1971, p. 33.
[3] Yusif Sayegh, *Free Palestine* (London), vol. 4, no. 10, October 1971, p. 1. [Retranslated from the French.]

seems to me that this analysis is not adequate to the reality of Israel. The Arabs are accustomed—and the habit is deeply rooted and sincere, there is no doubt about that—to considering the Jews a religious community. That used to be basically correct, and it still is as far as the Jews of the Arab countries in particular are concerned, and to some extent the Jews of the United States as well. I have always considered the structure of American society to resemble that of Lebanese society—for reasons I am not fully aware of, since I am not very well acquainted with the situation of that country. But I do know that there you are not simply American the way you are just French in France, but American through the intermediary of an ethnic or religious community, or an ethnic-religious community. We sometimes read in the press stories that we find astonishing, like that there is an alliance between the Italians and the Poles against the Jews and the Irish in the municipal elections in New York, for example.[4]

But let me return to our main subject. My point is that it is important for Arabs to analyse the situation of Jewry accurately and with subtlety. Naturally, this is not easy. In my view, the Israeli Jews in historic Palestine do not constitute a religious community. The sort of entity they do constitute is not readily defined: perhaps they represent a new people, or a nationality, or an Israeli-Jewish ethnic group (or a group designated by whatever other name) endowed with a common culture. Moreover, we cannot be sure that this community will continue in its present form for all time. We cannot claim to make predictions on this score. It is not impossible that it could disintegrate, for it was only recently formed; but we are talking now about present circumstances, and the essence of Israeli reality today is not religious. Many Israeli Jews are not religious and in fact suffer deeply from the domination of Israeli society by zealous religious elements.

If we recognize the existence of two ethnic communities with two different cultures, then the solution cannot be freedom of religious worship as put forward in the Palestinian programmes. Let us take, for example, the case of Cyprus, where there are two peoples (or two ethnic groups, or cultural communities, or whatever term you use),

---

[4][The example is obviously invented, but nevertheless typical of real situations.]

the Greeks and the Turks. Of course, they adhere to two different religions, but that is not the decisive element of the present conflict. It is quite clear that no guarantee of religious freedom (which no one dreams of denying them) would contribute in any way to resolving their conflict.

It is obvious that if there are two or more ethnic groups in the same country, and if the danger of the domination of one by the other is to be avoided, then both these groups must be represented as distinct communities at the political level, and each must be accorded the right to defend its interests and aspirations.

Let's take another example: the Soviet Union, in which more than two hundred nationalities, or something like that number, coexist. In no way am I suggesting—quite the contrary—that the question of the coexistence of these nationalities has been definitively resolved. But at least the Soviet state has sought to advance a theoretical solution. It has delimited the ethnic groups or cultural communities—though undoubtedly not in an ideal form—and has created a special parliament called the Soviet of Nationalities, alongside the other Soviet, in which the deputies are elected proportionally to population without regard to community or nationality. I repeat that in general this theoretical solution has not put an end to all the problems, but at least the fundamental one has been acknowledged and a solution sought. I see no sign of this in the Palestinian programmes.

Another point, with regard to another country: Lebanon. I know that many Arabs and Lebanese protest against confessionalism and the system of representation by communities both in parliament and throughout the administrative departments of the state. Fundamentally, I agree with them, although I wonder whether this situation does not reflect Lebanese reality and whether its sudden abrogation would not engender privileges for one community at the expense of another. This even though here we are in fact dealing with religious communities and not nationalities, since the Lebanese in their totality belong to a single Arab culture. This is obviously not the case in Palestine.

I have tried to think seriously about the problem of the Palestinian programmes. I ask myself this question: what is the aim of a programme? I have come up with four possible ways to define its function.

1. The programme may be meant to present the outline of an ideal solution. In that case, it follows from everything I said earlier that the solution proposed by the Palestinian programmes is not adequate to this aim. Indeed, it does not guarantee all parties the collective representation required to defend their interests and aspirations.

2. The programme may be meant to propose a solution that might actually be realized. In that case, it seems to me that the Palestinian solution is completely unattainable, at least in the present epoch. It is possible that the situation might change in the future, but as Gérard Chaliand, an author sympathetic to the Palestinians, has said, we are not so interested in what might happen twenty-five years from now, and we cannot hope to predict the future so far in advance. As far as the present period is concerned, as some Egyptians say, Israeli tanks are a few kilometres from Damascus and Cairo. Proposals calling upon these Israelis to constitute a state in which they will receive no overall political representation cannot hope to elicit any response from them. ...

3. The programme may present projects intended to contribute to mobilization and propaganda. From this point of view, in the sort of examination we are conducting here, we must distinguish between the influence of the programme among Palestinians and other Arabs on the one hand, and on the outside world on the other (I am referring mainly to Europeans, since I know them better than I do other peoples). As far as the Palestinians are concerned, it seems to me that the programme has in fact succeeded in mobilizing them effectively on quite a broad scale.

As for Arab peoples other than the Palestinian people, things seem less clear. Inasmuch as the realization of this programme, according to those who uphold it, is seen as the result of a total and very harsh revolutionary war that would undoubtedly entail considerable losses in human lives and property, I dare say that I doubt that the Arabs, whatever their fraternal feelings for the Palestinians, would be prepared to accept such a hypothesis. I know that many people suspect that those Arab organisms...which fear this eventuality represent the petty bourgeoisie, or reactionary layers, or something of the sort. Nevertheless, I think that the ordinary inhabitants of all these countries—regardless of the organizations of which they are members—would not be enthusiastic about a war of this kind. It is true that at certain moments they do get enthusiastic about it, especially if the danger is far removed—and that is quite common in the Arab world, which has not seen the kind of all-out wars that we have known in Europe, in which tens of millions of people have perished. In this respect I recall something Dr Lorand Gaspar said about the inhabitants of Jerusalem a few days before the beginning of the June 1967 war.[5] They were listening intently to the programmes broadcast by Arab radio stations, which were full of heroic appeals, but when he mentioned to them that it seemed to him that some preparations were necessary, the digging of trenches for example, they looked at him in blank astonishment, as though the war was going on in some far away region. It seems to me that when real military operations draw near, mentalities change—the events in southern Lebanon demonstrate this—and fraternity with the Palestinians is limited to visits to Palestinian camps by ladies from charity organizations.

Finally, as for the effectiveness of the programme in Europe, I think that it is virtually nil, except among the members of some far-left groups. This is because experience, both direct and indirect, has made us increasingly doubtful about the possibilities of the coexistence of ethnic-national communities [within a united state]. We have in mind the cases of northern Ireland and Pakistan. Apart from the members of revolutionary organizations imbued with ideology, almost no one believes that this programme is realistic. The average European thinks that in proposing such a programme, the Palestinians are either trying to dupe us or are fooling themselves.

4. The programme may be meant to be useful from the point of view of its broader political influence. Here again, we must distinguish between Palestinians, Arabs, and foreigners. In relation to Palestinians and Arabs, the subject would require a long and detailed study of the positions and reactions of the Arab states. Because of the complexity of the matter, and because I lack complete information about it, I will not dwell on it here. Among Europeans, as I have said, the influence of this programme remains limited to narrow

---

[5][The reference, obviously, is to the old city of Jerusalem, then Jordanian, which lay just a few metres from the Israeli 'border'. The short book by this author, *Histoire de la Palestine*, Paris 1978, is to be recommended: it is well documented, full of instructive details, and of a profoundly humanist orientation in the best sense of the word.]

circles: some right-wingers, for example, anti-Semites and sym-pathizers of the Arab cause. In Britain, for instance, I have en-countered not a few high-society ladies who see themselves as carry-ing on the spirit of T.E. Lawrence. In general, they support the Arabs while believing that the Palestinian programme is not sincere and that in the final analysis the Jews will be driven out of Palestine. There are also some far-left circles, Maoists for instance, who accept this programme.

That is why I ask Palestinians this question: are these the milieux that you want to win over? If you do win them over, do Palestinian politicians think they will have backed the right horse and that these groups will soon accede to power in Europe? For my part, I doubt the possibility that this might come to pass.

Q. How do you envisage the evolution of the Jewish question throughout the world (in the capitalist countries, the Soviet Union, occupied Palestine, etc.), especially as concerns the perpetuation of anti-Semitism on the one hand and the hegemony of Zionism over the Jewish groups on the other?

A. That is also a broad question, so I will take just a brief look at a few general problems. To begin with, it must be said that the role once played by anti-Semitism in perpetuating the Jewish entity, or the set of Jews, has now been taken over by Zionism. I use the terms 'entity' and 'set' and not 'confession' since in many countries, France for example, the term 'confession' does not fit the Jews. In France before 1940 people of the Jewish confession in the strict sense were a minority of the people to whom the word 'Jew' was applied. In other words, a significant portion of Jews did not adhere to the Jewish religion, and their links with the confession from which they had arisen had been severed, although some of them preserved some traces of this traditional affiliation to varying degrees. For sentimen-tal reasons, some continued to practice various Jewish customs, like not eating pork or refusing to work on the Sabbath. Others had lost any connection with Judaism as a religion and community, some had embraced another religion (Christianity, obviously), and some had gone so far as to adopt new names in an effort not only to forget every trace of their origins but to make others forget as well. There were even some who did not know that they were of Jewish origin, something that was not at all rare in Europe. It was then that anti-Semitism played a capital role in gathering together an entire group that was otherwise on the road to disintegration. Zionism played no significant role at the time, since before 1939 the number of Zionists in Jewish milieux was quite small. The Zionists were combatted by religious and irreligious Jews alike. Those who were genuine Zionists emigrated to Palestine and thus disappeared [from the French scene]. Naturally, there were some Jews who felt sympathetic to Zionism, but it never went beyond dropping a few coins into the collection-boxes set up in Jewish grocery shops (as was often the case for the Arabs as regards the Palestinians). No one had any clear idea of what the money collected in these boxes was being used for. Many thought it was earmarked for the legal and limited purchase of land. The donors did not believe that by dropping their coins in the slot they were somehow taking a definite position on Zionism.

In short, anti-Semitism acted to re-awaken Jewish identity among many of those who had drifted away from it. ...Then came the reaction of being 'Jewish despite oneself'. Some began to cling to their Jewishness once again and later rallied to Zionism. That position is comprehensible from a human point of view, although many Jews of my milieu and my friends had rejected this option and had declared for French nationality, for France as homeland first and last. We refused to consider ourselves Israelis, believing that it is, I think, difficult to mix two ethnic-national allegiances together, whatever the Zionists may claim.

Since the last world war, then, Zionism has become the unifying element of the set of Jews, or the Jewish entity. Jewish sympathy for Israel mounted after the birth of this state. In 1967 demagogic Arab propaganda contributed much to polarizing the Jews once again (and not only the Jews), and to presenting the situation of the Jews in Israel as resembling that of the Jews in Europe during the Second World War. Very few of them were aware of the strength of the Israeli army, or of its capacity not only to defend Israel but also to occupy the neighbouring states. It was then very difficult for us to present the situation as it really was. It was easy to call those who did so 'Nazi'.

In Eastern Europe the situation is different in several respects, among others the continuation of anti-Semitic sentiments among popular layers despite its supposed disappearance according to Soviet leaders. This was clearly manifested during the Nazi occupation of Soviet territories between 1941 and 1945. The Nazis strove to resuscitate anti-Semitism by employing old slogans portraying revolutionaries and the Communists themselves as Jews in disguise. This later led to the Communist leaders' doing all they could to expunge this image from the minds of the people. They did not want the Jews to look like a group that had been specially persecuted during the war. They tried to limit the proportion of Jews among intellectuals, and particularly among leading circles. This led to discrimination against the Jews. Here mention should also be made of Stalin's temperament itself, which inclined him to a sort of anti-Semitism.

But Zionism played a capital role in regenerating anti-Semitism. It implied at least the call for a double allegiance, and that could only lead to placing the Jews in a critical situation, especially in countries that insist on the obligation of ideological allegiance to the state. One of the events that excited Stalin's anti-Semitism was the enthusiastic reception enjoyed by Golda Meir (who is of Russian origin) among Soviet Jews upon her arrival in Moscow at the end of 1948 as the first Israeli ambassador.

On the other hand, in the case of the Jews, the Soviet nationalities policy, which was excellent *in principle*, led to the opposite of what was intended. It prevented the assimilation of the Jews by creating a Jewish nationality (which was in contradiction with the definition of nationality given by Stalin himself in 1913), although the majority of Soviet Jews lived in conditions favourable to their assimilation into the nationalities whose culture they had assumed (Russian, Ukrainian, etc.). The most recent statistics show that only 25 per cent of Soviet Jews speak Yiddish, which is officially considered their national language. This unusual situation encourages some Jews to look to Israel as an ideal country, somewhat the way many American blacks look at Africa. In my book *Israel and the Arabs* I mentioned an anecdote recounted by the French Zionist Elie Wiesel. During a trip he made to the Soviet Union, some old Jews nostalgically asked him to show them something that had come from Israel. He showed them an Israeli newspaper. Looking at the headlines—which were like the headlines of any world newspaper, featuring accidents, protests, strikes, robberies and crimes—they were convinced that their interlocutor was working for the Soviet secret police, which had fabricated forged Hebrew newspapers in an effort to present Israel in an unfavourable light. Thus it is that some Soviet Jews have been driven to support Zionist ideology, or at least to regard Israel with sympathy. Naturally, this arouses the animosity of the Soviet regime and leads to events of the sort with which we are now familiar.

The situation in Poland is somewhat different, for there anti-Semitism has been used as an instrument in the power struggle among various groups.

In conclusion, I would like to return to a point that often misleads Arabs, which is the question of the use of the adjective 'Zionist'. In Europe, there are Jews whose political opinions and attitudes vary enormously, but who, in most cases, are committed to Israel's continuing existence. Arabs therefore tend to call them Zionists. Nevertheless, some questions about the definition of Zionism ought to be asked. If the word denotes mere recognition of the state of Israel (which is undoubtedly the product of Zionist ideology), then the qualification 'Zionist' applies equally to Podgorny, Charles de Gaulle, and probably to many Arab leaders as well.

Naturally, one has every right to supply one's own definitions of the terms one uses, but it is no good closing your eyes to reality. In fact, there are very great differences among these various attitudes. ...By characterizing them all as Zionist, the Arabs take a facile position, but one that essentially hampers their propaganda efforts. Some of these people who support the existence of Israel do not hesitate, in other circumstances, to condemn the practices of the Israeli government and even to back certain Palestinian demands. I can tell you a significant anecdote to illustrate the point. A short time ago I received the text of a protest issued in Beirut against Israeli practices in Gaza. ...The petition condemned these Israeli practices—and there was no problem about that—but it concluded by demanding that Israel be expelled from the United Nations. Now, I doubt that this position got a very favourable reception on any serious scale, whereas if the petition had been limited to condemning the condemnable practices it could have gathered far greater assent. I would like the Palestinians and Arabs to understand that they cannot simply write off people who, at a given moment, have expressed sentiments of sympathy towards Israel and the Israeli people, and that they must not believe that such people are radically incapable of understanding the situation of the Arabs and Palestinians.

Remarks

by D. Talhami

Before commenting on Professor Rodinson's statements, it is indispensable to affirm the following point clearly. Professor Rodinson speaks as a friend of the Arab peoples and of the Palestinian people in particular. Those of us who knew him before 1967 are well aware of the efforts he made at that time to combat the influence of Zionism on the presentation of information in France, under difficult conditions. This made him a principal target of insults, as a symbol of 'betrayal of the Jewish people', 'rejection of the cultural patrimony', 'self-hatred', and so on. In our interview, we began on this basis of appreciation of his efforts to disseminate historical truths among the Western public and his steadfastness in the battle against Zionist propaganda. On this basis too, we asked him for permission to comment on certain points in his answers, convinced as we are of their importance, for they express the attitudes of a vast sector of 'friendly' public opinion, and not only in the West.

1. There is no doubt that the Palestinian revolution has not yet proposed a complete and detailed programme for the Palestine of tomorrow, despite some attempts to deal with this subject in some depth. Nor is there any doubt that revolutionaries must study scientifically—and objectively—the nature of Jewish colonial society in Palestine[6] and the totality of the Jewish question, which is linked, whether we like it or not, to the Palestinian question. But it is also indispensable to affirm two points that were mentioned briefly in Professor Rodinson's answers. The first is the depth of the evolution that the slogan 'democratic Palestine' represents compared with the previously dominant conceptions, which sought the elimination of the majority of the Jewish settlers (and these conceptions have not

---

[6][When Daud Talhami speaks of 'occupied Palestine' or of 'Jewish colonial society', he obviously means the state of Israel and the Israeli-Jewish *yishuv*.]

ceased to predominate to a wide extent, perhaps as a result of the lack of clarity of the slogan 'democratic Palestine' in the eyes of the masses and the lack of conviction of the cadres).

The second point relates to the present balance of military forces in the region, which to a large extent is favourable to Israel and unfavourable to the resistance and even to the Arab countries as a whole. No strategic programme, whatever degree of precision it attains, will get any response from circles of Jewish settlers so long as Israeli tanks—as Professor Rodinson says—are arrogantly poised a few kilometres from Cairo and Damascus. The legitimation of the existence of any revolution is the desire to accelerate the modification of the balance of forces. The nature of the violence suffered by the Palestinian people and by significant sections of the Egyptian, Syrian, and Jordanian peoples will certainly impel them to the struggle—however long and multifarious its forms may be—to overturn the present relationship of forces. In the circumstances that will develop, and under the influence of a military and political situation less one-sidedly in Israel's favour, the projects of Palestinian revolutionaries will find a broader response within the colonial society and throughout the world in general. All this absolutely does not obviate the necessity of defining essential positions right now, and that definition must rest on a deep analysis of Palestinian and Jewish colonial society, as well as of the experiences of peoples close to the Palestinian situation. ...

2. It is certain that war will cause many losses in human lives and will maim many healthy beings, not to mention the material losses. Here we can repeat with Mao Tse-tung: 'If it depended on us alone, we would not resort to war for a single day.' The Palestinian people is a peaceful and open people, as shown by the succession of many civilizations and the coexistence of many populations and religions on its land for many centuries. But any people in the world that had been confronted with attacks like those it has suffered would inevitably rebel. That is the case today with the Vietnamese people, known in the past for its peaceful nature, which is now giving the world lessons in revolution, in resistance to conquest and violence, whatever the sacrifices it entails. In the course of the past fifty years, the Palestinian people has shown itself capable of sacrifices and of enduring the consequences of rebellion to recover its rights. Recent

years have shown the extent of its readiness to sacrifice in spite of the avidity of many forces, both world-wide and, in many cases, local, and in spite of the setbacks it has suffered and will suffer again. Likewise, it is certain that only the language of revolutionary violence can answer the language of Zionist domination and arrogance. For revolutionary violence is a language that is understood throughout the world. The Palestinian people became 'an incontestable reality' only after they took up arms after 1965, and especially after the battle of Karamah [in 1968]. It imposed its existence on its enemy, and will see its rights recognized only by virtue of this language. It is also appropriate to affirm that the enemy is the Zionist apparatus of political-military domination, and not the individuals who established this colony as Jews. A great part of them will transform their present hostile position towards the Palestinian people and its demands. But as Professor Rodinson said, if the Zionist domination continues, the Palestinian question and Palestinian rebellion will also continue, so long as a single Palestinian remains on the face of the earth.

As for the other Arab peoples near to the field of battle, Professor Rodinson's remark, which reflects the present situation in the given circumstances and influences, requires two observations. The first is that the lack of experience of war of the present generations does not mean that they are incapable of arousing themselves to deal with repeated aggression and with the consequences of their reactions to it. The aggressive and expansionist nature of Zionist occupation suffices to place wider and wider sections of the Arab peoples in conditions similar to those of the Palestinians (as is the case today for the inhabitants of Sinai or the cities along the Suez Canal on the one hand, or the inhabitants of the Golan Heights and South Lebanon on the other). Here again, we can invoke the example of Indochina. The Laotian and Cambodian peoples—and perhaps tomorrow the peoples of Thailand and other countries too—have not had to face an immediate occupation as dense as the American occupation of South Vietnam, and they do not have the experience of a war of resistance over dozens of years as the Vietnamese people have. But in the course of the struggle they learned to respond to dominating violence with revolutionary violence. Today they are far along the road to liberating their countries from American occupation and the domination of its agents. The second remark is that the participation of other Arab peoples, despite their spontaneous sympathy with the Palestinian revolution, will be commensurate with their understanding of the fact that their destiny and their daily lives are linked to the battle. This means that we cannot ask these peoples to associate themselves with the battle for Palestinian liberation without considering the domination and oppression with which they are faced in their own countries, both on the part of the imperialists and on the part of their agents and the exploiters in general. The Palestinian struggle will find a genuine and lasting response in the Arab world only if it collaborates with all the struggles, throughout the Arab world, for the liberation of Arab man. This has perhaps been one of the fundamental lessons the resistance has drawn from its setbacks after September 1970. That is what we learn day by day from the experience of other peoples. The Arab character of the Palestinian battle does not mean that all the Arab combatants must move to the Palestinian region, but that the example of the Palestinian revolution must be extended through all the regions of the Arab world and must be adapted to the circumstances and situations of each country —without forgetting that the immediate struggle against Zionism is not limited to the Palestinian people, in view of what we said about the extension of Zionist aggression to other regions.

For our part, we hope, as does Professor Rodinson, that all this will occur with the minimum of sacrifices in lives and property, but we know very well that in the final analysis this depends on the oppressor and on the continuation of the state of oppression. Until that ends, people have no choice but to oppose it with all their might.

3. The remarks of Professor Rodinson about Western public opinion are important, given his knowledge in this domain. For our part, we can only affirm the need for efforts to broaden the circle of friends of the Palestinian revolution and increasingly to isolate the Zionist enemy to the circles of its natural allies, the imperialists and reactionaries in general. We know that the Palestinian revolution has precious allies in the world, in the form of the revolutionary movements and states (including the national liberation movements). We know that we cannot avoid the necessity of carrying the battle against Zionism into its bastions (in the Western countries and in certain eastern countries of the Third World alike), by striving to win

over the democratic elements capable of understanding the problems of liberation and of human dignity. There is no doubt that significant sections of the French people and of the peoples of the West in general are capable of understanding the demands of the Palestinian people and the Arab liberation struggle, if sufficient information is provided and if the means of transmission of that information are sufficient. For our part, if we note the enormous difference between Zionist and Palestinian or Arab possibilities in this domain, it is our duty to work with patience and perseverance, with the aid of our friends in the West, to change this situation. Our Vietnamese companions in struggle have succeeded in this before us, so our success is not impossible. The first condition for it, as the experience of recent years and of the Vietnamese people itself has shown, is the continuation of the struggle of the Palestinian people and the rise of the Arab liberation movement. Thus, if we renew our thanks to Professor Rodinson for his efforts in this domain, we hope that our discussion will enrich our common experience and will nurture our struggle to realize these objectives, the liberation and dignity of man throughout the entire world.

7
A Few Simple Thoughts on Anti-Semitism

This essay appeared in the autumn 1981 issue of the quarterly journal Revue d'Etudes Palestiniennes, *published in Paris by the Institut des études palestiniennes, formerly of Beirut, now based in Washington, D.C. Its content seems to me to be self-explanatory. Readers may note that while there is little in it likely to please advocates of what I have called the Zionist 'vulgate', by no means can it be considered an apology for Arab points of view either.*

1. The term 'anti-Semitism' is a modern European expression.[1] It signifies hatred of Jews and systematic hostility towards them. In itself it entails deformations of an ideological type, for implied in it are the concepts, common in nineteenth-century Europe, that humanity is divided into well defined 'races' to which people belong by birth and that these races coincide to a large extent with linguistic families. Hatred of Jews was considered to be aroused by their supposedly hereditary racial characteristics, which were regarded as either detestable in reality or of such a nature as to engender the hatred of others. Essentially, these characteristics were supposed to be features of the entire so-called Semitic race, which meant—in practice—all those peoples now speaking or once having spoken Semitic languages, and therefore the Arabs as well.[2] Christianity,

---

[1] The word 'anti-Semitism' seems to have been coined in 1873 by the German publicist Wilhelm Marr. It was rapidly adopted and adapted in all European languages. On the translations of this term in the Muslim East, see the appendix to this article.
[2] The term 'Semites' really ought not to be used, any more than the term 'Indo-Europeans' (or Aryans). These words lack any scientific justification. One can speak

having arisen from the Jewish religion, and having been created by Jews, itself bore the stigma of this Semitic origin.

2. European anti-Semites, in fact, were motivated primarily by hatred of Jews, and sometimes by hatred of Christian ecclesiastical institutions. They were not interested in the other so-called Semites. The futility of an argument often voiced in the Arab world is thus clear: 'We cannot be anti-Semites, since we are Semites.' Historically, the words 'anti-Semite' and 'anti-Semitism' express the idea of hatred of the Jews. Naturally, this hatred can be encountered among any people, including the Arabs.

3. Indeed, it is not a matter of just any hatred or just any hostility. Modern European anti-Semitism was linked to the notion of race. According to this notion, the Jews had always been and would always be endowed with a pernicious *essence* transmitted genetically just like colour of hair or blood group. Since this notion has now fallen into discredit, today's Judeophobes, the continuators of the anti-Semitic doctrine, have (in general) ceased to ascribe these supposed pernicious characteristics to genes constituting a patrimony transmitted by heredity from the ancient Hebrews, or even from the alleged original Semites. In principle, they may concede that these characteristics are not eternal. In particular, some of them believe that the existence of the Jews in the new Israeli nation has abolished at least many of their pernicious characteristics. Those who hold these positions are therefore both Judeophobes and Israelophiles.

---

only of peoples speaking Semitic languages, peoples speaking Indo-European languages, and so on. These groups of languages do indeed exist, and there is a family of related, Semitic languages. But peoples that speak related languages can be very different, and each of them, moreover, is profoundly heterogeneous. The expansion of languages normally occurs through assimilation, conquest, migration, and so on. The blacks of Haiti speak forms of French. Quite obviously, however, they have few genes in common with the French of France. The latter, in any case, speak a language derived from Latin, which was the tongue of a tiny minority of people from Italy who conquered Gaul in the first century before Christ. The Gallic language has been dead in France for more than sixteen centuries, although many more French people are descended from the Gauls than from Latin-speaking Romans. Examples are just about as numerous as peoples. 'For me', wrote the philologist F. Max Müller in 1888, the man who coined the word 'Aryan', 'an ethnologist who speaks of an Aryan race, or of Aryan eyes or hair, commits as gross a blunder as a linguist who speaks of a dolichocephalic or brachycephalic grammar.' (*Biographies of Words and the Home of the Aryans*, p. 120, cited by A.C. Haddon, *History of Anthropology*, Watts, London, n.d., p. 97)

Nevertheless, all of them proclaim that these characteristics have become features of the Jews as a result of conditions in which they have lived for many centuries (they may differ about the date of origin), and that they continue and will continue to be features of them for a very long time to come (at least in the diaspora).

In general, then, this modern form of Judeophobia is distinct from religious Judeophobia, which holds that the sole cause of the supposedly pernicious characteristics of the Jews is their religion. According to this latter concept, a Jew converted to another religion would be radically purged of these defects, and thus regenerated.

As in many ideologies of hostility, it is supposed that the set of individuals or groups against which the ideology is directed are endowed with great unity, with a single centre on which these individuals and groups depend. It is imagined that this centre elaborates a programme, strategy, and tactics, which the individuals and groups then proceed faithfully to implement in an effort to attain their detestable goals, most often the absolute domination of the rest of humanity. It is an occult conspiratorial centre.

4. This sort of essentialist ideology of hostility has attained extreme degrees with respect to the Jews. But it has also arisen, to a greater or lesser extent, in very many other cases. Hostility among human groups (ethnic-national groups and religious confessions in particular) has clearly been a constant feature of human history, even though the relations between any two given groups most often include phases of hostility, neutrality, and amity. Hostility of any durability, however, tends to lead to an essentialist ideology. The adversary is ascribed a perpetually evil essence of which the conjunctural hostility is said to be merely a manifestation. Naturally, the group issuing this judgement regards itself through the prism of a no less essentialist ideology, but one that characterizes the group as the embodiment of a perpetually good, laudable, and generous essence —one endowed, in short, with all possible good qualities. Alongside the negative essentialism that characterizes the other groups, in particular those that are adversaries for a given period, there is therefore a positive essentialism that is more or less indistinguishable from ethnocentrism.

Ethnocentrism consists in viewing all other ethnic-national groups through the prism of the presumed superiority of one's own group.

It has been a universal phenomenon since the origins of human society. To believe that one's own group (or the set of groups among which this group is classed) has escaped ethnocentrism or an essentialist view of itself and others is to accord it an astonishing privilege connected to its essence, and is therefore a manifestation of essentialist ethnocentrism.

The universalist religions normally think of themselves as the exclusive guardians of the truth about the Hereafter, the World, and Man. They are therefore naturally drawn to a view that approximates the ethnocentric one. Nevertheless, some advanced theologies may attenuate the excesses of this concept to a greater or lesser extent.

Since the groups that develop ethnocentrist ideologies consider themselves endowed with an essence of a superior quality that should normally be expected to arouse only admiration and love, these ideologies perceive any hostility to which they are subjected as the consequence of gratuitous wickedness on the part of others, a kind of universal jealousy. Like the paranoiac at the level of individual psychology, they adopt an attitude that I propose to call *panekhthrist* (from the Greek *ekhthros*, or 'enemy'). The entire universe is thought to be wickedly in league against the group in question. This concept is quite frequent, carried to more or less extreme lengths, and takes hold in more or less lasting and spontaneous fashion, theorized to varying degrees of elaboration.

5. Over the past three thousand years, the word 'Jews' has been applied to the members of groups and formations that differ to some extent but among whom there has been some continuity [see chapter 1]. In the West today, the term is normally used to refer to descendants of members of these groups even when they are not themselves members, or are former members who have departed from them. In the Muslim East, on the contrary, the Jews are the members of a 'community' sharply defined by its proclaimed loyalty to a given religion, Judaism. It matters little whether the individual members feel total adhesion, partial adhesion, total indifference, or even repulsion for this religion, provided that they have not joined another religion. Such is the general concept of religious community that prevails in these countries, for historical and sociological reasons. All citizens must belong to one or another community, as to

a sort of sub-nation.

The groups that may be called Jewish, like many others, have often been the target of hostility. For two thousand years, these groups, having been encompassed within societies upholding hegemonic ideologies, and being minorities within them, have been objects of scorn, disparagement, and often hatred, and on many occasions have suffered persecution of varying degrees of cruelty. For complex reasons, this has been the case primarily in Christian Europe, in which they formed the only minority religious community, and a small one at that. These persecutions were often atrocious. They grew much worse when the Jewish religious community was on the way to dissolution following the secularization of the state. At that time the persecutions, sustained by a racist ideology, targeted all those who, as descendants of members of the Jewish community, were supposed to be carriers of the wicked genes that were claimed to be characteristic of them.

European Jews became the victims of a set of hostilities of different kinds, directed against different sorts of groups:

a) Religious hostility from Christians as adherents of a religion which, according to Christian ideology, they should have acknowledged as obsolete, as lapsed, on the authority of their own sacred texts, which are considered holy by Christianity as well; according to the same ideology, they were primarily responsible for the crucifixion of Jesus, one of their own, whom they should instead have recognized as the Messiah whose coming had been forecast by their prophets and as the Son of God, God Himself incarnate.

b) The secular hostility of many anti-clericalists and anti-Christians of Christian stock who held that the Jewish religion— supposedly more or less the expression of the Jews' essence—was the root of what they considered the pernicious characteristics of Christianity, or at least of the Christian church as an organization.[3]

---

[3]People from Muslim countries—and notably Arabs—often fail to realize how old and deep are anti-religious (and in practice therefore anti-Christian) tendencies in Europe, especially in France. They often assume that irreligion in European society was born with Marx and Marxism. This is a misunderstanding that has added much confusion to many an analysis. On this point Marx no more than took up the ideas of the French and English deists and atheists of the seventeenth century, which German philosophers had already given a more sophisticated twist. He merely extended them and made them

c) The social hostility of those wronged or injured by the activities to which Christian regulations long confined the Jews: the collection of taxes or ground rent, money-lending, etc., activities which, as a result of family traditions and customs, persisted among many of them—or rather, among those that attracted the most attention—after the abolition of the regulations in question; likewise, hostility from those who were offended by their preference for life-styles and professions to which these traditions had predisposed them (in the final analysis, results of those same regulations): urban life, intellectual and liberal professions, etc.

d) Quasi-ethnic hostility towards groups whose daily lifestyle differed in part from that of the great majority of peoples among whom they lived, since they thus appeared as foreigners in many respects; this perception was reinforced when persecutions brought to Western Europe very many Jews from faraway countries—primarily Eastern Europe—who were indeed foreigners in all senses of the word, at least for the first generations after their migration.

6. The Jews themselves had very naturally developed an ethnocentric and panekhthrist ideology representing their group as superior to others, which is generally what happens. For a long time this ideology was exclusively religious. It thus located the secret of this super
·iority in a religious notion: that the Jews were the 'chosen' people, divinely selected among all others as the repository of the supreme truth. The general hostility that surrounded them was likewise considered a consequence of this superiority. The other humans—the 'nations' (*goyim*[4]), as it is put traditionally—were jealous of the people of Israel and of its privileges. God wanted to purify his people through trials, and so on.

---

more consistent, following Ludwig Feuerbach. His personal contribution had to do with the philosophical and sociological explanation of religion more than with the attack on it, which was a commonplace phenomenon throughout the European, especially socialist, left.

[4]The word *goy* ('people', 'nation') was used in ancient Hebrew to designate any people, including that of Israel. But the plural, *hag-goyim*, 'the nations', eventually came to designate all other peoples. In post-biblical Hebrew, the expression 'a goy' came into fashion to designate an individual member of these other peoples, in other words a non-Jew. The Hebrew word is related to various Semitic terms that signify the interior of a thing, in the Arabic dialect of the Fertile Crescent *juwwa* (in Egypt *gowwa*); hence the idea of 'community'.

Exceptionally, these conceptions were partially shared, in certain respects, by the Christian world itself, from which the persecution or enforced inferior status of the Jews emanated. According to Christian religious ideology, for more than a millennium the Jews had indeed been the people chosen by God, the only earthly repository of the Revelation.[5] This Revelation was superseded with the arrival of Jesus Christ on earth, but remained valid in many respects; in particular, it allegedly contained proofs of the Christian revelation, in prophecies that were claimed to have heralded the coming of Christ. The Jewish people had been the nucleus and initial agent of the Christianization of the world. Their kings had been the ancestors of the Christ 'in the flesh'; his mother and all his first disciples had been Jews; these disciples acted in a Jewish world, and sought first of all to convert Jews with arguments drawn from Jewish dogma. If God had not allowed all of them to join Christianity, that 'heresy' that had arisen among them, then there must have been some deeper design that we could seek to comprehend.

One Christian argument, for example, was that the Jews had to remain Jews because by remaining faithful to Scriptures which, according to Christian ideology, clearly condemned their rejection of Christ, they thereby attested all the more to the truth of those Scriptures. The text of these writings—the Old Testament—which were originally intended to prophesy the final victory of the Jews over their enemies and the return to their country of origin of those who had been deported by these enemies (mainly in the sixth century before Christ), were reinterpreted. From them it was deduced that the end of time, the Last Judgement, would begin with the 'return' of the Jews to Palestine and their conversion.

Alongside heinous stereotypes and partially intermingled with them, there had therefore been stereotypes attributing great privileges to the Jews. These were developed mainly in the Protestant world from the sixteenth century onwards, because of the primacy accorded the Bible by Protestantism. Within the Bible itself, many Protestant communities were more attached to the Old Testament

---

[5]Although they are not exactly accorded the same exclusivity of the Revelation before Muhammad, the ancient Jews—most often called the *Banu Isra'il*, or children of Israel, in the *Koran*—nevertheless have great privileges from this point of view according to Muslim tradition as well.

than the New, since the books of the former often evoked the concrete conditions in which these communities found themselves.

Jewish panekhthrist ethnocentrism, additionally stimulated by echoes of those Christian stereotypes that accorded the Jews 'privileges', began to be secularized with the epoch of the Emancipation (eighteenth and nineteenth centuries). Although in Western Europe the institutional groups proclaiming themselves Jewish had been steadily withering for a whole period, more or less mythical ideas about the Jews continued to flourish. Among many descendants of the members of these Jewish communities, these ideas perpetuated their sense of somehow belonging to this Jewish stock and made them proud of it. In the 1880s, when verbal assaults, harassment, and persecution underwent a resurgence, and when, after a long period of relative quiescence, they reappeared far more grievously in the 1930s, with their atrocious culmination of 1939–45, a great number of 'Jews' (in all senses of the word) inevitably became convinced that the whole world was, had always been, and would always be, in league against them, and that the only valid reaction was mutual solidarity, self-defence, and withdrawal into a coherent formation that would possess all the necessary resources of self-defence, and perhaps of attack as well. The Zionist appeal for an ingathering of the Jews, for the formation of a true nation (since in any event the others treated the Jews as a nation), endowed with both a national ideology of its own and a state, would inevitably meet with increasing favour in these circumstances. Because of European ethnocentrism, which was shared by the majority of Zionist Jews, the decision to locate this state in Arab Palestine in no way troubled those who supported these options, as I have explained elsewhere.

Panekhthrism and ethnocentrism are mutually reinforcing. Ethnocentrism is very sweeping, ascribing to the people of which one is a part a value superior to others. In the context of a religious ideology, it is easy to proclaim a people 'chosen', since it is necessary only to invoke the highly free will of a god or God. It is more difficult to justify such alleged superiority with secular arguments. But there is no hurdle before which the virtuosity of ideological thought draws back. There is not sufficient space here to elaborate an analysis of the various fantastical constructions to which devotees have resorted. Minds of philosophical training—and I am not alluding to real philosophers—have distinguished themselves with the gratuitous abstractions permitted by speculation in a vacuum. The superiority of the Jews has been discovered in various domains, in different ways, and under contradictory aspects. In each case, this superiority is said to have been the motivation for the persecutions.

It should be emphasized that these myths have been reinforced by significant borrowing from the Christian ideological arsenal. Earlier I referred very rapidly to Christian conceptions of Judaism and the Jews. These can be used to justify a hostile attitude toward the Jews, and for a long historical period they were generally oriented in this direction. But conclusions favourable to the Jews and Judaism can equally well be drawn from them. A strong current of this type has recently been in evidence. Some of these Christian arguments were susceptible to being adopted by Jews, and so they were.

7. It is the convergence of all these factors that explains the rise of a mythified conception of the real Judeophobias encompassed under the name anti-Semitism (itself borrowed from the anti-Semites).

According to this conception, for one reason or another (here variations appear depending on political and philosophical orientations), the Jews have been, are, and always will be the object of a hatred that is to their honour and augments their value. Any suggestion that this hostility—or rather, these hostilities—had causes rooted in the concrete conditions that have shaped relations between Jews and non-Jews is vehemently rejected. Any sign that some societies have not experienced and are not experiencing this hatred, or that some historical periods were free of it, is ignored (and mention of it often denounced as itself the product of an 'anti-Semitic' effort).[6] The tendency is to include in the concept of anti-Semitism all manifestations of special hostility towards any Jewish group or even towards any given Jewish individual, regardless of their gravity. Harmless cracks or ironic quips are sometimes exaggerated and presented as signs of hostility. Above all, any suggestion that these

---

[6]See, for example, what S.W. Baron, a great historian of the Jews, has to say about this reaction in his article 'Emphases in Jewish History', *Jewish Social Studies*, 1939. The peoples of China and India, among whom there are Jewish communities, have never manifested any especially hostile behaviour towards them. It is well known that modern Italy was free of any anti-Semitic attitudes until the pressure of Hitler on his ally Mussolini impelled the latter, despite his own reluctance and that of the population, to decree laws of this type and to try to propagate anti-Semitic ideology.

manifestations of hostility could be of the same kind as those also directed against other peoples or other human groups is rejected. Moreover, the very idea that quite similar phenomena directed towards other peoples or other groups might be manifested among the Jews themselves is cause for indignation.[7]

It is therefore understandable why the majority of Jews, as well as Christians and others, who were alarmed by the crimes of Nazi Judeophobia, felt varying degrees of guilt for not having reacted strongly enough against them, and were unaware of the real conditions of Zionist settlement in Palestine, simply saw Arab reactions to this settlement as new and particular manifestations of eternal anti-Semitism. Any attempt to explain these Arab reactions as caused by genuine wrongs inflicted on the Arabs by *some* Jews (who claimed to represent all Jews) was characterized as yet another indication of anti-Semitism, even when it came from individuals—like the author of these lines—whom the accusers themselves would label as Jews. It was then sufficient to introduce the concept of 'self-hate' (*Selbsthass* in German), which reduced the matter to a pathological phenomenon that could be treated by psychoanalysis.

8. This mythical concept of anti-Semitism must be rejected. Hostility to Jews carried to the extreme pitch of ascribing a pernicious essence to these human beings arises neither from mystical factors nor from divine will. It does not arise from reactions to a genuinely pernicious Jewish essence, for no people is endowed with an invariable essence, whether good or bad, and many Jews, and many Jewish groups too, have evinced undeniable and sometimes exemplary moral qualities, in the past and present alike. Nor does it arise from reactions to an eternally benign Jewish essence or from the alleged fact that the Jews were and remain the bearers of noble truths, and thus arouse the jealousy and hatred of others. Indeed, many Jews, and many Jewish groups, have *also* exhibited defects and deplorable behaviour, have *also* made contestable, erroneous, or blameworthy assertions. No, this hostility arises from the con-

---

[7] I have long criticized the attitude of Léon Poliakov, a historian of anti-Semitism, from this point of view. These criticisms are condensed in a short article which, liberally, was accepted for the 'Mélanges' published in his honour: 'Quelques thèses critiques sur la démarche poliakovienne', in *Pour Léon Poliakov, Le racisme, mythes et sciences*, Brussels 1981, pp. 317–22.

vergence of various factors that can be historically and sociologically explained, factors that may be noted in relations between human groups everywhere, and in particular among formations of an ethnic-national type or among religious communities. In this case, however, these factors combined in their most virulent form, the duration and intensity of the atrociousness exceeding that which has been seen elsewhere.

The idea expressed in the preceding paragraph presently wins scant acceptance in the European world, and particularly in the Jewish world. I have often argued strongly in favour of it at times when it was especially unpopular (as it still is). As a result of this polemic, for many years I met with serious difficulties, multifarious lack of understanding (even among friends), and violent hatred.

On the other hand, objections to the mythical concept of anti-Semitism can win ready assent from Arabs, at least as concerns rejection of the image of the Jews as eternally and essentially victims and never able to be anything but victims. I therefore risk receiving copious applause from that quarter. Since some of those who will read this article will be inclined to applaud for this reason, I would like to clarify certain points straightaway, possibly at the risk of moderating their applause, or even of transforming it into catcalls.

I did not undertake these polemics and put up with the consequent difficulties in order to produce apologies for the Arabs or for anyone else. I did not expend such efforts to demonstrate that the Jews are not a saintly people only to proclaim instead that it is the Arabs who hold that distinction. No people is saintly. No people is intrinsically good or bad eternally and by their essence. No people is destined always to be victims. All peoples have been victims and executioners by turns, and all peoples count among their number both victims and executioners.

I do not seek applause from those who say, in effect: 'Bravo for your courage in denouncing the iniquities and deceit of those who can be considered your own people. As for us, however, we see only virtue, magnanimity, and truth on our side. Above all, do not count on us to denounce the iniquities, errors and deceits of our own people.' As the inmate in the asylum says in the old joke, 'That lunatic thinks he's Napoleon. He's completely out of his mind! I'm Napoleon!' About twenty centuries ago a famous Palestinian Jew had something to say about people who saw the mote in their neighbour's eye but not the beam in their own. Well, whether it be two motes or two beams, blindness towards oneself remains a permanent feature of human psychology—used, exploited, and magnified by ideologies of combat.

I would therefore like to emphasize a number of important points.

a) To deny that the hostility to which the Jews have been subjected arises from any essentialist factor, from any eternal characteristic quality as victims, does not mean to deny the reality or intensity of the hostilities unleashed against very large groups of Jews in the past and present. It is psychologically understandable that exasperation caused by the mythification of these Judeophobias, by the use that has been made of them, by the absurd conclusion drawn from them that all Jews are incapable of evil thought or action, has led many in the other camp to deny or minimize the wrongs suffered by the Jews. But it is no less stupid for being understandable.

Jewish communities have suffered persecution and often massacre on various occasions in history. The mass massacre of the years 1939 to 1945 in Germany and the countries occupied by the Germans was an enormity and an atrocity. There were millions of victims. There are no valid reasons for denying the reality and scope of this massacre (even if one could argue about the exact figures and the details of the extermination process), on the pretext that many Jews and Jewish groupings have drawn unwarranted conclusions from it. All such denials—whether by declared or disguised anti-Semites (Arabophiles included) who believe that they are thereby aiding the struggle against Zionism, or by leftists who, since they denounce the capitalist system or colonialism as criminal, desire that these be the only criminals—are contradicted by the obvious events from which many, including the author of these lines, have suffered so cruelly, and by millions of witnesses who survived. They have been demonstrated as invalid by the criteria of historical research.[8]

---

[8]See especially the decisive refutations by Nadine Fresco, 'Les redresseurs de morts' (in *Les Temps modernes*, June 1980, pp. 2150–2211), and by Pierre Vidal-Naquet, 'Un Eichmann de papier' (in *Esprit*, new series, no. 45, September 1980, p. 52), reprinted in his book *Les juifs, la mémoire et le présent* (Paris 1981, pp. 195–272), with very useful appendices. The same issue of *Esprit* contains instructive exposés and criticism of similar approaches as applied to Cambodia. Motivated by his ardour in striving to

b) Contrary to what has been said and written in Arab and Muslim circles, the condition of the Jews in the world of Islam was not idyllic. It is quite true that the negative aspects of the Jewish situation in Muslim countries have been much exaggerated by Zionist propaganda. It is quite true that unwarranted conclusions have been drawn by such propaganda. It is quite true that on the whole the situation of Jews in Muslim countries over fifteen centuries has been better than in the Christian countries.

But this does not alter the fact that the status of *dhimmi*[9] applied to Jews and Christians was inegalitarian and that it kept them in positions of inferiority, which was in any case perfectly natural at the time. Judaism and Christianity were tolerated religions, 'protected' in a certain sense and enjoying a special status. But their believers were none the less considered enemies of the true faith. Appreciations of them were disparaging, suspicious, and scornful. In the case of the Jews, these attitudes were able to find support in many passages from the Koran dating from the time when the Jewish tribes of Medina constituted Muhammad's main adversary, passages that can readily obliterate the favourable attitude towards Jews and Christians reflected in other, earlier passages. The entire collective psychology of the Middle East still bears the stamp of the judgements of the Middle Ages, an epoch whose conditions persisted for a very long time in certain regions. At that time, the Christians of the Muslim countries were considered linked to their powerful co-religionists in Europe, in general in a state of war with the world of Islam. The result was much hostility, but also a certain esteem. The Jews, on the other hand, like the Zoroastrians and Mazdeans, were considered enemies within, cunning and sly, seeking to damage the True Faith in a secretive fashion. It was easy to think that, subjected to Muslim domination with no hope of requital, they would seek secretly to avenge this submission by whatever means were necessary.

---

undermine the self-satisfied good conscience of the rulers of American society, a man as admirably lucid and logical as Noam Chomsky employs the worst paralogisms in his effort to reject an image imposed by solidly attested facts: the systematic massacre of millions of people by the Khmers rouges, in accordance with a plan resulting from an uncontrolled and demented theory run amuck. It is as if the denunciation of the vices of one society required that all the enemies of that society be innocent!
[9]The *ahl al-dhimma* were non-Muslim subjects in Muslim countries who paid a special tax and were granted protection and safety in return—*Translator's note.*

These suppositions were further inflamed by the ire of the Muslim popular masses against these minorities, whom princes often favoured since they were more readily at their mercy, being less protected by society as a whole. They therefore often became powerful and grew rich, and the bulk of true believers found it difficult to forgive them for this: a 'poor white' type reaction on the part of masses who considered themselves the legitimate recipients of state favour and felt frustrated to the advantage of merely tolerated interlopers who should at least have eschewed insolence. The princes sometimes yielded to this wrath of the masses, temporarily allowing them to take their revenge. The same processes unfolded in the Christian West, at the expense of the Jews alone, the sole non-Christian minority generally tolerated.

Many instances of disparagement and suspicion of the Jews, and of slander against them, therefore exist in the Muslim tradition, especially at the popular level. Many proverbs testify to this, for example. The accusation of ritual murder, for instance,[10] may be found in the *Thousand and One Nights* (a charge levelled against Christians and Mazdeans as well), and the origin of Muslim sects which the 'orthodox' majorities consider as undermining Islam from within is often ascribed to converted Jews. Extremist Shi'ism in the

---

[10]There is a hoary slander that certain Jewish religious ceremonies require that the Jews kill a Christian (sometimes a Christian child is specified) for the ritual use of the blood. It is a variant of similar accusations against Christians by pagans in Antiquity. From the twelfth century onwards, anti-Jewish slanders were often bandied about in the Christian world to account for missing or murdered children. The falsity and stupidity of such accusations were often demonstrated—by many Christian sovereigns, Jewish and Christian scholars, and at least five popes. It is therefore all the more distressing to have to note that during a solemn session of UNESCO in honour of Arab rights to Jerusalem, held at the beginning of 1981, the Syrian politician Ma'rouf Dawalibi cited as a proven truth just such an accusation made in Damascus in 1840 under extremely suspicious circumstances: primarily by Christians supported by the French consul, with regard to the disappearance of the Italian superior of the Capuccine monks, one P. Tomaso. The falsity of the accusation was demonstrated even at the time (see the detailed study by S. Poesner, *Adolphe Crémieux*, Paris 1933-34, vol. 1, chapter 8, pp.198-247). It is no less deplorable that none of the organizers of this meeting felt it appropriate to protest or to set the record straight. The audience came away with the impression that Arab opinion as a whole considered such slanders natural. Little incidents of this sort help to shape opinion, and do the greatest damage to the credence afforded legitimate Arab grievances. Does anyone believe that the European public can thus be encouraged to participate in such demonstrations?

early years of Islam and Fatimid Isma'ilism later are two examples.[11] In various Muslim countries, public signs of contempt are attached to the Jews, and the most difficult and repugnant jobs are reserved for them.

All these phenomena are perfectly explicable by the sociological and historical conditions of the time. There is no reason to portray them as crimes with which to stigmatize Islam, the Arabs, or both—as the Zionists and their friends often do. That betrays an anti-historical approach that ultimately would treat practically all people of the past, even the most admirable, as criminals, beginning with the ancient Greek thinkers who countenanced slavery. But there is no reason to deny such facts either, as Arab and Muslim ideologues often do. When they paint an unreasonably idealized portrait of a Muslim society in the Middle Ages in which justice, benevolence, and harmony alone prevailed—against the testimony of millions of Arab sources—they merely arouse the incredulity of non-Muslims and lead them to suspect that the situation was worse than it actually was. Like many propagandists, they therefore ultimately achieve a result opposite to the one they had sought.

All this inevitably has its effects on collective psychology. It should be emphasized, however, that at the end of the nineteenth and beginning of the twentieth centuries this legacy of the past was on the road to liquidation, especially in the countries of the Middle East. The judgements of the past were revivified somewhat by the slender influence of European anti-Semitism here and there. But it was primarily Zionism that stoked these smouldering embers. It could not have been otherwise when a group of Jews loudly claiming to be the sole true representatives of the Jewish world laid claim to an indisputably Arab land, declaring that they intended to wrench it from the Arab world and turn it into a foreign state. It could only

---

[11]Cf. I. Goldziher, *Muhammedanische Studien*, vol. 1, Halle 1889 (reprinted Hildesheim 1961), pp. 204 ff.; M. Canard, the entry for 'Fatimids' in the *Encyclopaedia of Islam*, second edition, vol. 2, 1965; Lacy O'Leary, *A Short History of the Fatimid Caliphate*, London 1923, pp. 33 ff. On 'Abdullah ibn Saba', supposedly the founder of extremist Shi'ism and said to be a converted Jew, see M.G.S. Hodgson, *Encyclopaedia of Islam*, second edition, vol. 1. On the image of the Jews in the *Thousand and One Nights*, see the thesis of Oskar Rescher, *Studien über den Inhalt von 1001 Nächte*, Berlin 1919, pp. 79 ff.

have been aggravated when this group of Jews realized its designs by force and with the aid of the powers of the Christian world.

The Arab anti-Zionist struggle, like all ideological struggles, uses all the weapons it can find. It is wonderful that this ideological struggle has so often foresaken the weapons of racial and religious hatred, and that its attacks have so often targeted only those directly responsible for the alienation of Arab Palestine, namely the followers of the Zionist movement.

But it was inevitable that in the ardour of the ideological struggle against Zionism, those Arabs most influenced by a Muslim religious orientation would seize upon the old religious and popular prejudices against the Jews in general. It was inevitable that certain fundamentalist Muslim organizations would link Zionism to the supposed general pernicious character of the Jews and Judaism. It was inevitable that the Muslim popular masses, once mobilized against Zionism, would call to mind popular traditions about the Jews and associate them with this combat.

I recall all this as a warning. Zionist propaganda does its work by arguing that all the anti-Zionist efforts of the Arabs and others are motivated by anti-Semitic propensities, by hatred of the Jews in general. The Zionist propagandists know very well that, for the time being at least, anti-Semitism arouses great revulsion among the majority of European and American public opinion. To denounce an action or assertion as anti-Semitic is thus to rally public opinion against it.

The Arabs and some of their friends ought to understand that they are in effect aiding Zionist and Arabophobic propaganda whenever they denounce a Zionist act or thesis while explaining it, or appearing to explain it, by the eternal maleficence of the Jewish people, while accordingly seeking analogies for it in Jewish history, or while suggesting that the persecution of the Jews was deserved, or did not actually take place, or was minimal.

It does not help to conclude or preface such arguments with the proclamation: 'We are not anti-Semites, the Arabs have never been anti-Semites, and they will never be anti-Semites.' How many people have I seen who have at first believed such proclamations, only later to hear critical, mocking, hostile, malevolent, disparaging, or slanderous remarks against Jews *in general* in Arab circles? They have concluded that they had been deceived by Arab propaganda and that the Zionists were right after all, at least in part, when they claimed that this propaganda was motivated at bottom by anti-Semitism. They have then decided that the Zionist offices that organize bulk mailings or sales of translations of anti-Jewish pamphlets that circulate in the Arab countries were revealing the truth of the matter after all.[12] Every time an Arab government, for example, prints and distributes the *Protocols of the Elders of Zion*, the forgery of the Tsarist secret police well known as such in Europe and America,[13] every time Arab publicists adopt such fabrications, they proffer effective aid to Zionist propaganda, which makes no mistake when it gives maximum publicity to all these acts. The question is whether the Arabs want to continue to accord Zionism such valuable assistance.

c) It is understandable that the Arabs are exasperated by the extent of solidarity with Israel on the part of Jews around the world. The phenomenon may be deplored, but is inevitable to a greater or lesser

---

[12]By way of example: the 'Centre d'information et de documentation sur le Moyen-Orient' (Geneva) once distributed a pamphlet in English and French containing the most flagrant anti-Jewish extracts from the minutes of the Fourth Conference of the Academy of Islamic Research (of the Azhar mosque), held in Cairo in September 1968. These minutes were said to have been published in Cairo in 1970, in a three-volume Arabic edition and an English edition of a single volume. The French abridgement is entitled *Les Juifs et Israël vus par les théologiens arabes* (Editions de l'avenir, Geneva 1971), the English *Arab Theologians on Jews and Israel* (same publishers and date). Some of the texts cited are actually only anti-Zionist or are merely religious criticisms of Judaism from a Muslim point of view. But there are also many that preach general hatred of all the Jews of all times and all places, claiming that they are endowed with a maleficent essence. The non-Muslim reader of these texts, who has no acquaintance with the obscurantists who drafted them and is unaware of their place in society, the degree of their influence, the circumstances, and so on, can only conclude that the Arabs in general harbour a violent hatred for the Jews in general and dream of their extermination.

[13]This document is a fantastic account of how a group of Jewish leaders supposedly concoct a conspiracy to conquer the world. It was shown long ago that it is a forgery fabricated by the Tsarist secret police on the basis of a pamphlet having nothing whatever to do with Jews and written by a French publicist named Maurice Joly against Napoleon III, the *Dialogue aux Enfers entre Montesquieu et Machiavel* (1864). For the entire history of this forgery, see the excellent book by Norman Cohn, *Histoire d'un mythe, la 'conspiration' juive et les Protocoles des Sages de Zion*, Fr. trans. Paris 1967. Arabic translations of the *Protocols* are distributed in Arab countries, sometimes by governments, and are often cited in the Arab press and by Arab publishers as though referring to a genuine document.

extent. Most Jews are unaware of exactly how Zionism was implanted in Palestine (for that matter, how many Arabs or others know it well?), and most still remember the painful persecutions of the past; they believe Zionist propaganda when it says that the existence of a Jewish state is a guarantee against any repetition of them, and they are suspicious of any attack on Jews. Any population with a minimum of features in common would be capable of similar reactions. As Ilya Ehrenburg once said somewhere, if some dictator took it into his head to persecute redheads, all redheads would come to feel a mutual solidarity. And I would add: they would also suspect that any assertion whatever that might seem critical of redheads, or even of any slightly rusty-haired man or woman, was a falsification.

Although Arab exasperation is understandable in the face of such a phenomenon, which would diminish in intensity if circumstances were favourable, the Arabs must also understand that any assertion that targets the Jews in general on the contrary can only reinforce it. How can any Jew—in any of the many senses of the term[14]—remain indifferent to Arab assertions claiming that all Jews are maleficent, and how could such assertions fail to incline them to lend a more favourable ear to Zionist theses?

This too, unfortunately, is an inevitable phenomenon to some extent. Unlike many European societies, and in particular unlike France, Middle Eastern society is institutionally multi-confessional. Jokes, jeers, and more or less ironic, scurrilous, or critical remarks about members of other confessions have been common for centuries. Hardly anyone pays any attention to them any more, and their profoundly noxious effects become evident only on certain occasions. In Europe, however, they seem maleficent in themselves.[15] That they are currently fashionable only makes it even more necessary not to aggravate an already bad impression by spoken and written flourishes that are indeed Judeophobic, even if their authors claim otherwise.

---

[14]See above, p. 175, and chapter 1, 'A Bit of Clarity at the Outset'.
[15]In France it was long felt that even to call someone a 'Jew'—or an 'Israelite', a locution long employed to avoid the injurious connotations of the word 'Jew' bequeathed by tradition—was impolite, or was even an attack in and of itself. In principle—but only in principle—any distinction among French people based on religion (present or ancestral) had been abolished. Moreover, an atheist or someone who positively re-

Appendix
Oriental Translations of the
Word 'Anti-Semitism'

Obviously, the word 'anti-Semitism' is a relatively recent European invention. Non-European peoples have therefore had to find some word to designate this concept, which played such an important part in European politics, whether or not they felt any hatred of Jews and even whether or not they knew who the Jews were. In accordance with the usual practices of linguistic borrowing, they soon adopted the European word in one of its forms, either altering it to conform to indigenous phonetics (like the Russian *antisemitizm*, taken as is from French, or the modern Greek *antisemitismós*) or trying to translate it.

The latter procedure itself revealed ideological inflections. Without detailed and arduous research, however, it is not easy to determine which variant the language adopted and when. In Arabic, for example, the word *anti-Semitism* was translated as *la-samiyya* which literally means 'non-Semitism', a bizarre and awkward translation. It would be interesting to find out who was first responsible for it and what he had in mind.[16] Perhaps the author of this neologism understood European anti-Semitism as a demand for the exclusion of the 'Semites' (the Jews, that is) from important social positions or from society in general. It was indeed that, but only in

---

jected the established religions could not belong to any of them, Judaism or any other. This situation is completely beyond the ken of anyone who has internalized the Middle Eastern attitude, and of some others as well. To them, someone descended from Jewish ancestors but who declares himself or herself 'without religion' appears to be guilty of a shameful repudiation, whereas from the general French point of view he or she is merely registering an objective fact. Albert Memmi tells of Jewish artisans in Tunisia poking fun at their European customers who, when asked whether they were Jewish, replied, 'Well, of Jewish origin'. They called them 'the of-origins'. Each side saw matters according to the viewpoint of their own society. A great many non-religious French citizens can in fact be correctly designated only as French of Catholic (or Protestant) origin.

[16]The only chronological reference I have been able to locate is the presence of *la-samii* and *la-samiyya*, in Léon Bercher, *Lexique arabe-français..., contribution à l'étude de l'arabe moderne*, 2nd edn, J. Carbonnel, Algiers 1942, which is based on surveys of the Arabic press of the preceding years (see pp. 101 and 189, the roots no. 764—and not 706, as the index on p. 19 incorrectly says—and 1364).

part. Perhaps he was inspired by similar 'calques': *la diimuuqraatii*, *la-taa'ifiyya*, literally 'non-democratic', 'non-confessionalism', but in practice meaning 'anti-democratic' and 'anti-confessionalism'.[17] In any event, it is the only term currently employed in Arabic, and as is the case with 'anti-Semitism' in Europe, its visible etymology affects the idea that Arabic-speakers have of the concept.

Hebrew translated the European words in just as striking an ideological fashion. It is true that modern Hebrew dictionaries often list a simple adaptation; for the adjective 'anti-Semitic' the adjective suffix – *ii* is affixed to an apocope of the European term based on the latter's etymology: *antishemii* (and hence, with the addition of the suffix denoting abstractions, *antishemiyyuut* for 'anti-Semitism'). But there were also—before the creation of the state of Israel[18]—the terms *soneh Yisrael* and *sin'at Yisrael*, or 'enemy of Israel' and 'hatred of Israel' respectively. One may well imagine the ambiguity of the connotations these terms could arouse.

---

[17]Cf. V. Monteil, *L'arabe moderne*, Paris 1960, pp. 138 ff. Contrary to a suggestion of Monteil's that is dubious, in this case at least, the neologism is not a calque of innovations from Ottoman Turkish, however common these are. The Arabic term is unknown in both Turkish and Persian, in which 'anti-Semitism' has generally been translated by expressions signifying 'hostility to the Jews'.

[18]Cf. Abraham Elmaleh, *Nouveau dictionnaire complet française-hébreu*, Jerusalem 1933, col. 2242.

8
Arab Views of the Israeli-Arab Conflict

*It was Pierre Vidal-Naquet who suggested that I include this old arti-
cle (written in 1969), which I had almost forgotten, in this collection.
Rereading it, I find that it might indeed be useful to give it a new
lease of life. There is no escaping the fact that Jewish problems today
are closely linked to the repercussions of the Israeli-Arab conflict,
itself born of the realization of the Zionist project. As a result, every
Jew in the world is compelled to take some attitude towards the Arab
people, the Arab states, and Arab political movements. Logically, it
would seem that this should encourage every Jew to try to understand Arab reactions. But many all-too-human psychological and
sociological factors work in the opposite direction. All these reactions tend automatically (and also all-too-humanly) to be classed as
instances of eternal anti-Semitism, a concept whose deficient explica-
tive value I have sought to demonstrate elsewhere in this volume. It is
always facility that triumphs. They hate us, and they always have
(with the variant favoured by Judeophilic goyyim of Christian stock:
they are hated and have always been hated, the proof being that we
have always hated them). Who needs go any further?*

*The article that follows is meant to show that there is good reason
to go further. It was published in the review* Economie et Human-
isme, *no. 190, November-December 1969, pp. 60–74.*

In the way the Israeli-Arab conflict is commonly understood in
Europe and America, the Arab point of view is generally unknown
or rejected from the outset. There are a number of reasons for this,

and it would be quite interesting to examine them in detail. I have tried to do this to some extent elsewhere, but much more remains to be said about it, and I will not be able to go much further in the compass of a brief article. Let me therefore simply list these reasons.

The first of them has to do with the common images of Jews and Arabs in European consciousness. These images have been shaped by the entire history of Western mentalities at least since the Middle Ages, partly under the influence of the relationships between Latin Christendom and Jews and Arabs, but also under the impact of waves of ideas that have successively broken over the West. In any event, they have only a very tenuous relationship to the realities of the conflict, realities of which most people are profoundly ignorant. Another factor is the impact of Zionist and Israeli propaganda, generally cleverly conducted, but which in any event has found receptive ground for reasons unconnected to its content or form. Furthermore, we must take account of the negative impact of Arab justifications, pleas, and propaganda, which present the cause they are defending cloaked in myths that are scarcely acceptable, if not downright repugnant, to average European public opinion, and which also manifest the greatest ignorance of the sources of that opinion and consequently act with extreme clumsiness. Let us add that the so-called under-developed character of Arab societies—actually the existence within them of broad sectors unadapted to the modern world—is reflected in the government apparatuses in charge of propaganda, just as it was strikingly reflected in the conduct of the war [of 1967] and in military organization. Finally, in reality there is not one single Arab point of view, but divergent and often contradictory points of view expressing the conceptions of particular layers and sectors of opinion and varying according to country and historical phase. These contradictions can only confuse outside opinion, ignorant as it is of the complex problems of the Arab world.

A very great effort is therefore needed for most Europeans to take the steps required to arrive at a clear-sighted view, one as objective as possible, of the division of responsibilities, the reciprocal wrongs committed, and the stakes of the struggle: one must rid oneself of stereotypes bequeathed by centuries-old tradition and reinforced by recent experiences, sometimes justified by European conditions inapplicable to the circumstances of the conflict in the Middle East; one must disregard the arguments and myths of propaganda, or at least reduce them to their real value; and, one must discover the kernel of truth that lies enveloped in these myths. All this obviously requires knowledge of facts that are ignored or distorted by apologetics and by ideological attacks. It is not surprising that this sort of effort is rarely attempted, and that it even more rarely leads to valid conclusions.

Arab Critique of Zionist Myths

The Arabs often see through—and this is quite understandable—the misinterpretations given credence by adverse propaganda based on the stereotypes of European-American consciousness. They do not recognize themselves in the image that is presented of them: noisy and lazy incompetents, bloody and cruel fanatics, pillaging and half-savage bedouins, sensuous and opulent potentates. They are very often quite clear-sighted about their shortcomings. Some—among them the 'angry young people', dissidents, and far-left revolutionaries—may admit that certain features of this portrait are real. But they vehemently deny that it depicts the essence of the Arab people, immutable and everlasting. To the extent that they believe that some of these defects (or others) are real, they ascribe them to transitory socio-historical circumstances, which the revolutionaries intend precisely to eliminate. With equal vehemence they insist that no feature of the Arab character, whether good or bad, can account for the conflict with Israel, any more than it can justify the enforced amputation of a territory that was Arab in the usual sense of the word.

The Arabs likewise readily see through the misinterpretations peddled by the usual themes of Zionist and Israeli propaganda and generally accepted by European and American public opinion. They can see that the usual rules of judgement are not applied to them, but are bent for the Israelis. Another people's right to Palestine is proclaimed on the basis of the fact that this people inhabited the country in Antiquity, whereas this concept has never been used anywhere else, except in western Poland, when the Germans took possession of it while invoking the Slavic occupation of this territory in the High Middle Ages. But that argument is never presented without being accompanied by a statement of German guilt towards both the Poles and humanity in general. Clearly, ancient inhabitation was regarded as insufficient justification. And collective guilt cannot honestly be charged against the Arabs.

Arguments drawn from Jewish and Christian holy books are often used: the election of the people of Israel; the promise of Palestinian territory to the posterity of Jacob (which is enough to make someone like Jacques Maritain say that no people's right to its national territory is more firmly attested than that of Israel to Palestine); St Paul's thesis that God never abjures His promises. I leave aside the question of the validity of the exegetic interpretations of these texts, in particular as they concern the present epoch. But even supposing that the exegesis most favourable to Israel were perfectly valid, since when is a people deprived of its right to a territory on the basis of the religious ideas of other peoples?[1] Suppose the Gypsies carried their veneration of the sanctuary of Saintes-Marie-de-la-Mer to the point of considering the Camargue a sacred territory in which their race, dispersed for a millennium and a half, must now be ingathered to constitute a state of the Gypsy language. Suppose further that this belief were perfectly attested to down through the centuries by books that the Gypsies held sacred. How many French people would accept these beliefs as valid justification for the establishment of the Camargue as a Gypsy state? And what would have been their attitude had the Gypsies tried to realize this dream without consulting the French and with the support of an occupying power, say, Germany?

It is understandable that the Arabs are particularly exasperated when people who have opposed policies, attitudes, and acts of even their own national community in the name of universal principles of conscience, and who have fought for the application of these principles in reality, suddenly refuse to apply their own criteria because the community at whose expense these principles would act is Jewish.

---

[1] It is true that the texts in question are also holy to Christian Arabs. But from the very outset, traditional Christian exegesis has purged them of any 'Zionist' interpretation that could be valid after the Redemption—the only exception being certain Protestant sects like the one to which Michael Rohen belongs, the man who set the fire in the Aqsa mosque. The mind may wander where it wills, but no one will be surprised that such sects have few adherents among the Arabs.

These people—of the left according to the established designation—have sharply condemned the occupation of the territory of one people by another, and the extension of privileges to one ethnic element over another within the same state. They have vigorously combatted such practices—in word and often also in deed—even when they gave advantages to members of their own national community, indeed even considering it a particular duty to act against these injustices when they were being committed by their own fellow citizens, to put their own house in order, as Lenin said. On those occasions they rejected colonial justifications based, for example, on the labour that had been expended in these neglected territories, on the introduction of a new order, the raising of living standards, the model offered by a civilization considered more highly developed. But they seem not to consider any of their criticism of these sorts of arguments applicable when it comes to Jews occupying the territory of another people and claiming special rights in it for themselves. In this case, they seem to believe that arguments about the 'benefits of civilization' and colonization are overwhelming and ought to prevent the Arabs from complaining.

Our leftists have also almost always understood and most often excused terrorism as a method of struggle against colonialism. Some have even collaborated with it. That was their attitude towards Jewish terrorism in Palestine against the British occupation forces between 1944 and 1948. At that time, humanitarian objections about innocent victims were brushed aside with disdain, since 'any war causes innocent victims', and so on. But the same people often condemn Palestinian terrorism against Israel quite severely, as they suddenly rediscover a dormant sensitivity to the human agony thus caused. Either of these two attitudes may have its advocates and ethical justifications, and discussion of them is to be welcomed. But what about consistency and impartiality? I have been told, it is true, that certain pro-Israeli philosophers, making good use of the remarkable aptitude of philosophical (like poetic or mystical) discourse to deck out any irrational assertion in acceptable colours at will, are hard at work elaborating a remarkable theory of good and bad terrorism—the latter, obviously, being that practised by others.

Our leftists have always protested against the undue generalization to an entire movement of acts of atrocity committed by extremists on the fringes of that movement. They denounced the use of the carnage of Melouza as an argument against the entire movement for Algerian independence. In Palestine itself, they applied that same principle to the massacre committed by the Irgun and elements of the Stern Gang at Deir Yassin in 1948. Had not the massacre been condemned by the leadership of the Jewish state, they argued, by Ben-Gurion himself? Very well. But then, why blame the Palestinian movement as a whole, much less all Arabs, for the actions of the PFLP commandos or others, and consider them proof of the intrinsic perversity of the Arab soul?

European Myths About the Jews

These are some of the observations the Arabs can make, and it seems clear that they can readily contest, with quite valid arguments, the rules of judgement that are applied to them.

But one great argument stands against them. Their rejection of and resistance to Israel is based on the application to the Jews of the normal criteria of judgement they have seen applied to other human groups. They want the Jews to be treated as people like any others (further on I will qualify this assertion somewhat). For a good part of European consciousness, however, the Jews are not people like any others.

I will not say much about the mystical exaltation of the Jews that has supplanted the scorn and hatred so long practised by some Christians. There is no doubt that the former attitude is better than the latter, which at the very least made a big contribution to bringing about the horrors of which we are so well aware. If this new attitude could at least act as a guarantee against any resurgence of Hitlerite anti-Semitic cannibalism, then it could only be applauded, at least as far as its application to Europe was concerned, whatever one's reservations about its exegetic validity or rationality. But nothing is less certain. The child praised as a model for his fellows earns only their hatred. If the transition is readily made from mystical Judeophobia to equally mystical Judeophilia—one has only to compare the arguments (if they can be called that) of Maurice Clavel[2] with those of the confirmed anti-Semite Léon Bloy—nothing would be easier than the return journey. Let us leave aside how unhealthy such adoration is for the Jews themselves. The question is, why should such an attitude carry any weight with the Arabs?

But the events of recent decades have given rise to other myths about the Jews, secular ones far more widespread than Christian religious myths, though sometimes intermingled with them. At their root lie very real facts and quite laudable sentiments; but such is humanity that all good sentiments are inextricably entangled with more dubious motives, and any reaction of repugnance to barbarity can lead, at least potentially, to complicity with some other barbarity.

The human mind has a fatal propensity to slide continually from the concrete to the metaphysical. In the Christian world, the Jews have often been despised, harassed, discriminated against, persecuted, tortured, massacred. The fact is undeniable and deplorable. It is just for the Christian world to make its self-criticism, fortunate that it deplores its errors, fruitful for it to analyse their roots, and infinitely laudable that it should seek ways to avoid the repetition of such aberrations and should proclaim its rejection of the ideas that served as their basis. It is excellent for correct notions about the Jews, their history, their traditional religion, and their culture to be disseminated among masses of people still influenced by these ideas. Given the contempt that has been showered upon them, it is quite salutary to recall not only that the Jews are people like any others, but also that they have given humanity a significant number of great figures in all domains: scholars, philosophers, people of rich and pure life, saints.

But to go beyond this recognition of reality and enter the realm of essences is pernicious. That is the road of racism, which, Albert Memmi to the contrary, is not only oppression, but initially the at-

---

[2]His articles in the *Nouvel Observateur* (nos. 252, 8–14 September 1969, and 254, 22–28 September 1969) may serve as classic texts for the study of the mechanism of metaphysical alienation. They are definitely worthy of Karl Marx's example of the analysis of the pear, and they have the additional merit of being genuine. It is to be hoped that no Jew was able to read without embarrassment these articles meant to deify the Jews.

tribution of a good or evil essence to an ethnic group. A high proportion of Jews have been intellectuals, they have very often been most barbarously oppressed, and they have often formed the most disadvantaged layers of various societies. But they are not endowed with an intellectual, oppressed, or proletarian essence. They have also had their manual workers, oppressors, and capitalists. In the proper conditions, groups of Jews may have quite a different structure and engage in quite different activities. Like all other peoples and groups, they too have on occasion massacred, oppressed, and exploited. There is nothing astonishing or paradoxical—unfortunately—about the assumption of such attitudes by Jewish groups or individuals in the present or future, for they have already been encountered in the past. Jewish or Christian theologians may accord the Jews, considered as a whole down through the centuries, an eminent part in the designs of God, in the economy of salvation of humanity. But these doctrines must be reconciled with the observed fact that in their practical everyday existence actual Jews are people like any others, with only slightly variant proportions (which change from group to group) of good and bad, saints and sinners, geniuses and fools, sharp operators and simpletons—proportions that vary, moreover, depending on the concrete conditions in which Jewish groups have been or are placed. It therefore cannot be considered sacrilegious to criticize (and if necessary to combat) the attitudes, acts, or ideas of particular Jews or of a given group of Jews.

The tragedy is that in the European-American world it is both indispensable and dangerous to enunciate this simple principle, that Jews are people like any others. The same propensity to ascribe essences can quickly shift from rejection of the myth of the Jew who is good in essence to the adoption of the myth of the Jew who is perverse in essence. We have seen this happen in Eastern Europe (where, naturally, other factors are at work too). I myself have been abused innumerable times for having enunciated and applied this principle. Some of my adversaries were right to see dangers in this attitude, and it is quite true that these dangers are serious, that they often cause me to hesitate. In criticism, as in combat, there is a natural pressure to generalize, and others could readily take up my arguments, extrapolate them, and carry them in the direction of essentialization, even if in a less elaborate form.[3] But can anything be said or done that is not dangerous, in one respect or another, in a situation that is so terribly complex and difficult? Is not the truth the least parlous of choices?

But in any event, there is no point whatever in answering the Arabs with European myths about the Jews, as is commonly done. The Arabs feel no sense of guilt with regard to the Jews, and if there is an Arab myth, it will take quite another form. Many pages would be required to trace an accurate and properly shaded portrait of the conditions of the Jews in the Arab countries in the past, for they varied in time and place. Neither the idyllic image presented by Arab propaganda and Muslim apologetics nor the hellish tableau painted by Zionist and pro-Israeli propaganda is accurate. Since the prophet of Islam considered the Jews models at first and enemies later, the Muslim sacred texts contain words of praise and malediction, tolerance and combat. The Jews, like the Christians, constituted minority and subordinated communities in the societies dominated by Islam. The latter accorded them a status of conditional protection. These communities were often quite comfortable, but sometimes persecuted, or at least harassed. In the countries and epochs in which archaic, authoritarian, traditionalist sorts of society held sway, they were sometimes reduced to the status of pariahs. But on the whole, the situation of Judaism was a hundred times better than in the Christian countries. Abjuration was very rarely demanded. The best proof of this is that tens of thousand of Jews from Christian countries 'voted with their feet', seeking refuge in the lands of Islam at various epochs, notably under the Ottoman Empire. And during the nineteenth century an evolution towards secularization, or

---

[3]Much has been made of Arab anti-Zionist caricatures, which are often anti-Semitic, sometimes consciously, sometimes not. During the colonial epoch, for instance, Indian caricatures depicting the English (complete with the distinctive features then ascribed to them by the current stereotypes) being cast into the sea were not apt to excite anyone. They served a limited objective, the decolonization of India, and were not likely to have any other effects (or hardly any others). But the Arab caricatures, while they aim at the goal of the decolonization of Palestine, can indeed serve to attribute an essence to the Jew as a pernicious being. Too often they evoke too many terrible memories to be regarded with equanimity by Europeans. The Arabs thus find themselves violently criticized and taken to task for engaging in practices of psychological warfare which, while quite deplorable as a general rule, are willingly pardoned by world opinion when used elsewhere, against different enemies.

at least towards equality of confessions, was quite evident in the most developed countries of the Muslim world, those of the eastern Mediterranean.

It is therefore understandable that the Arabs or Muslims scarcely feel any responsibility for the misfortunes of the Jews in Christian lands, that they refuse to allow themselves to be the only ones forced to make restitution at their own expense, that they recognize no obligation to abstain from criticizing or combating Jewish acts or attitudes that wrong them. Why should the massacre of Jews by the Germans require the surrender of an Arab land to *some* Jews? If the Europeans feel guilty, the Arabs say, let them make restitution at their own expense. The Arabs could perhaps contribute a reasonable pro rata share of international reparations, and if anyone had taken the trouble to solicit their point of view, they might perhaps have contemplated concessions. But what happened in practice? The Europeans said, in effect: 'Some of us have massacred these people, and many others passively allowed the massacre to occur or somehow aided the executioners. We cannot even be absolutely sure that we will not massacre them again. So move aside and make a refuge for them. And suffer the punishment you deserve for not having acquiesced automatically and immediately to this surrender of territory that has been imposed on you.'

It is quite possible that in rejecting this argumentation, the Arabs have failed to measure up to ideal Christian (or Buddhist) behaviour, forgiving abuses and manifesting complete self-denial when confronted with the misfortune of others. But what Christian or Buddhist national or ethnic group would have done so in these same circumstances? Where is the Pharisee who would cast the first stone?

Demythization and Arab Myths

The Arab refusal to accept Israel therefore has a foundation perfectly grounded in rationality and ethics, for the basic Arab argumentation seems difficult to refute. The constitution of an Israeli people and state has definitely meant—as I have explained at length elsewhere, with, I think, all the necessary justification[4]—the establishment of a new element of population imposed, without their acquiesence or even consultation, on an Arab people thus forced to choose between exile and subordination. This does not necessarily mean that the Arab rejection has always been opportune from the standpoint of the ultimate interests of the Arab peoples, nor that it still is. Nor does it mean that the basic Arab argumentation has not, on occassion, also been enveloped in myths, which have sometimes gone so far as to obliterate the Arab case itself, to the great detriment of its credibility in the eyes of world opinion. It is the lot of humanity to warp even the most just of causes with inept myths, to extrapolate the most correct of ideas to the point of rendering them absurd, to employ the most dubious means in the defence of demands that are justified, at least in part, and to dilute without end the sacrifice of martyrs with the manoeuvres of the malicious.

The Jews as a Middle Eastern Community

To begin with, and at a very low level of conceptualization and theorization, the Arabs have a normal tendency to think of the Jews in terms of their own categories and experience. Just as Europeans automatically assimilate Israelis to the category of oppressed and massacred Jews so well known to them, just as they see the Arabs in terms of those Arab groups with which they have been in contact in history and with which they think they are well acquainted, so the Arabs of the East—those directly concerned—think of the Jews as members of one of the 'communities' of their multi-communal society. A lengthy dissertation would be required to explain in detail the structure of this traditional society, dominated by a ruling Muslim layer but with its roots stretching back to the ancient, pre-Islamic eastern civilizations. Contrary to medieval Christian society, in which the Jews formed practically the only non-Christian community—tolerated but considered as standing outside the social norm, at least in theory—Muslim society was legally considered

---

[4]Cf. Maxime Rodinson, *Israel: A Colonial-Settler State?*, New York 1973, and *Israel and the Arabs*, 2nd edn, Harmondsworth 1982.

multi-communal, theoretically including only monotheistic communities (of *ahl al-kitab*, or 'people of the Book', those endowed with a holy scripture revealed by God[5]) but in practice also including other communities that did not fit within this framework. Christians and Jews—who were considered the repositories of a true divine Revelation which they had only misunderstood and distorted in places, wrongly failing to admit that it had been superseded and partially abrogated by the Muhammedan revelation, though remaining faithful to prophets also considered holy and venerated by Muslims[6]—were 'protected' provided they paid a special tax and occupied a position inferior to that of the Muslim community. Each community, virtually autonomous in many respects, had its own personal code, judged its own members according to its own laws, and obeyed its own authorities. Christian patriarchs and grand rabbis were personages venerated by the state itself, admitted to the court with high honours alongside the Muslim religious authorities. With the trend towards inter-confessional equality that was slowly developing in the nineteenth century, both Christian and Jewish festivals, for example, were recognized as public holidays by the state. It is understandable that a man like Albert Memmi, who comes from the Tunisian Jewish community, finds it intolerable, a sign of oppression, that only Christian festivals are public holidays in France. With the development of nationalistic ideology during the same period, Arabic-speaking Christians and Jews came to be considered Arabs of non-majority faiths.[7] Jews played an important role in the Arab nationalist movement.[8] This situation was institutionaliz-

---

[5] But considered distorted by posterior transmitters, Jewish or Christian, who are claimed in particular to have deleted any passages heralding the Muslim revelation.

[6] Many Muslims, for example, have borne the names Musa (Moses) and Issa (Jesus), and still do.

[7] There have been, especially in recent years, more or less veiled instances of suspicion about the Arabism of the Christians (not to mention the Jews, obviously compromised by Zionist action). This is not at all due to old confessional struggles, but to the fact that for obvious reasons the Christians, like the Jews, have historically been the first to collaborate with their European co-religionists and to profit from this co-operation. The phenomenon thus grows out of the logic of nationalism.

[8] The most famous example is the Egyptian Jacob (Ya'qub) Sanu' (1839–1912), one of the pioneers of nationalism, primarily in its Egyptian form. His satirical publications in the spoken Egyptian Arabic dialect were immensely popular in the Nile Valley. He was one of the companions of the great Muslim nationalist agitator Jamal al-Din,

ed in a particularly clear fashion under the Ottoman Empire, which encompassed the great majority of Arab countries from the beginning of the sixteenth century, with an increasingly egalitarian tone in the contemporary epoch, especially immediately after the Young Turk revolution of 1908. After the dissolution of the Ottoman Empire, it led to a marked inter-confessional egalitarianism, both in Lebanon, where the Christians and Druzes formed more than half the population, and in Palestine under the British mandate, where the Christian occupier organized all of society along these lines.

Accustomed to such a situation, and considering the Jews to be members of a particular community, the Arabs—especially in the East, where relations were almost egalitarian—could not understand the desire of the Jews of Israel to form a separate state of their own, any more than Richelieu could yield to the desire of the French Protestants to constitute a community that would escape the common laws of the Kingdom of France to some extent, although in this latter case the term 'state within the state' was a slightly exaggerated metaphor in essence. They could not understand the reaction of European Zionist Jews, who claimed to constitute not a religious community but a people, claiming a right to a state of their own like all other peoples, protected by their own institutions, including an army of their own, against any interference by non-Jews, such interference in general being felt as oppression naturally capable of leading to persecution. One line of reasoning often heard from Arabs of the East is based on the oddness of this behaviour, since without a state the Jews could have played a role in all the Arab countries far more easily, whereas reduced to the few Palestinian cantons constituting their state, they would have to limit their activity to those areas.

The programme adopted some two years ago by the Palestinian resistance organizations is based on this perception of matters, which can be tailored not only to the traditional concept, simply tilted towards egalitarianism, but also to a modernist secular concept of the French type. That is the origin of the project of an egalitarian, secular Palestine in which all confessions would be accepted as full

known as al-Afghani. On Sanu', see the book by Irène L. Gendzier, *The Practical Ideas of Ya'qub Sanu'*, Cambridge, Mass. 1966.

participants. It represents an ideal that is particularly attractive to all those who would like to overcome the present situation of mounting hatred between Jews and Arabs. It could be particularly attractive to Jews outside Palestine who do not want to be drawn into a struggle that seems not to concern them, like the French Jews, for example, who are accustomed, although by a different cultural situation and historical evolution, to conceptions of the same type—to the extent that recent events have not convinced them to abandon these conceptions, at least in part. There are only two difficulties—but they are sizeable. First, although the Jews of the world do not constitute a people in the strict sense, the Israelis constitute not a religion but a group of an ethnic type, a nation at least in formation. Second, this Israeli ethnic group was formed precisely under the impetus of those of the Jews who were more concerned with the state than with the formation of a nation in itself, in order to achieve total independence of decision-making and to create a defence force (or possibly an attack force) of their own. A very large number of Jews of the diaspora who were initially hostile to this idea later came, under the impact of the persecutions of 1939–45, first to excuse this option, then to accept it, and finally to support it, for others.

Here it may be of interest to remark that the programme of a secular Palestine now being advanced by the Palestinian organizations, while it does represent an important innovation at the level of public commitments and to some extent at a quantitative level as well, is not a fundamental, so to speak qualitative, change. Let me explain what I mean. I do not believe that the Arabs of Palestine struggling against Zionism have ever preached the complete elimination of the Jews from Palestine (except perhaps at moments of excessive excitation by some leaders). They have always acknowledged the existence of a Jewish religious community among others. What they denounced was the unlimited growth of the Jewish element through organized immigration. They saw this, correctly, as a political design, or at least as the beginning of a chain of events liable to overturn the traditional structure described above: formerly dominance of the Sunni Muslim community, more recently a balance among communities. It was obvious that the Zionists wanted, through immigration, at least to exert decisive weight as an autonomous political element in Palestinian society as a whole and at most to create a Jewish state in Palestine, which was, no one had forgotten, the initial programme and reason for existence of their movement. Hence the kinds of programme advanced with more or less coherence by various Arab leaders in the past: to accept only Jews who had immigrated before 1880, or before 1917, or before 1932, or before 1948, and so on. In each case, the point was to maintain the Jewish element in its 'normal' role as a community of the Middle Eastern type, in a balance with the others. This state of affairs would be compromised by the existence of a Jewish majority created by immigration, especially in the light of the declared political ambitions of Zionism. It seems clear that the European character of the mass of the Jewish population prior to 1948, foreign to the Middle East, as well as its evident inspiration by motives that were anything but religious, played a role in this apprehension of matters. Let us recall a somewhat similar situation in neighbouring Lebanon, regulated up to now [1969!] by far more peaceful means, which facilitates the common membership of the many Lebanese communities in the Arab ethnic group, their attachment to an identical type of society and culture. In Lebanon population statistics broken down by community are simply avoided, so as not to compromise the painfully established balance between the set of Christian communities and that of Muslim communities. This balance was founded on the supposition, more or less accurate in 1920, that the two groups were numerically equal. Since there is no doubt that the majority is now Muslim (as a result of greater emigration among Christians and a higher birth-rate among Muslims), it is feared that public proclamation of this fact would lead to Muslim demands for political predominance; the fiction of equality is therefore maintained at the expense of statistics, and despite universal awareness of its fictive character.[9]

The innovation introduced by the Palestinian programme thus consists essentially in: 1) acceptance of the Jewish presence, whatever its numerical weight (that this acceptance in itself is courageous may be seen by referring to the Lebanese example); 2) resignation to past

---

[9][Written in 1969! The massive Palestinian immigration to Lebanon, with its independent political and military structures—an indirect consequence of the Zionist victory—brought about the rupture of the equilibrium.]

Jewish immigration, which thus acquires a sort of legitimacy, whatever its date of origin (whereas previous programmatic drafts sought to register the illegitimacy of the massive immigration imposed by foreign administrative apparatuses, first British and later Israeli); 3) solemn proclamation in responsible declarations of what until now had been set forth only in secret negotiations by some organizations devoid of generally recognized authority. It must be added—and it is important to note this—that formally the Lebanese-type community structure, in which each community is more or less autonomous and institutionally endowed with political power of its own, is rejected. The Palestinian programme (as it has been formulated up to now by the most numerous resistance groups) views the Jews of Palestine as a religious community, but one stripped of its specifically Middle Eastern characteristics, solely in the manner in which one may speak of Catholic or Protestant communities in France (I leave aside the Jews of France, who are now allowing themselves to drift precisely towards a rather Middle Eastern—or American—type of community; but this will take a long time). In the eyes of the law, Muslims, Christians, and Jews would be, as they are in France, no more than citizens[10] holding different metaphysical views. This would, of course, pose the problem of the very large number of Jewish atheists, but it must be said that even in the state of Israel—itself also the legatee of the Ottoman Empire through the British mandate—these atheist Jews have allowed themselves to be encompassed within the framework of a Middle Eastern community that is defined by religion, even if it is not practised or believed—in short, by the religion of one's ancestors. Thus, from a modernist standpoint, after defining the Jewish entity in Palestine in accordance with the norms of a Middle Eastern type of community, the Palestinian movements then reject precisely this sort of community, as most of the Arab states have also done in principle. Such an evolution seems clearly desirable, provided, however, that it is not limited to theory, that the after-effects of the community situation are really eliminated. Otherwise the result would be to deprive the minorities of any means of protecting their collective interests. I will return to this point later.

---

[10]Palestinian citizens, of course, and hence Arabs, at least according to the Fatah programme.

The Two Myths: Towards the Rightist Arab Myth

This primitive concept of the Jewish group as a religious community is the necessary starting point, but the Arab theories contain much more, whether implicitly or explicitly. Very generally and crudely, one may say that Arab demands are presented to the world within the framework of one of two different myths, depending on the tendency concerned, although each myth contains admixtures of the other.

The first myth, that of the right, is that Israel constitutes religious aggression against Islam (and in the Christian variant, aggression against Christianity[11]). Historically, it was the first to develop. The initial Arab reactions to Zionist penetration of and claims to Palestine had been varied, not uniformly hostile. Before 1914, hostility came primarily from local politicians, who were more sensitive to the disquiet of the Palestinian masses, and more strongly from Christians than from Muslims, since the Christians feared that the Jews might begin to compete in activities that were primarily the province of Christians in Palestinian society at the time, under the rule of the Ottoman Empire. Others, however, accustomed to the settlement in the lands of Islam of newcomers from abroad, wondered if it might not be good policy to ally themselves with these foreigners, who possessed European technology and culture and were presumed by public opinion (and by Zionist diplomacy at the time[12]) to command considerable financial resources. Various Ottoman parties and some currents of embryonic Arab nationalism toyed with this idea. At one time, it was even the view of Sharif Husain of Mecca, theoretically the commander of the Arab revolt of 1916, and of his son Faisal, the prestigious leader of Arabist policy in the years that followed. In this the Arab nationalists were strongly encouraged by their English protectors, and some of them were not insensitive to the Zionist theme of return to the ancestral homeland.

---

[11] A Christian editor of a Lebanese journal confided to me last year [in 1968, that is]: 'Do you really believe in Israeli expansionism? No, what they want is not land, but to combat Jesus Christ.'

[12] In its early stages, Zionism made systematic use of the anti-Semitic myth of Jewish financial power. The Zionists also managed to make use of the element of reality that had shaped this myth—and the state of Israel has continued to do so.

But the incompatibility of Zionist and Arab claims became increasingly clear after 1920. The anti-Zionist attitude of the Arab national movement grew ever more radical and irreversible. This attitude had to be theorized for world opinion.

The simplest theory—the one that conformed most closely both to the reality of the facts and to the ethical rules that were fairly generally acknowledged at the time (at least in theory)—emerged from the very outset. It was simply to protest against the control of a territory by a foreign population element. The resolution of the General Syrian Congress held in July 1919 is already perfectly clear on this subject:

'We reject the claims of the Zionists for the establishment of a Jewish commonwealth in that part of southern Syria which is known as Palestine, and we are opposed to Jewish immigration into any part of the country. We do not acknowledge that they have a title, and we regard their claims as a grave menace to our national political and economic life. Our Jewish fellow-citizens shall continue to enjoy the rights and to bear the responsibilities which are ours in common. ...The basic principles proclaimed by President Wilson in condemnation of secret treaties cause us to enter an emphatic protest against any agreement providing for the dismemberment of Syria and against any undertaking envisaging the recognition of Zionism in southern Syria: ...The lofty principles proclaimed by President Wilson encourage us to believe that the determining consideration in the settlement of our own future will be the real desires of our people; ...'[13]

This theme, while it never disappeared, was nevertheless insufficient to rally all the desired and potentially available assistance both inside and outside the country.

Internally, it quickly became only too clear that that the Wilsonian principles of self-determination were a rickety foundation. English and French 'protection' was imposed on various Arab countries (in the hypocritical form of 'mandates'). The leaders of the nationalist movement of the time more or less resigned themselves to this development, striving only to play on the contradictions between the

---

[13]The text is translated in George Antonius, *The Arab Awakening, The Story of the Arab National Movement*, London 1938.

two imperialist powers, and also on their internal contradictions and their liberal principles, in an effort to loosen the leash somewhat. The Zionist movement was being very coy at the time, still keeping in mind the ultimate goal of a Jewish state, but mentioning it as little as possible, deleting it from its short- and medium-term programme and being content with the slow and patient establishment of a base that would someday permit the supreme claim. Many of the Jews settled in Palestine, among the rank and file and sometimes even in the leadership, contemplated sticking to that level of limited presence in Palestine as a serious possibility, although the ever subjacent fundamental ideas of Zionism would often conflict with this perspective, implying quite a different dynamic.

In this situation, the Arab masses themselves, oscillating between the ever-present objective of independence and resignation to at least a long period of foreign rule, however relaxed, did not always manifest an unfailing anti-Zionist ardour, especially outside Palestine. Zionism sometimes looked like a nationalist movement similar to those of other non-Arabs settled in the Middle East—the Armenians, for instance—of no great immediate danger for the indigenous inhabitants. This was especially true in that Jewish immigration to Palestine remained feeble, assuming worrying dimensions only after 1933 (and even then it never raised the Jewish component of the population to more than a third of the total), since Britain, the mandatory power, was becoming increasingly hostile to Zionism's ultimate claims, and since no power seemed ready to play the part of a modern Cyrus. Zionist bookstores were therefore open for business in most Arab cities, and in Egypt—a country in which aspirations for complete independence, which had long been present, were only belatedly formulated in the context of Arab nationalist ideology—the local Zionists even had a headquarters in the centre of Cairo, their flag flying from the roof. The Zionist youth organizations were able to parade through the streets without arousing appreciable reactions from the populace.

The Rightist Arab Myth

The necessity for summoning up reinforcements through other fac-

tors of mobilization is thus comprehensible. Alongside the conception of the Jews as an alien people, which was especially noticeable in
Palestine, the idea of the Jews as a religious community was still
deeply rooted everywhere. As we have seen, in the context of that
concept, the Zionist movement tended to appear primarily as an effort by the Jewish community to upset the balance of the various
communities, to its own advantage. A mobilization against that objective could therefore draw upon all the age-old well-springs of
inter-religious conflict, which had most often been contained within
rather peaceful limits. Both Koranic invective against the Jews of
Medina as enemies of the prophet and Christian literature against
this stubborn people guilty of deicide and of insulting the Virgin
(which has its reflections in the Koran as well) could be used—and
was, abundantly. The question of the holy sites was also exploited. It
was argued that although the Muslims recognized the sacred
character of the Jewish and Christian holy sites, there was no
reciprocity on this score from the Jews (and partially from the Christians). Control of these sanctuaries therefore could not be ceded to
the Jews. The Catholic church, and to some extent the Protestant
churches too, were quite sensitive to this argument. Finally, this
purely religious theme was increasingly accompanied by the European anti-Semitic argument that the Jews sought world domination,
which was in growing favour in Europe with the rise of Hitlerism.
The anti-Semitic myth, forged in Europe and exported to the Orient
(it is no accident that caricatures of the Jew in Arabic anti-Semitic
literature faithfully reproduce features whose evocative value
depends upon European circumstances), was able to acquire an eminent mobilizing power in the Middle East, which logically should
have been greater than in Europe, since in the East the threat of the
hegemony of certain Jewish groups was real and not mythical. It is
remarkable that genuine anti-Semitism[14] did not develop there more
than it actually did. But it is possible that, with Israel's aid, it will be

---

[14]Naturally, I am using the word 'anti- Semitism' in the usual sense of hatred of Jews
in themselves, considered as endowed with a pernicious essence. This usage conflicts
with etymology, but etymology has never been a reliable guide in the semantic use of a
word. Hence the futility of the argument of certain Arabs: we cannot be anti-Semites
because we are Semites too. It is true, however, that Hitler's theory was directed
against the Arabs as well.

just a matter of time.[15]

Outside Palestine, recourse to the myth of a Jewish assault on Islam succeeded in winning considerable sympathy between the two world wars. Anti-Semitism was then on the rise and was to triumph horribly. The Catholic church, which in any case was not immune to clearly anti-Semitic orientations on occasion, was anti-Zionist for reasons that have been explained. On the other hand, an orientation of this kind alienated potential support from any forces that were at all progressive and liberal. It reinforced the already powerfully rooted stereotype of 'Muslim fanaticism' with weighty arguments. After the Second World War, the reaction of guilt and horror on the part of European and American public opinion was to deprive any propaganda conducted along these lines of most of its effectiveness, although some Arab propagandists continued to stay the course. For in oriental circles[16] it is often imagined that European opinion is shaped in the image of that of the Middle East, with its deep schisms and bitter rivalries between communities. The Jewish peril to the other religions is therefore still invoked on occasion, perhaps enjoying some resonance among certain Europeans, but generally appearing rather anachronistic in an epoch in which ecumenism is becoming a palpable trend. It is not surprising that those Arab efforts still directed along these lines reinforce European stereotypes about the Muslim world and fall as manna from heaven for the propagandists of the other side, intent as they are on identifying anti-Zionism with anti-Semitism.

Arab Nationalist Myths

Arab nationalist myths are less at variance with reality and more closely attuned to generally recognized values and profound currents

---

[15]The *Protocols of the Elders of Zion* have been distributed in the Arab countries on various occasions and now, it appears, with particular success. It must be said that the unconditional solidarity of many Jews throughout the world with Israel and its policy confers an apparent plausibility upon the fabrications of the forgers of the Tsarist Okhrana about the Jewish mobilization for world conquest.

[16]And also among the Jews of the Arab countries. The reinvigoration and even renewal of French Jewry through the massive influx of Jews from Algeria has had significant consequences from this point of view.

among the Arab masses; in principle, they could have drawn greater sympathy from world opinion. Little by little, strictly nationalist ideas in the East have gained much ground on religious ideas, and above all on the 'patriotism' of religious communities, although not without difficulties, contradictions, and backward lurches. The sentiment of solidarity in the struggle for independence is a reality among the Arab masses, and the right of peoples to self-determination has become a nearly unanimously respected value throughout the world, at least in theory.

Nevertheless, nationalist ideology in the Arab world has suffered contamination and has not yet entirely detached itself from traditional Muslim religious (or rather, communitarian) ideology. Within Islam, the Arabs possess the privilege not only of having been the people from which the prophet and the first propagators of the new faith emerged but also of speaking the language of divine revelation. Among Muslim Arabs there is often a great temptation to amalgamate themes drawn from both sources, and outside the Muslim world confusion is frequent between Arabism and Islam. This has often been prejudicial to the coherence of Arab propaganda, internally and externally alike. It has also facilitated various efforts on the part of the right wing of Arab nationalism, as we shall see.

Moreover, Arab nationalism is an ideological movement, and as such subject to the general laws of this type of movement[17] and to the particular laws of nationalist movements as well. Naturally, it includes many shades and tendencies. Those that respect truth and justice for all are not always the ones that carry the day, which is unfortunately quite natural in a period of heated struggle and ardent activism. Ideological movements tend rather spontaneously to a certain totalitarianism, as the aims, objectives, methods, and initiatives of the movement come to be held sacred, the adversary turned into a kind of 'devil', and any criticism rejected with impatience. Most often, a given nationalism has little understanding of any other nationalism whose aspirations may conflict with its own. An apologetic 'holy history' comes to render the entire past of the people concerned sacred.

---

[17] I have tried to adumbrate some laws of this type in various articles, most recently in 'Sociologie marxiste et idéologie marxiste', *Diogène*, no. 64, 1968, pp. 70–104. [See also my book *Marxism and the Muslim World*, London 1977.]

For instance, Arab nationalists who protest vigorously (and validly, in my view) against English, French, or Zionist encroachments on Arab territories at the expense of Arab populations are quite embarrassed by Arab encroachments on the rights of other peoples, such as the Kurds or the blacks of southern Sudan. While they (rightly) appeal, in the name of universalist principles, for solidarity with their struggle, even from people who more or less belong to a group that benefits from these encroachments at Arab expense, a rather slender number of them adopt a similar attitude towards those peoples who have suffered from Arab encroachments. Many excuses are found to rationalize this reluctance, and although they sometimes have some foundation (though only in part), they excuse nothing. Cynical manoeuvres in support of the Kurdish or south Sudanese movements are held up, and indeed some such manoeuvres are real. History and ethnography are reconstructed so as to claim, for example, that the Kurds are Arabs. Other reconstructions portray the Arabs as a people that has always done right by its neighbours, just as Muslim ideologues idealize Muslim society down through the centuries—and just as Zionist ideologues idealize and sacralize the people of Israel of all ages and lands. This subject could be discussed at great length.

The attention of the outside world has been drawn to these repellent aspects of Arab nationalism more than to its justified motivations. Zionist and pro-Israeli propagandists have naturally contributed to this, but the Arabs have given them considerable aid. This has become increasingly perceptible, for the nationalism of others is often displeasing. The nationalism of the colonial countries succeeded in attracting sympathy because its justifications were only too visible, and the Arabs benefitted from this; Israeli nationalism mined the sympathy engendered by the factors we discussed earlier. But Arab nationalism often appeared (especially as it increasingly attained its objectives) as the nationalism of a dominating people who desire their freedom only in order to subjugate others. The very term 'pan-Arabism' used so often, first by the imperialist powers and then by Israel, has contributed to this view of matters by recalling pan-Germanism. Nevertheless, the objective of the unification of peoples speaking the same language, even if utopian or inopportune because of differentiations, ought to arouse revulsion only if it is accompanied by the will to expand at the expense of other peoples.

In the enumeration of the factors that have damaged and are still damaging the Arab point of view, mention must also be made, even if only in passing, of how maladroit Arab propagandists have often been. Let us note just one essential dilemma in this respect. There are many Arabs who are very well acquainted with European society, who have sometimes settled in the West and have even been assimilated. But they are very often hostile or indifferent to the Arab nationalist movement. The real advocates of this ideology are recruited primarily among just those layers least in contact with Western culture and society, who know it only through translations, articles in the Arabic press, films, and so on. Like all militants of an ideology transported into a milieu that does not share it, and that even rejects its implicit assumptions, they speak a language that inevitably has a repellent effect on their audiences.

The Leftist Myth

It has been shown in recent years that the Muslim, and even purely Arab nationalist, interpretations of the Palestinian conflict are laden with dangers for the left elements of the movement, and even for Palestinian activist elements, whether of the left or right. Because of the nature of the opposition forces it has faced, Arab nationalism has been led by circumstances into conflicts both with the structures that maintain the power of pro-Western oligarchies ('feudal' or bourgeois) and with the Western powers which in practice have not only impeded evolution towards complete independence of decision-making and self-reliant modernization, but have also evinced great active complicity with Israel, to say the least. Gradually, an alliance with the Communist world came to appear as the only reliable one (within certain rather broad limits). As against this tide, which was difficult to resist and was engendering enthusiasm among the masses, recourse to Islamic sentiments quickly became a powerful weapon in the hands of the pro-Western regimes of the region. One of the rightist currents of Arab nationalism, itself preaching sacred egoism, distrustful of the Communist bloc, and consequently against any categorical and definitive break with the Western bloc, pressed for a change of course, and hesitated at the alliance, to the advantage of powers guilty of greater or lesser complicity with Israel. This became increasingly intolerable as the struggle sharpened, especially with the June 1967 war, the Arab defeat, and the occupation of new Arab territories.

The left elements were then driven to resort to the left myth to which I alluded earlier, situating the conflict in the perspective of world struggle against imperialism. I want to emphasize that I am using the term 'myth' in the Sorelian sense of a mobilizing representation, without in any way denying that the myth may contain a kernel of truth of greater or lesser importance. The representation of Israel as a mere bastion of an evil world force called imperialism could have permitted, and in fact did permit, the sympathies of the left (and especially the 'far left') to be aroused in many countries. Finally an effective counterweight had been found to the left Zionist propaganda that had awakened so great a response by invoking the supposedly 'socialist' character of Israeli society. Among the Arab masses, an organic bond was thus forged between the anti-Israeli objective and the general mobilization for the independence of decision-making power and for a self-reliant modernization that would enable living standards to be raised, a mobilization that has aroused a very deep response. Although, in accordance with the natural laws of ideological movements, clearly mythological representations were therefore generated (at least at the propaganda level)—economic dynamic of capitalism leading automatically to political and military expansion; single centre of political decision-making, quite imprecisely situated, automatically reflecting an economic impulse in a single direction; assimilation of the capitalist system to evil and selfishness in itself—there were sufficient elements of reality in this ideological synthesis to render it quite plausible as a whole.

It must be emphasized that the left myth, situating the local Palestinian conflict in the perspective of a revolt of the Third World against 'imperialism', also gained centrist and even rightist advocates—sometimes temporary, vacillating, or even hypocritical, but sometimes profound and quite sincere too. Indeed, this perspective can be garbed in purely nationalist dress. Any American or Western gesture in Israel's favour inevitably enhances the attraction of this opinion. The adoption of the view that the Palestinian movements are the vanguard of the fight for anti-imperialist demands, called upon to mobilize the entire Arab world along this line, may thus subtly lead some towards a socialist or socialistic position in which imperialism is denounced as a consequence of the economic dynamic of capitalism itself; but it can also supplant any criticism of the established regimes of the Middle East, whether they be 'state capitalist' (the difference from the 'state socialist' regimes is not readily detectable, but revolutionaries prefer this term), capitalist, or pre-capitalist to varying degrees. Some have seen the danger of this exclusive 'Palestinianism' (see the French-language review *Études arabes*, for example), which has led, for instance, to seeking the support of Saudi Arabia, a friend of the United States and the beneficiary of copious Aramco royalties, against 'imperialism'. The Palestinians and their supporters oscillate among these tendencies. Only, or almost only, the Democratic Popular Front for the Liberation of Palestine (see note 19 below) has taken a clear position of intransigent anti-imperialist revolutionism.

Arab Myths and Israeli Reality

As is natural from a socio-historic standpoint, Arab views thus present themselves as shrouded in myth. It would be too simplistic to reject them on the grounds of this mythical character. All movements develop in this manner. Before arriving at a judgement, then, it is only fair to examine whether or not these myths have arisen on a real foundation. Elsewhere I have shown in detail that in my view Arab grievances are in large part justified, that no impartial ethical attitude which applied to them the same principles as are virtually universally recognized as valid elsewhere could honestly declare their cause inadmissible or pronounce them guilty for rejecting the Israeli conquest.

The Judaization of a portion of Palestine seems to me to have been a clear infringement of Arab rights, which are as deserving of respect as anyone else's. But there is also no doubt that an Israeli people now exists. This people, forged of disparate elements united only by the genealogical bonds of descendence from relatives adhering to the Jewish religion, was created only with difficulty. It also has difficulty holding itself together, the principal cement being Arab hostility. It is not impossible that in certain circumstances the national bond could unravel. But for the moment it exists, and is even backed by considerable military strength.

The Arabs perceive the existence of this Israeli people, indeed in a way that is quite harsh for them. But they apprehend it in mythified forms: as a religious community endowed with a will of exceptional force; as a local bastion, lacking any will of its own, of a wicked international economic and political force.

Many Arab governments have long been prepared in practice to accept the *fait accompli* of the Israeli state, provided they are not also compelled to renounce the advantages of theoretical non-recognition. Others would even accept theoretical recognition, if only the Israelis would facilitate matters for them through transitional forms that would (perhaps) enable them to get their people to swallow this bitter pill. In the past they have often disguised any step in the direction of recognition by bellicose declarations intended for internal consumption, threats about the future, or counter-steps in the opposite direction—and they continue to do so today. They thereby invite the incomprehension of European and American public opinion, and open themselves to charges of incoherence, trickery, intransigence, and hypocritical bellicosity. The Israelis (for most of whom Arab public opinion has always been a myth) have never understood or accepted this process, instead demanding solemn and irreversible commitments from the very outset. Their fear of Arab reversals has always induced them to advance utopian demands unacceptable to their interlocutors. The result has been the successive wars and the present situation, in which any agreement has become impossible.

The world powers are trying to reach agreement to impose the acceptance of Israel by constraint, within certain limits and in exchange for certain compensation. We do not know whether they will manage to agree on the limits, the compensation, and the nature of the pressure to exert. The practical application of a plan of this sort would have unpredictable consequences. A new situation would emerge, one that would entail all kinds of readjustments. Unless one is blessed with the gift of prophecy, it is better to refrain from trying to predict them.

In the long run, however, everything depends on the deeper reactions of the peoples concerned, and from this point of view there are not an infinite number of possible prospects. On the whole, Arab public opinion remains irreconcilable with acceptance of Israel as a state. But many Arab states are resigned to allowing the imposition of this acceptance in reasonable forms and within reasonable limits. It is probable that some layers of the Arab populations would also resign themselves to it. Many Lebanese Christians, while feeling no sympathy for the Israelis, would not view with disfavour this counterweight to predominantly Muslim Arabism, within the framework of the communitarian conception described earlier, which is far from having entirely disappeared. But few dare openly to set themselves against a very general, profound, and ardent national sentiment that has swept away many an obstacle in vigorous struggle during recent decades. On the whole, the Arab world will remain irredentist. It is also unlikely that Israel, intoxicated with its victory and facing proclamations and actions more bellicose than ever, will do very much to facilitate any revision of this attitude.

At the same time, it does not seem that Israel is destined soon to suffer the fate of the medieval Latin states of the Crusaders. Its continuing presence may arouse—as many Arab revolutionaries, especially Palestinians, hope—a general mobilization of the Arab masses in an anti-imperialist revolutionary struggle throughout the entire Middle East, taking increasingly socialist forms. The cool analyst can foresee the cost of such a possibility, but the outcome, or outcomes, are far more difficult to predict.

The Palestinian movement is acquiring an increasingly profound and sophisticated knowledge of its enemy.[18] It is also trying to disintegrate Israel from within. Armed with this knowledge, and seeking formulas capable of attracting at least a part of the Israeli population, some elements of the movement may possibly come to

---

[18] Hebrew lessons are now on the agenda among the Palestinians, and among some of their friends in other Arab countries. It is characteristic that the Institute for Palestinian Studies in Beirut, a Palestinian organization whose publications are generally of high quality, published an Arabic translation of the *Israeli* contributions to the special issue of *Les Temps modernes* devoted to the Israeli-Arab conflict. The intention was to make available the various points of view prevailing among the enemy, while the Arab contributions were neglected as expressing ideas already well known and frequently rehashed in the Arab world.

revise, to varying degrees, their view of the Jewish entity as a religious community of the Middle Eastern type, and to alter the parts of their programmes and concepts that are tainted by this view. Perhaps one day they will consider the Israeli Jews an ethnic group and will draw the logical consequences. Certain indications—highly tenuous, it must be admitted—point in this direction.[19]

Things may therefore be moving—but much depends on the general political context, a function of the relationship of forces—towards prospects that are both more realistic and more agreeable to the observer concerned with justice and peace. In any event, any solution that did not move in the direction of the egalitarian coexistence of the ethnic groups on the scene would conflict violently with collective Arab consciousness (for inequality, in the present circumstances, could only be at the expense of the Arabs) and would have little chance of lasting.

---

[19]It seems that the small Marxist Palestinian group known as the Democratic Popular Front for the Liberation of Palestine, which is making an intense effort to educate a solid core of militants in depth, has taken this sort of position. So far it has remained isolated among the Palestinians (and is not to be confused with the Popular Front for the Liberation of Palestine, or PFLP, responsible for the attacks in Athens, Zurich, etc.).

9

The Conditions
of Coexistence

This brief article was written for a new magazine sympathetic to the French Socialist Party (called Intervention) *and was published in its first issue, dated November-December 1982. My intention was to explain that if Israel is ever to coexist with the Arab world, recognition of the fundamental justice of Arab rejection of the effects of the implementation of the Zionist project will be required. In the past few years, the grip of the Zionist 'vulgate' on European and American public opinion has slackened somewhat—partly because of the change in the importance of the Arab world in international politics, partly because of the actions of the Israeli government since Begin came to power. As evidence that it still has its advocates, however, I have included a letter received by* Intervention *from a reader deeply offended by my warped view of history. His letter is followed, in turn, by my answer. It is to be hoped that the day will come when exchanges like this will no longer be necessary. That, in itself, may well be one of the conditions of coexistence.*

No one is unaware that peaceful coexistence between the state of Israel and the Arab world remains a goal very difficult to attain. It is easy to take offence at this state of affairs, but more intelligent to try to understand the reasons for it. European—and in particular Jewish—ethnocentrism is usually content with a primitive explanation. 'The Arab mentality', 'Muslim fanaticism', and 'eternal anti-Semitism' are usually cited. Particular facts are invoked that seem to support these accusations. Unfortunately, however, these facts are enveloped in the mystifications of ideological constructions. Nations that were enemies for centuries now manage to coexist peacefully, like France, Germany, and Britain. Why can't Israel and its neighbours do the same?

There is a reason, and it is not at all mysterious. But a flood of publications, a mountain of clever and brilliant speeches, sometimes attaining the very heights of intellectual virtuosity, stubbornly obscure, deny, and strive to make people forget this fundamental cause, of which every Arab is well aware. Hence the gap between the two perceptions.

History of a Confrontation

This fundamental cause is simple. At a congress held in August 1897 in Basle, Switzerland, 197 delegates of Jewish associations from all countries adopted a programme: the creation in Palestine of a country for the Jewish people (or of a homeland, *Heimstätte* in German, the language of the congress), so defined by public law. Probably not more than 5 per cent of these delegates (or of those who had elected them) had any idea of conditions in Palestine at the time. It is estimated, however, that there were then some six hundred and fifty to seven hundred thousand inhabitants in that country, of which some sixty to seventy thousand were Jews. The statistics for the time are highly inexact and uncertain.

Palestine was then at least nine-tenths an Arab country.[1] It was under Turkish domination, part of the Ottoman Empire, but that changed nothing in its ethnic composition. It was Arab just as much as Lombardy and Venice were Italian during the time of their incorporation into the Austrian Empire, between 1815 and 1859 and between 1815 and 1866 respectively.

Now, these foreigners proclaimed that this Arab country had to be transformed into a Jewish homeland. Although the exact connotation of this term was not very clear, the Congress insisted on calling for it, under the inspiration of Theodor Herzl, the congress president. He had attracted much attention as a result of his book

---

[1] Indeed, it must be remembered that many of the Jews of Palestine spoke Arabic, were 'indigenous', and were considered simply adherents of a religion that encompassed a minority among the local population, and not members of another people.

published the previous year, entitled simply The Jewish State, or rather, The State of the Jews (*Der Judenstaat*). The goal of political Zionism, the movement created in Basle, was clear to everyone, and especially to the Arabs of Palestine: to transform Arab Palestine into a Jewish state.

Twenty years after Basle, on 2 November 1917, a government no less foreign to Palestine, that of Britain, pledged in the Balfour Declaration to organize 'a national home for the Jewish people' in Palestine—despite the opposition of Edwin Montagu, the only Jew in the cabinet. Another thirty years passed, and on 29 November 1947, the General Assembly of the United Nations voted by 35 to 13 (among the latter were the 10 Arab or Muslim states that were then members of the UN), with 10 abstentions, for the creation of a Jewish state in Palestine. On three occasions, then, foreigners decided to alienate an Arab territory in favour of groups of people who claimed to be descended from its ancient inhabitants of twenty centuries past but who, in the eyes of the inhabitants of this territory, could only have been considered yet other foreigners.

This manner of the creation of a state by foreigners for the benefit of other foreigners despite the unanimous opposition of the population differs strikingly from the conditions of origin of other states. Immediately upon the UN vote of 29 November 1947, the representatives of Saudi Arabia, Syria, Iraq, and Yemen declared that their governments did not consider themselves bound by this decision. In this they expressed the unanimous attitude of the Arab peoples. To accept such an amputation is difficult for a people. Instead of taking offence at what I have called 'the Arab rejection', instead of expressing astonishment at its sometimes brutal and often unrealistic forms, one must rather seek to understand the profound repugnance of a people at a painful amputation that was imposed by force.

Indeed, it would take too long to present here—as I have done elsewhere[2]—the details of the manner in which the Zionist project was realized. Whatever the responsibilities for each particular event, the most elementary logic demonstrates that the replacement of one people by another on a given territory can occur in just one of two

---

[2]For example in the articles collected in my book *Peuple juif ou problème juif* (see the present volume), in *Israel: A Colonial-Settler State?*, New York 1973, and in the new edition of my book *Israel and the Arabs*, Harmondsworth 1982.

ways: subordination or expulsion. And this is just what happened, through a long process with many ups and downs. A large part of the Arab people of Palestine found themselves driven from their homes and expelled from their country: only about a tenth of the population of the state of Israel, in its 1948–1967 borders, was Arab, whereas on the eve of Israel's creation, the Arabs formed more than two-thirds of the population.[3]

It would also take too long to recount the vicissitudes through which the state of Israel expanded beyond the 1948–49 borders that had been assigned it by the UN to attain those from which, in 1967, it conquered both the rest of Palestine west of the Jordan River and Sinai (subjugating a numerically large Arab population to which it denied the right of self-determination), or those from which, in 1982, it invaded Lebanon, which country it is inclined to evacuate possibly only in part and after having imposed its demands. But it is impossible not at least to mention these events, systematically distorted or passed over in silence as they are by the Zionist vulgate diffused in nearly all countries by clever and multiform propaganda and taken for good coin by the mass of the European and American population.

What Coexistence?

Coexistence between the two peoples is possible. There has been no lack of projects designed to bring it about. At first, from around 1920, it was a matter of the coexistence of two communities within the same state. That was the plan of those of the Jews of mandatory Palestine who dreamed of a bi-national state. Much later, it was the plan taken up by the PLO (the united democratic secular state called for in its 1964 Charter). The inspiration may be admirable, but the plan has long since become unrealistic. Now it is a matter of two peoples, two nations, and not two religious communities, as the Arabs long said and believed because of their difficulty in discarding modes of thought suggested by situations that have now been

---

[3] Jewish colonization under the aegis of the British mandate had increased the Jewish population from 10 or 11 per cent of the total to nearly a third in the space of twenty years.

superseded. In our epoch, two peoples cannot coexist within a single state unless each commands its own political structures. Especially when recent history has set them violently against one another.

For at least a protracted historical period, then, one can speak only in terms of the coexistence of two states. This coexistence is difficult. Nevertheless, I believe that it is possible. But some minimal conditions are required. Can a significant proportion of men and women in each camp be found to accept it (a proportion significant both from the standpoint of numbers and from that of the strategic position they occupy within each community)? Indeed, there is no point in trying to disguise the fact that in the best of cases a more or less powerful residue of intractable extremists will remain on both sides. It would be necessary only that they not be in a position to effectively sabotage the decisions assuring coexistence.

On the Arab side, the legitimacy of a specifically Jewish political structure, of an Israeli state, would have to be accepted. I hope I have succeeded in explaining why that is difficult, why the Palestinian, and more generally the Arab masses and their leaders are imbued with profound repugnance for this abandonment of all their rights to a portion of Arab national territory, a symbolically important part into the bargain. Because of this, there will always be dissidents opposed to resigning themselves to this renunciation. The rearguard battle waged by realistic Arab leaders conscious of the necessity of this abandonment, who have tried many equivocal and sophisticated formulas one after the other, may be compared to the positions taken by General De Gaulle between 1958 and 1962 in his attempts to get the French, above all the French of Algeria, to acknowledge that independence had to be granted that country.

It is difficult, but possible. Israel's military superiority is evident. Its internal structures and the state of mind of its inhabitants (with all their nuances), while previously completely unknown, are now perceived with increasing clarity in the Arab world. Underground contacts, secret or semi-secret, have proliferated over the past several years. Israeli reality has been brutally imposed; hence mounting hatred, but hence also greater knowledge.

It is a fact, perhaps difficult to explain, but observable on a number of occasions, that the Arabs willingly reestablish good, even excellent, relations with those from whom they have been divided by apparently inexpiable struggles. Mutual embraces among leaders who have just been cutting each other to pieces, often with considerable loss of blood, are well known. At the end of the ruthless war in Algeria, the French were greeted amicably, even fraternally, by the Algerians. The warmth of this welcome has steadily increased since then, even with regard to those who had once been hostile to independence.

Subterranean links exist between Israelis and Palestinians, who have long coexisted and have learned to know each other in myriad ways. It was futile to hope, as certain leading Israelis did, that these links would heal the breach between two peoples in struggle. But in conditions of peace, they can play a great part in rapprochement.

The conditions of coexistence also appear difficult, even impossible, on the Israeli side, unless a turn is taken under the pressure of internal or external forces. To start with, the limits of the Zionist project would have to be defined once and for all, and solemnly declared definitive. Need it be recalled that at the outset Zionism based its claim to Palestinian land on the fact that between the thirteenth century BC and the second or third century after Christ the country had been peopled in its majority and ruled by the Hebrews, in principle the ancestors of the present Jews? A glance at any historical atlas will show that this ancient habitat included not only the entire territory that was Palestine under the British mandate (in other words, present-day Israel and the territories it now occupies), but also a good part of what is now the Kingdom of Jordan and a small border region now part of Lebanon. In 1920, the first Zionists who concretely broached the problem of the territory of the 'Jewish national home', dealing with the question on the diplomatic level, demanded (quite logically) this entire territory for the settlements of Jewish population that were to furnish the human material for a future Jewish state (this was not referred to openly, but it was in everyone's mind). When, under British pressure, the leaders of the movement formally renounced the prospect of colonization east of the Jordan River (then called Transjordan), an opposition movement sprung up within the Zionist ranks.

This movement called itself 'revisionist Zionism'. Its purpose was to revise the limits imposed by the British mandate. Its chief was Vladimir Jabotinsky, a complex and often realistic personality. He insisted that the Arabs would never agree to abandon their rights to Palestine unless forced to do so. It was therefore necessary to prepare to conquer 'by blood and iron' the ancient kingdom of Israel, the entire land known in Jewish tradition as *Eretz Yisrael*, the 'land of Israel', both east and west of the Jordan.[4]

'Secure and Recognized' Borders

Some Zionists, and later Israelis, often religious Jews, have voiced even more sweeping territorial claims, deduced from the promises God made to His people, according to the Old Testament. Taking note of the military strength of their state, some Israeli strategists have dreamed of a sphere of preponderant influence extending throughout the Middle East. General Ariel Sharon, for instance.[5] In 1982 he was even able to take a few steps towards the realization of his dreams.

Will this project be realized, and if so, to what extent? Only the future will tell. In any event, the Arabs note the constant expansion of Israeli ascendancy since the UN partition plan. The 1948 war itself saw a palpable enlargement of its borders. In 1967 all of the West Bank came under Israeli occupation, as did Sinai (later evacuated to obtain the peace treaty with Egypt) and the Syrian Golan Heights. In 1982, it was Lebanon's turn for occupation. God knows when it will be evacuated.

The Arabs observe this constant expansion and fear that it will continue, justified by 'historic rights' to Jordan or southern Lebanon, or by 'imperatives of security', or some other pretext. Peaceful coexistence will be possible only when this fear is eliminated by solemn declarations and unequivocal acts by the Israelis. Let us

---

[4]See, for example, Walter Laqueur, *History of Zionism*, London 1978. This work, by a pro-Zionist who seems to be somewhat disabused, is naturally biased, but reliable on the whole; it is based on considerable documentation.

[5]An address prepared by Sharon for a strategic studies colloquium at the University of Tel Aviv, published by the Israeli newspaper *Ma'ariv* and commented on in the newspaper *Al Ha-Mishmar* of 24 December 1981, stated: 'Beyond the Arab states of the Middle East, the Mediterranean, and the Red Sea, the Israeli sphere of strategic interest in the 1980s ought to include states like Turkey, Iran, and Pakistan, and regions like the Persian Gulf and Africa, principally the states of north and central Africa.'

recall that neither the fundamental laws of Israel nor any other document or treaty set definitive limits to this state. Another condition for coexistence is that Israeli leaders show greater understanding and patience with respect to Arab public opinion. Instead of always harping on the rights of the Israeli people, or of the Jewish people as a whole—whether they be based on the ancient habitat (a principle difficult to admit in international law), the sufferings endured by the Jews (for which the despoiled Arabs are hardly responsible), or the labours accomplished on Palestinian soil over the past several decades (the only argument of any validity)—they will have to acknowledge once and for all, in word and deed alike, that the Arabs of Palestine had primordial rights to this land, which they inhabited and cultivated. Their renunciation of these rights can be negotiated, but it cannot be expected that they will acknowledge that they never existed.

To recognize that it will be difficult for the Arabs of Palestine and elsewhere to accept this renunciation of their rights is to cease to make use of any Arab reaction, however violent and contestable, to justify a fresh attack, a fresh conquest. In short, the Israeli leaders will have to recognize (and demonstrate that they recognize) that the security of Israel lies above all in the ability of an alien body—for in practice the new Israeli populace is just such an alien body, despite its claims to be indigenous—to gain admittance to, to be accepted by, the Middle Eastern environment, which means, first of all, by the Arabs. It is here that the lasting peaceful solution lies, and not, as Israeli leaders have imagined for thirty-four years now, in the blows delivered, the 'lessons taught' their neighbours, to use their terminology.

It may be argued that these blows, whatever their moral value, have succeeded. They eventually persuaded Sadat to conclude peace with Israel (he was unable to do so until he had raised his prestige with a partial victory in 1973); they have just now destroyed the centres of the PLO in Lebanon; and they threaten to turn a good portion of that country into an Israeli protectorate. That is true. But can anyone fail to see that these 'successes' have been won by sowing seeds of hatred that make the desired pacification even more difficult and engender thousands of future combatants eager to struggle for the destruction of Israel? Bismarck was also 'right' in 1870 against the German pacifists. His 'success', the Treaty of Frankfurt and the resignation of France, proved him so. But a few decades later the judgement was reversed. It seems clear that the conditions of coexistence will not easily be brought about, especially at a time when one of the protagonists is savouring the intoxication of victory. But force and victory do not forever remain on the same side. Thus did the Hebrew prophets of Antiquity ceaselessly warn the kings of Israel and Judea, overconfident in their own strength. One day, as David Ben-Gurion feared, some leader and organizer could mobilize the accumulated thirst for revenge among the Arabs and unite them. And the ancient prophecies could then acquire a touch of topicality.

Paris, 8 December 1982

Dear Editor,

Let me first of all congratulate you on the excellent general quality of your review, which notably has the merit of providing its readers with valuable documentation on the subjects with which it deals.

Nevertheless, one of the articles that appeared in your first issue, signed by Mr Rodinson, shocked me deeply because of its systematic legerdemain, even its distortion of historical facts that are nevertheless incontestable. I would add that my letter is not motivated by any partisan spirit: I respect the positions of Mr Rodinson on the problem of the Middle East (although I do not share them), but I deny his right to 'revise' history in a fantastical and sometimes mendacious manner, and it is with the aim of establishing certain historical truths that I take the liberty of writing to you.

Indeed, how can Mr Rodinson write on the same page that the 'goal of the Zionist movement, created in Basle, political Zionism, was clear...: to transform Arab Palestine into a Jewish state', while a few lines earlier he affirmed that less than 5 per cent of the Zionist delegates to this same congress were aware of the reality of the Arab populace of Palestine.

A little further on, citing the three landmarks of the Zionist Congress of Basle (1897), the Balfour Declaration (1917), and the UN decision to partition Palestine (1947), Mr Rodinson, conjuring away the reality of the continuous Jewish peopling of Palestine since 1880 (despite the prohibition of Jewish immigration imposed by the

British in 1939), reduces the creation of the state of Israel to three punctual decisions, isolated and taken thirty years apart, and by 'foreigners' to boot:

'On three occasions, then, foreigners decided to alienate an Arab territory in favour of groups of people who claimed to be descended from its ancient inhabitants.' He is wilfully blind to the fact that these decisions did no more than note the desire for autonomy of the Jewish population, its presence on the soil of Palestine alongside the Arab population.

Mr Rodinson then has the audacity to go so far as to affirm that the creation of this state was accomplished 'despite the unanimous opposition of the population', which suggests that this population was exclusively Arab. Now, all sources, including Arab historians, agree in estimating the Jewish population of Palestine at some six hundred thousand souls (in 1947).

A little further on, Mr Rodinson's words reach a pinnacle of mendacious amalgam (I would have used the word 'grotesque' had this conflict not spilled so much blood), when he claims that the PLO charter of 1964 only takes up 'the plan of those Jews of mandatory Palestine who dreamed of a bi-national state'. I know that one is accustomed to read in the press that the PLO charter does not reflect the current positions of the PLO (which remains to be proved), but since Mr Rodinson alludes to it, let us refer to it in our turn. First of all, it must be noted that *at no time* is there any question of a bi-national state in this charter (which would be to recognize the Jewish national fact). Article 16 mentions only the creation of a state open to all religions, without further specification. But who will the citizens of this multi-confessional state be? Article 6 answers unambiguously: 'Those of the Jews settled in Palestine before the Zionist invasion of 1917 will be considered Palestinian.' It is now 1982. Which means that this measure amounts to the expulsion of virtually the totality of the Israeli population. I strongly doubt, Mr Rodinson, that this was the desire of the Jews of mandatory Palestine, and I am astonished that a specialist on the Arab world as famous as yourself is so ill-informed about the charter of the PLO.

Another transformation of the historical facts, this time by omission: referring to the eve of the creation of the state of Israel, Mr Rodinson affirms: 'Jewish colonization under the aegis of the British mandate had increased the Jewish population from 10 per cent of the total to nearly a third in the space of twenty years.' Now, anyone even slightly cognizant of the history of the Middle East knows that in 1939, in the face of pressing Arab discontent (notably the anti-Jewish riots of 1929 and 1936), the British implemented the 'White Paper', which in practice prohibited any Jewish immigration to Palestine. Mr Rodinson's omission is an insult to the memory of the passengers of hundreds of clandestine embarkations similar to that of the *Exodus*, who, intercepted by the British, suffered the tragic fate of return to Europe, to the Nazi camps, or perished on the high seas.

I hope that this letter attains its goal, which is to reestablish the historical truth where Mr Rodinson has twisted it. I dare to hope that despite its length you may publish certain significant passages of it, in order that readers unacquainted with the history of Palestine and of the state of Israel may be made aware of the fact that Mr Rodinson's version is adhered to only by its author.

Thanking you, sir, for your kind attention to this letter.

Yours sincerely,

Henri Carasso

Mr Henri Carasso wants to rectify historical truth as against my 'distortions'. Obviously, his intention is to defend the vulgate of the Zionist ideological movement, so widespread in all circles (traces of its influence may even be found in the same issue of *Intervention*). Similarly were the Stalinists deeply shocked, for example, to hear talk of the historical role of Trotsky, in contradiction to the 'historical truth' expressed by the official *History of the Communist Party (Bolsheviks)* and a hundred other publications.

He is astonished that I affirm simultaneously that as early as the Basle Congress of 1897 the Zionist movement meant to turn Arab Palestine into a Jewish state and that less than one delegate in twenty had any idea of the real situation in Palestine at the time. Where is the contradiction? On the one hand, these delegates were not the slightest bit interested in the indigenous inhabitants of contemporary Palestine whoever they might have been, since all they had to know was that this country had been the home of the ancient ancestors of today's Jews and had played a cardinal role in Jewish 'mythology' ever since. On the other hand, Palestine was then (1897) an Arab country in the usual sense of the word. Ignorance of the ethnic situation of a country was no obstacle to the legislation of its fate, especially in those days. Colonial history is full of such instances.

I did not 'conjure away' the reality of the flood of Jewish emigration to Palestine beginning in 1880, even before the Basle congress, that is. But I insisted on the incontestable fact of capital importance, ignored by Mr Carasso and by Zionist ideology, that this immigration did not occur in a vacuum, that it was able to take place only by virtue of institutional protection established from the outside. In Basle, Herzl won recognition as the head of a new movement directed towards the realization of the project he himself had outlined the previous year: the Jewish state. 'Without him', the pro-Zionist historian Walter Laqueur has written, 'Zionism would have remained a movement of very narrow scope aiming at a cultural renaissance while also concerning itself with subsidiary philanthropical and colonizing activities. ... Herzl laid the foundations of the subsequent achievements of the Zionist movement and can with good reason be called the architect of the Balfour Declaration' (*History of Zionism*, London 1975).

Equally, without the Balfour Declaration, and in particular without the incorporation of its promises into the text of the mandate over Palestine that Britain was granted by the League of Nations, it would have been impossible for sufficient immigration to have occurred to have brought the Jewish share of the population from 11 per cent towards 1922 to 32 per cent towards 1940. The British were enjoined by the mandate to protect this immigration. Mr Carasso fumes with indignation, citing the impediments established by the White Paper of 1939 (which *limited* the annual quota to seventy-five thousand immigrants for five years before halting it completely). This is a confusion of chronology typical of the mechanism of ideological thought.

The reluctance of British functionaries prior to 1939 and the limitation and halt to immigration called for after that date do not alter the importance of what took place under British protection between 1922 and 1939. A third of the population was Jewish by the latter date, and this alone permitted the claims and struggles leading to the Jewish state. The UN decision of 1947 alone afforded that state an international legitimacy.

Who can believe that any Palestinian state, any Arab state, any Middle Eastern state, would ever have permitted such an occurrence if they had been masters of the destiny of Palestine during that period? There were indeed, then, three fundamental decisions without which Jewish immigration could have occurred only on a reduced scale or not at all. And in that case, how could a Jewish state have been formed? It is significant that public opinion is so conditioned by Zionist propaganda that merely to recall these incontestable facts, still not clear in the public mind, to say the least, is to expose oneself to insults.

Indignant at my sacrilegious dissent from the Zionist vulgate, Mr Carasso also chides me for formulations that he wilfully refuses to understand.

I wrote (laconically, in view of the lack of space) that various projects envisaged the coexistence of two communities, that certain Jews of Palestine under the mandate interpreted this coexistence in the form of a bi-national state (meaning a state encompassing two nations), that the PLO charter (of 1964, amended in 1968) again took up this idea of coexistence. I explained in the next sentence that the Arabs were wrong to understand this as the coexistence of two religious communities. It is indeed precisely that conception which underlies Article 6 of the said charter, which Mr Carasso quotes: 'The Jews who resided normally in Palestine before the beginning of the Zionist invasion [when?] shall be considered Palestinians.' (See the text in Olivier Carré, *Le Mouvement national palestinien*, Paris 1977, p. 153, and compare the 1964 text, in *The Israel-Arab Reader*, Walter Laqueur, ed., 2nd edn, Harmondsworth 1970.) I discussed the mistake that lies at the root of this conception, and its causes. Mr Carasso does not even notice this. He proclaims that I have confected a 'mendacious amalgam'. Had he not assumed a priori that I am capable of the most evil designs, he would have readily been able to understand that I simply meant to show the (very slow) evolution from projects of coexistence of two communities towards one of coexistence of two nations, while emphasizing, moreover, that the Arabs were wrong to adhere too long to the first conception. But my sin is to try to explain the historical reasons for this delay instead of simply denouncing it as a crime for which the entire Arab people must atone.

Likewise, when I spoke of the unanimous opposition of the population to the creation of the Jewish state, I was quite obviously referring to the Palestinian situation as it has evolved since 1880 or 1897. This evolution moved towards the creation of this state by laying a basis for it through mounting immigration, sheltered by structures gradually established from abroad, against the unanimous opposition of the original indigenous population, the proportion of which within the total population was thus steadily reduced (although it was still a majority towards 1940: two-thirds as against one-third). Perhaps I did not express myself clearly enough. But whatever Mr Carasso may think, I am not so ignorant of the problem as to be unaware that in 1947–48 the Jews of Palestine formed one-third of the population (in fact, I said so explicitly), and I am not so idiotic as to try to suggest that they were against the Jewish state at that time.

Maxime Rodinson

Index